STATE BOARD FOR
TECHNICAL AND
COMPREHENSIVE EDUCATION

STATE BOARD FOR
TECHNICAL AND
COMPREHENSIVE EDUCATION

THE HERRING GULL'S WORLD

THE NEW NATURALIST

THE HERRING GULL'S WORLD

A STUDY OF THE
SOCIAL BEHAVIOUR OF BIRDS

by

NIKO TINBERGEN

Illustrated with
51 Photographs taken by the Author
58 Drawings and Diagrams

BASIC BOOKS, INC. PUBLISHERS
NEW YORK

© 1960 Revised Edition by Niko Tinbergen

Published in the United States of America

by Basic Books, Inc., 1961

Library of Congress Catalog Card Number: 61-5466

Printed in Great Britain

CONTENTS

CONTENTS

CONTENTS

*A full list of plates will be found at the end of the book
on page 242.*

EDITORS' PREFACE

THIS INTERESTING BOOK represents somewhat of a departure from *New Naturalist* procedure because all previous monographs that we have published have been of the comprehensive kind, dealing with every or nearly every aspect of the biology of a particular species or group.

THE HERRING GULL'S WORLD is not a comprehensive monograph on the Herring Gull. Dr. Tinbergen's researches on bird behaviour during the last two decades have been by observation and experiment, and it is his findings about the mind of this interesting social bird, the Herring Gull, that form the subject of this book. We did not want to circumscribe the development of Dr. Tinbergen's ideas on this subject by demanding that he should deal (for instance) with the Herring Gull's complicated systematics or geographical distribution, subjects which (in this particular case) are so vast that they almost deserve a monograph to themselves.

THE HERRING GULL'S WORLD is thus dedicated wholly to the exploration of what (before Dr. Tinbergen brought his logical mind to bear on them) were the mysteries of gull sociality. Dr. Tinbergen would be the first to admit that mysteries remain, for the victories of research simply breed new questions for new other researches, but his critical work has shed an entirely new light on a fascinating problem. Dr. Tinbergen draws a picture of the senses with which the Herring Gull perceives the external world and responds to its stimuli, and the signals by which it communicates with others of its kind. He then takes us through all the stages of the Herring Gull's breeding life, from the early spring settling-down of the colony with its concomitant fighting, through pair-formation, pairing and nest-building, to the incubation of the eggs, the hatching of the chicks and the defence of the brood. He describes the family life of the Herring Gull and gives a fascinating analysis of the chick's world. His researches on " sign stimuli " are as ingenious as they are important and it is here that he makes his most important comparisons between the world of the Herring Gull and that of man and other animals.

The work of Niko Tinbergen is characterised by a strictly objective approach and by a balance between observation and experiment. While remaining strictly biological he does not indulge in the mental gymnastics indulged in by some students of animal behaviour in order to avoid any suspicion of anthropomorphism. Tinbergen is a " common-sense " biologist in his methods of work as much as in the language he uses to communicate them to his fellows. He believes in simplicity, in the need of inductive work (in the present state of our knowledge of animal behaviour) as well as of far-reaching hypotheses and deductive reasoning. He also believes in devoting equal attention to those three different aspects of behaviour—its apparent purpose or biological significance; its physiological causation; and its historical evolution.

Niko Tinbergen has been a naturalist ever since boyhood. His years of childhood were much occupied in watching birds, collecting sea-shells, studying fresh-water and sea animals in aquaria, identifying flowering plants. At first, like many others, he had not much use for laboratory and museum zoology. What started him on a professional zoological career was a visit to the Rossitten Bird Observatory in Germany. He says that he would have been a bad student if he had not been inspired by the example of Jan Verwey and the writings of Oskar Heinroth and Julian Huxley to see the possibilities of serious research on the behaviour of animals, particularly birds.

When still a young man Tinbergen went on an arctic expedition to East Greenland, where he made what are now classic studies upon the Snow Bunting and the Red-necked Phalarope. On his return he was entrusted with the building up of a department of animal behaviour-research and behaviour-teaching at

Leiden University, and this is when his main work began, not only on birds but also on fish and insects.

This book on the Herring Gull can be said to have begun in those Leiden days. In 1936, Tinbergen got in touch with the remarkable Austrian naturalist Konrad Lorenz and worked with him in 1937. Lorenz, whose novel ideas were then only beginning to gain wide acceptance, had a great influence on Tinbergen's thinking, and ever since then the two have worked closely together.

After he had held the Chair of Experimental Zoology at Leiden University for some years, Tinbergen, in 1949, came to Oxford at the request of the Linacre Professor of Zoology, A. C. Hardy, who asked him to organise behaviour-research on the same lines as at Leiden; and with a number of pupils he is now continuing and expanding his work on the behaviour of gulls, sticklebacks and insects.

We regard THE HERRING GULL'S WORLD as one of the most remarkable and unusual books in the *New Naturalist* series, and are confident that it will not only have a well-deserved success but exercise a considerable and important influence on the development of the young and vigorous study of ethology or, as we in Britain mostly call it, animal behaviour.

Because of his close association with Tinbergen's work we asked Professor Lorenz to write something by way of preface to this book : the result is the accompanying Foreword.

THE EDITORS

FOREWORD BY KONRAD LORENZ

MUCH OF THE BEAUTY and wonder of nature is based on the fact that organic life is directed towards goals—towards survival, reproduction, and the attainment of higher perfection. This very directedness of life, impelling evolution from the amœba to ourselves, and, we may legitimately hope, to something beyond our present selves, is indeed something very wonderful. It is, therefore, intelligible and pardonable if many naturalists, particularly many students of animal behaviour, have become so fascinated with its directedness, with the question "What for?" or "Towards what end?" that they have quite forgotten to ask about its casual explanation. Yet the great questions "Why?" and "How?" are quite as fascinating as the question "What for?"—only they fascinate a different type of scientist. If wonder at the directedness of life is typical of the field student of nature, the quest for understanding of causation is typical of the laboratory worker. It is a regrettable symptom of the limitations inherent to the human mind that very few scientists are able to keep both questions in mind simultaneously. It is a fact that organic life in general, and animal behaviour in particular, is "directed"; but it is also a fact that it obeys the laws of natural causation, just as much as inorganic nature. It can, accordingly, only be understood if both these facts are equally kept in mind. One of the few people who really do this is Niko Tinbergen. It is also characteristic that he cannot be classified either as field observer or as laboratory man: he is both at once.

But primarily he is a hunter. He likes to stalk and watch and sit in hides. Unlike myself, he does not want to keep and breed animals, but prefers to study them in their wild haunts, the wilder the better. In him, the hunting instinct has been sublimated into the search for a deeper understanding of nature. The question, what a particular type of animal behaviour is for, what is its function and its biological advantage, must be settled first, and can best be answered by studying the animal in its natural habitat. But when we ask how that particular behaviour pattern is brought about, then the laboratory method of experiment must be brought into play. This does not by any means imply that the hunt must then proceed to the laboratory: it is amazing what an immense amount of precise and cogent experimentation Tinbergen has carried out in the field. He knows exactly how to ask questions of nature in such a way that she is bound to give clear answers; and he owes this knowledge to his habit of using his binoculars for a long time before formulating those questions. Also, he has a remarkable knack of choosing, for his observations, such objects as are favourable to his special methods.

One of these objects is the gulls and their behaviour. I put the gulls first and their behaviour afterwards, though the latter is the real object of his studies. It takes a very long period of watching to become really familiar with an animal and to attain a deeper understanding of its behaviour; and without the love for the animal itself, no observer, however patient, could ever look at it long enough to make valuable observations on its behaviour. If Karl von Frisch's name will, for all future time, be associated with the honey-bee, Niko Tinbergen's will always call to mind his work on gulls.

He has been observing and analysing the behaviour of the gull family for decades. Recently, he organised a well-concerted investigation of as many gull species as possible. In Britain, in the United States and on the Continent, pupils of Tinbergen are sitting in their hides and watching gulls of different species. Much of the outcome of his and their work is contained in this book. It is not only a book on gulls: it is a book, written with charm, clarity and precision, on those animals whose behaviour is, in the present state of our knowledge, perhaps the best analysed behaviour of any animals on this planet.

KONRAD LORENZ

PRELIMINARY AND ACKNOWLEDGMENTS

HAVING HAD the good fortune to spend my boyhood and much of my later life in Holland by the sandy shores of the North Sea, I have naturally come under the spell of its most familiar bird, the sturdy and yet graceful Herring Gull. The beach is simply unthinkable without these ever-present fellow-beachcombers. I have spent many happy days watching them. At low tide they foraged in large flocks on the broad flat beach, and their gatherings indicated to us boys the places where multitudes of interesting and mysterious sea animals were washed up. Wildly screaming, the gulls followed the fishing boats just beyond the surf, quarrelling with each other about the titbits thrown overboard, and snatching them away even from the fishermen's hands. In rough weather, when the westerly winds pushed the surf far up on to the beach, an endless procession of gliding gulls would pass along the windswept range of dunes, sailing without any effort on the airlift provided by the impact of the sea wind upon the sand hills.

In spring we followed the gulls into the sand dunes, where they settled down on their traditional breeding grounds. Throughout the years of my boyhood watching the life in the large gullery was complete happiness; and I derived a vague but intense satisfaction from just being with the gulls, feeling the sun upon my skin, enjoying the scents of the lovely dune flowers, watching the snow-white birds soaring high up in the blue sky, and assuming, or rather knowing, that they were feeling just as happy as I was.

It was this sentiment that sent me back to the gulls in later years, when I returned with a matured scientific interest, intent on exploring the secrets of their community life, so well known to me in one way, so unknown in its sociological implications.

Since the awakening of my scientific curiosity, few seasons passed in which I did not manage to spend time in watching them, for hours, days, and weeks, and I kept it up all through the years when, as a busy zoology professor, I should perhaps have given priority to other tasks, considered by many to be more urgent. . . .

Soon after starting such a study of a social bird's community life, one begins to realise how little one knows. Even an hour's careful observation of the goings-on in a gullery faces one with a great number of problems—more problems, as a matter of fact, than one could hope to solve in a lifetime. We see the birds fight each other. Why do they fight, for they seem to have been tolerant of each other for a long time? What is the use of this fighting? Why do these particular individuals fight each other? Why do they fight here, and not somewhere else? We do not know. We do not even know who they are. We do not even know whether they know each other! We don't even know whether they know their own young!

In spite of our ignorance, it soon becomes evident that a gull colony is not a haphazard accumulation of gulls, but that it must be an intricate social structure, organised according to some sort of plan. The individuals are connected to each other by innumerable ties, invisible in the beginning, yet very real and very strong. Step by step, by observation and experiment some of this social structure becomes visible, and slowly a picture of the social pattern begins to take shape. This gradual development of our understanding, resulting from the accumulation of many discoveries, minor and major (though mostly minor), gives intense satisfaction, but it has, at the same time, an entirely contrary result. Starting, on the first day, realising that we know next to nothing, and expecting that intense study would add to our knowledge and take away our ignorance, we discover that the feeling of ignorance does not decrease but rather is intensified, and that our ignorance actually grows at a much greater rate than our understanding, because each problem that is solved discloses a number of new problems. Yet in another way this development satisfies, because awareness of ignorance is in itself the result of some sort of understanding, the understanding and knowledge of problems to be solved. One feels as if, after a laborious climb, one has reached a mountain summit offering a commanding view of vast stretches of entirely new country, with new and much higher peaks to be explored. Every traveller knows the intense satisfaction and thrill such a moment brings; the joy of getting a first hazy view of wide new territory to be explored is not less than, and may often surpass, the joy of exploration itself.

Much of the work reported in this book is not my own. In the years I spent at Leiden University it was my good fortune to have a Herring Gull colony within an easy hour's bicycling distance. This made it possible to include gull-watching in the programme of a practical course in behaviour study given to biology students. During several years, the Herring Gull was used as a means to demonstrate to young zoologists how patient observation leads, first to discovery of puzzling phenomena, then to suppositions and hypotheses, and finally to well-planned observation and experiment. Some students returned in later years to do some special research on one of the many problems offered by the gulls.

From all my companions whose work has contributed to this monograph, I want to mention especially Prof. and Mrs. Baerends, Dr. H. L. Booy, Dr. D. Caudri, P. Creutzberg, Mrs. G. Duym, G. Paris, J. J. ter Pelkwijk, A. C. Perdeck, and Dr. A. Quispel. Our thanks are further due to the Director of the Municipal Water Supply Service at the Hague, to the Committee of the Hague Society for the Protection of Birds, and to the State Department of Forestry for their kind permission to work in the Herring Gull colonies near Wassenaar and on the isle of Terschelling. Help of many kinds was received from Messrs. Klein, Parlevliet, Remmerswaal, De Vries and Zorgdrager, bird wardens of these two colonies, to whom we wish to express our thanks.

We were, of course, not the first to study the Herring Gull's behaviour. In the ornithological literature several more or less monographic studies had already appeared when we began our work, such as Strong's paper in the *Auk* (1914), and the most valuable paper by Portielje (1928). Later, Goethe's monograph (1937) appeared. Also, numerous papers of a more fragmentary nature, and a multitude of short notes can be found scattered through the many ornithological journals. Yet all these publications together did not nearly exhaust the subject, and they certainly were not sufficient to enable one to get a more or less coherent picture of the structure of a Herring Gull community. There remained many gaps, some at important points, and many phenomena were not interpreted, or opinions about the interpretation differed, or the interpretations offered did not satisfy us. On the other hand, our study is far from " complete " either, and therefore the literature has been used to complement our narrative as much as possible, though I cannot claim to have used the literature exhaustively.

It may be clear, therefore, that it has not been my aim to give anything like an exhaustive treatise of Herring Gull sociology. It rather is an attempt at a sketch of the problems as I see them now. Here and there, it is true, I will be able to report about discoveries giving some insight into the gulls' social organisation, but the picture offered will be patchy and often vague, and it is exactly this incompleteness of my account that, I hope, will urge others to join in the effort and to continue the work. On the other hand, there are only a few species that are better known sociologically, and therefore, some of our conclusions and suggestions are, I think, new and it might be worth while to test their validity in other species.

I am indebted to Dr. David Lack and to James Fisher for much valuable criticism and advice. I also want to thank Dr. Lack and W. B. Alexander for cordial hospitality in the Edward Grey Institute and in the splendid Alexander Library.

PART ONE

Introduction

CHAPTER I

AIMS OF FIELD WORK ON BIRD BEHAVIOUR

An understanding of an animal's behaviour, including its social life, is impossible without first knowing something of the means and instruments which it has at its disposal. These means are threefold.

(1) First, the behaviour is continuously influenced by the outer world; in other words, much of the behaviour is reaction. For instance a gull may be dozing quietly on the nest with its eyes closed. All at once, a sharp alarm cry is uttered by a neighbouring gull who has spotted a human visitor in the distance. Immediately the sleeping gull will jump up, and walk or fly from the nest. Again, a gull may be flying a few feet above the surface of the sea, pointing its head downward and continuously turning it around in search for food. When the gull sees possible food it stalls, makes a sharp turn, and dives down in order to pick it up. In the first instance, the bird's behaviour was changed because it heard something; in the second case because it saw something. This is typical of the way in which environment influences behaviour: it usually (if not always) acts on the sense-organs, and the stimuli received by the sense-organs are passed on to the nervous system, and then on to the muscles, which carry out the movements and could therefore be called executive organs.

In order to understand the influence of the environment on behaviour, it is therefore necessary to know the capacities and the limitations of the bird's sense-organs. This is essential because, through work done in the last few decades, it is now known that so many animals have sense organs quite different from our own. On the one hand, stimuli which we are able to receive may be non-existent to the animal. A starfish, for instance, will never show a reaction to sound, for it is completely deaf. On the other hand, many animals are sensitive to changes in the environment which our sense-organs cannot receive at all. Honey bees can see ultraviolet light, which is entirely invisible to us, and in fact would still be non-existent to us were it not for fairly recent discoveries in physics. Bats are sensitive to sounds of a pitch far beyond the highest pitch we can hear; in avoiding obstacles, they do not use their eyes as we would do, but locate them by the echo of the " ultrasonic " sounds they produce themselves. It would of course be impossible for us to understand the dependence of these animals on external stimuli if we did not know about the sense-organs which they use and the stimuli to which they are sensitive. And although birds do not differ nearly so much from us as do bees or bats, a survey of their sensory capacities is an essential part of the study of their behaviour.

(2) The sense-organs and their functions are of course only one aspect of behaviour. Their stimulation often results in movements, and therefore we have to study these movements, and the executive organs which make them possible. These executive organs involve in the first place the muscles and the parts moved by them, such as the bill, the legs, the wings, etc. The influence which the animal exerts on the environment through these executive organs is often very obvious, for instance when legs, wings, body and bill move in the process of catching prey. However, there are also more subtle but no less important effects of movement, for instance the visual effects of movement and posture on a fellow member of the same species, or the auditory effects of call-notes upon other individuals. And there are even executive organs that work without the help of movement at all, merely through their colour. As I hope to show, the red patch on the lower mandible is an executive organ of this type.

(3) The two lines of approach indicated above, however much they may contribute to an understanding of behaviour, are not enough. The study of sensory functions tells us something about external influences, the study of executive organs shows us what an animal can do. It does not show, however, *how* it does it. It is now a matter of common knowledge that the muscles are made to contract by impulses from the nerves, and that sense organs pass their messages on to the nervous system. The nervous system is indispensable as an intermediate; without it no behaviour is possible. Whereas it is relatively easy to study the functions of the sense-organs and those of the executive organs, it is much more difficult to approach the nervous system, which works mysteriously inside the animal. Its functions can be revealed only by highly specialised and complicated methods, usually of an indirect nature. One of the methods used is the analysis, both in the field and in the laboratory, of normal behaviour patterns. In this book the field method is described. It is an attempt at a consistent pursuit of two problems: (*a*) what are the causes underlying the observed behaviour? and (*b*) how does behaviour help the animal in maintaining itself or its offspring? Further, it is sometimes possible to detect the origin of a movement, and thus to see a glimpse of the evolution of behaviour.

As I hope to show in this book, the behaviour of Herring Gulls can tell us highly interesting things about the functioning of their nervous system. Their innate behaviour shows wonderful adaptations, but also astonishing limitations. It is wonderful, for instance, to see a gull take a shellfish up into the air and drop it in order to crush it, and to know that this is an innate (or inherited and unlearnt) capacity, provided for in the nervous system. But it is equally astonishing to see that the bird never realises that it has to drop the shellfish on something hard, and it may go on dropping it on soft mud again and again. It is wonderful, again, to see how a gull rolls a misplaced egg back into its nest, but it is amazing that it does so in such a clumsy way, by balancing it on the narrow underside of the beak, instead of by a simple sweep of the wing, which would seem much easier. It is wonderful, again, to see how every parent gull learns to distinguish its own young individually after about five days, but it is disappointing to see that it never learns to distinguish its own eggs from those of its neighbour, however different their colour may be. These limitations in behaviour are not due to limitations in the sense-organs or in the effector organs, but to limitations in the nervous system. It never " occurs " to the gull to drop shellfish only on rocks, or to roll an egg in with its wing. This psychological expression, incidentally, is just another way of saying that the nervous system has limited powers.

Plate 1a. Gales at spring tide carry the surf over the Herring Gulls' feeding grounds

b Herring Gull in first winter, foraging

Plate 2a. The trumpeting call

b. Herring Gull preening

CHAPTER 2

THE EXECUTIVE ORGANS

General remarks

By a consideration of the executive organs alone, gulls can easily be distinguished from all other types of bird. Because they are cosmopolitan in distribution, and live in very diverse environments, one might have expected to see many diverse types among them, but in fact they form a rather close group of similar forms. The amount of adaptive radiation, such a conspicuous feature in many other animal groups, is surprisingly small.

The only other type of bird that shows a resemblance to the gulls is the family Procellariidæ, the petrels, shearwaters and albatrosses, but this is not due to close family ties, but to convergent evolution as sea-birds. In this, the Procellariidæ have been more consistent and uncompromising than the gulls, for most gulls have not become real oceanic birds but have filled another niche, that of the coastal fishers and scavengers. The main character of the gulls is lack of specialisation; they are many-sided and their organisation shows signs of compromise. On the one hand, they are not over-specialised gliding fliers like the shearwaters, which as a result have to crawl from their nesting places to the steep cliffs before they can take off. On the other hand, they are not over-specialised swimmers like divers, penguins, and the extinct Great Auk, nor are they purely walkers, like the Kiwi and Ostrich. Gulls walk, fly and swim equally well. In general, they do not venture far out from the coasts, although there are, in this respect, striking differences even between closely related species. Even the Herring Gull which is a more strictly coastal bird than its close relative the

Lesser Black-backed Gull (it is not the fault of this most elegant bird that it is blessed with such a name)—even the Herring Gull occasionally wanders far out into the ocean. Though no specialist, its skill in flying is sufficient to arouse admiration and, perhaps, envy. Recently a remarkable instance of its agility in flight was described. In a Guillemot colony at Bempton, Yorkshire, a Herring Gull was seen to steal a Guillemot's egg. While flying away with the egg in its bill, " it was beset by another Herring Gull, which so pestered the first that it released its booty. The second gull immediately stalled and with a rapid manœuvre seized the egg by its pointed end as it fell and flew off with it." The egg was still intact and was eventually consumed by the second gull. The whole manœuvre took place in a vertical distance of about 50 feet (Hazelwood, 1949).

Excellent fliers though they are, gulls are not specialised for any particular type of flight, nor for gliding like the albatrosses, nor for extremely fast flight like some falcons, nor for a quick take-off like the Magpie or Partridge, nor for quick turning like the Sparrow-Hawk and Goshawk, nor for hovering like so many small birds. Yet they can do all these things to some extent. Their wings have evolved somewhat in the direction of a glider's wing, having a long " arm," but in this respect they are far less extreme than the albatrosses.

The feet are webbed. But the adaptation to swimming has not gone so far as in divers, for the tarsi are scarcely compressed laterally. Like the webbed feet of geese, the feet of gulls are also well adapted for walking, and as a matter of fact, most of their foraging is done on foot.

Each toe has a sharp little claw, which can be bent downward at right angles. Probably these mobile claws are very useful on rocky coasts, but on the sandy shores of Holland the gulls could do very well without them, and, as the Dutch Herring Gulls are very much attached to their breeding colonies, returning to the same place year after year, this presence of claws which do not seem to be of any use to this population offers an interesting evolutionary problem.

The bill is strong, compressed at the sides, and long. It gives access to an enormous gut, so large in fact that when a gull opens its mouth, one can scarcely believe that there is more in a gull's neck than just this wide gut. The size of the food it can swallow is amazing; moles and rats are forced down whole.

Posturing

In a social species such as the Herring Gull, numerous movements of the individual are " understood " by its companions, who react to them in special ways. Some of these movements and postures are not difficult even for the human observer to appreciate, though the detection of most of them requires careful study. There are a multitude of very slight movements, most, if not all, of them characteristic of a special state of the bird. The student of behaviour is to a high degree dependent on his ability to see and interpret such movements. In the beginning, he will notice them unconsciously. For instance, he will know very well on a particular occasion that a certain gull is alarmed, without realising exactly how he knows it. Upon more conscious analysis of his own perception (an important element in behaviour study), he will notice that the alarmed gull has a long neck. Still later, he will see another sign, the flattening of the whole plumage, which makes the bird look thinner. Upon still closer study, he will see that the eye of an alarmed bird has a very special expression, due to the fact that it opens its eyes extremely wide. A study of the plates and text-figures will show some of these points.

In general, the movements playing a part in posturing are based on flattening or raising of the plumage as a whole, on eye movements and on the attitude of head, neck and wings. The various types of posturing will be discussed in later chapters, where an attempt will be made to understand their origin and their function. I will first consider voice as a means of affecting other individuals.

Voice

The voice of a Herring Gull is wonderfully melodious. Of course I am biased, but I think there is no finer bird-call than the clear, sturdy, resounding cries of the Herring Gulls, carried away by the wind along the wide beach or over the undulating dunes.

To what extent do these calls influence other individuals? As I hope to show, there is good reason to assume that most if not all calls have a communicative function.

Like many colonial birds, gulls are very vociferous. The tendency to make sounds is a curious one. What urges them to call? Our insight into these matters is only slight, though it is growing, and the less one knows, the longer it takes to explain what little one knows. Yet I will try to make clear what I think I know.

One often gets the impression that birds call when they are strongly activated by an internal urge, and yet cannot satisfy that urge by performing the activities to which it drives them. An aggressive bird, for instance, calls most noisily before or after a fight, but not during actual fighting. A hungry nestling calls most intensely before, not during feeding. A song-bird sings especially before it has a mate. Psychologists often say that calling indicates strong emotion. This is, I think, only part of the truth. The strong urge that drives a bird to action, and which is supposed to be accompanied by a strong emotion (a not improbable supposition based upon the fact that we humans feel strong emotions when under the influence of a powerful urge), does not always urge the bird to call; as a rule it does so only when there is, for one reason or another, no possibility of "venting" the urge in adequate movements. Calls are "outlets," through them an animal can "get rid" of impulses if there is no other way open. Sometimes there is action and calling at the same time, but this is always an indication that the action is not of the highest intensity, or that the drive is exceptionally strong.

Because of this, there is, in the life of birds, plenty of cause for calling. Further, many calls are typical of certain states of the calling bird, such as a sexually active state, or a state of readiness to feed young; and there has therefore been a social advantage in the development of selective responsiveness in individuals of the same species, such as the mate in the first case, the young in the second case. Exactly how this " understanding " of the calls of companions has originated, we do not know; but it is a fact that many calls elicit special responses in fellow-members of the same species, and the social advantage which this brings has probably been the cause of their differentiation and development. I hope the point will become clear in later chapters.

Not all species of birds are as vociferous as the Herring Gull. Especially in small birds, every call is a potential danger, as it may attract the attention of a predator. This is doubtless the reason why, through the action of natural selection, many species use their vocal powers only sparingly. The absence of loud calling is a feature of the behaviour of many small birds, especially in the nesting season. This is not immediately obvious, but one becomes aware of it when one notices that large and gregarious species, being less vulnerable than small and solitary birds, do not show any such inhibitions with regard to vocal expression.

Summing up, we get the following picture of the essence of vocal expression in birds: calls are an outlet of motor impulses, or, psychologically speaking, of emotions and related subjective phenomena. The development of a differentiated system of calls, notes, and song, is enhanced by the benefit that the species gets from it in the sphere of social co-operation. At the same time, noisiness tends to be suppressed because each call is dangerous. As always, natural selection has created, in the species that have managed to survive, a compromise, loud calls being preserved only when the resulting dangers are equalled by the benefits. This picture of the nature of vocal expression, gradually acquired through long study by many observers, fits very well with our observations on the Herring Gull.

Inventory of the calls

Here follows a list of the most common calls of the Herring Gull. At first, the variety of calls seems endless. This is due in part to the fact that the voices of the individual gulls differ so much. In part also it is due to the fact that an individual gull may utter the same call in various grades of intensity, and further that a bird may be in a complicated, blended or ambivalent state, and may utter calls more or less intermediate between two different calls, each indicative of a simpler state. Long and consistent watching enables one to see that there are certain basic calls.

The " call-note "

This call is a monosyllabic, moderately loud *keew* or *kleew*. I have not been able to connect it with any special instinctive state in the bird. It is heard at all times of the year, but much more often in the breeding season than in winter. Like many other calls, it is " contagious," i.e. when one bird calls, others do the same. The function of this call is not clear. Calls of this type are often considered to be a means by which social individuals keep in touch with each other, but the evidence for this in the case of the Herring Gull is nil. In other species, in tits for instance, there is evidence of this function : a bird separated from the flock will utter its call-notes persistently, and it will react to the call-notes of others.

The charge call

When a gull is attacking, or about to attack, a predator near the nest, a modification of the *keew* is heard, distinguishable by its loudness and its staccato character. I will call it the charge call. It is an expression of the readiness to attack a predator, and it instantly releases in the other gulls the same state.

The trumpeting call

The most elaborate call of the Herring Gull's repertoire is the multisyllabic call, named " the challenge " by Strong, and " trumpeting call " by Densing (1939). It can be heard all through the year, but its frequency and intensity increase strongly in early spring, and it is very frequent throughout the reproductive season, declining again in late summer. The trumpeting call consists of three phases. First, one or two low calls are given with the head stretched a little forward. Then, some subdued, high notes are forced out, the head being pointed down. Finally, the head is thrown upward with a jerk, and a final series of loud, resounding screams is given, during which the neck is stretched far forward and the mouth is opened wide. With each call, the body shakes; the bird is truly calling with its whole body. Each syllable is much like the basic *keew*; the trumpeting call therefore could be considered as a series of modified *keews*.

The mew call

This is another generalised call. It is a long-drawn note, produced with the neck stretched forward and sometimes downward and the bill usually opened very widely. The sound of this call very much reminds one of the human voice, and it has a wailing, " plaintive " character, but in the Herring Gull it has nothing to do with sadness; it indicates breeding activity with the emphasis on the friendly attitude toward mate, territory, nest and young. As I will show later, the young gull has an innate tendency to respond to it, especially when it is hungry, or when it is cold and needs brooding.

Choking

When the birds of a pair make a nest-scrape together, as will be described later, they make a queer rhythmical sound, something like *huoh-huoh-huoh-huoh*, during which the tongue bone is lowered, which gives the face a very curious expression. There are also pronounced movements of the breast in time with the calling. This sound and the accompanying movements are used not only in nest-building but also in aggressive situations, a fact missed by most authors on Herring Gull behaviour, and yet of great importance for an understanding of social relations. Noble, describing it in the American Laughing Gull, called it choking.

The alarm call

This is known to all who have visited a Herring Gull breeding colony. It is a hoarse, rhythmic *hahaha!—hahahaha!* This, like the charge call, is a reaction to a predator at the breeding place, but the emphasis is not on attack, but on flight. As a matter of fact, I have heard the same call three times in a situation where no predator was involved and where it was actually connected with escape. Two birds had had a prolonged fight, and one of them gave the other a thorough thrashing, so that we thought the results might be fatal. When the beaten bird finally managed to get out of its opponent's grip, it escaped, uttering the alarm call. This, together with the fact that gulls utter the charge call and not the alarm in the instant at which they are actually attacking man, shows that what I have called the alarm call is really expressing the tendency to escape. When a predator is on the breeding ground, the tendency of the gull to flee is always counteracted by a tendency to defend its nest, and that is why a gull calling the alarm-note does not normally fly away and alternates the alarm call and the charge cry.

Begging

At the beginning of the breeding season, the female is often fed by the male. This behaviour is begun by food-begging by the female, which is exactly similar to the food-begging of the grown-up young to his parents, though the sound uttered now has the clear ring of the adult voice and not the harsh, squeaking quality of the calls of the young. The soft, sweet-sounding *klee-ew* which I am calling the begging note, is also used by both sexes before coition.

The male's copulation note

During actual coition the male utters a rhythmic call, more or less intermediate in character between the choking and the alarm call. This is the only call which is exclusive to the male; all the other calls can be given by either sex.

Colour

Apart from its behaviour and its voice, an animal can influence other animals by its colour. For instance, some insects scare off predators by flashing conspicuous colours at

Plate 3a. Male in immature plumage: a bout of preening while guarding the nest

b. Female (*left*) begging for food from the male. Note the swelling in the male's neck

Plate 4a. One of the stretching movements: wing, foot, and half of the tail, all on one side

     b. The same movement in a half-grown chick

them, such as the so-called " eye-spots " used in defensive display
by the Eyed Hawk-moth and many other insects. During
experiments that I have carried out with these moths I have
seen Jays and Chaffinches jump high up in the air at such a
display, and avoid the moth from then on. Many birds, fish,
and other animals have conspicuous colours the only use of
which is to elicit a response in another member of the same
species, such as the sex partner, the young, or the social partner.
Thus the colour of the cere of a Budgerigar, which is blue in the
male and brown in the female, is the only characteristic by
which the bird can " recognise " the sex of a stranger. A male
Budgerigar tends to fight a newcomer with a blue cere, but it
courts a newcomer which has a brown cere. In such ways as
this, colour can act as a " social releaser " by releasing a response
in another individual just as a call often does.

Finally, many colour-patterns have the same negative effect
that stillness has in the domain of sound: they serve to conceal
the animal from predators. Whereas stillness is just absence of
sound, concealing coloration is an intricate specialisation, involving principles of patterning of a most refined kind, and also
corresponding behaviour.

Now, since the Herring Gull is a strikingly coloured bird,
with its silvery mantle, its snow-white head, neck, and body,
and its yellow bill with the bright vermilion colour-patch at the
tip of the lower mandible, it is well worth examining whether
any of these colours, or the pattern as a whole, have any function.
It may be added that the eggs and young have quite different
coloration, and *a priori* it would be hard to believe that none of
these patterns had any function.

As I hope to show in Chapter 22, there is experimental proof
of the releaser function of the red patch on the lower mandible
of the adult Herring Gull. Further, circumstantial evidence
scarcely leaves room for doubt concerning the cryptic (concealing)
function of the colour of eggs and chicks, although in this case
there is no experimental proof.

Several principles are involved in the cryptic coloration of
the eggs and the chicks which are also well known for many

other cases of cryptic coloration. First, there is a general resemblance in their colour to the colour of the background. The eggs are brownish or olive-green; the young are more khaki-coloured. In any cryptically coloured animal, the general resemblance to the background has always to be a kind of *passe-partout*, because it has been selected in relation to a variety of backgrounds. Except for animals that confine themselves to very special backgrounds, as for instance a caterpillar associated with one particular species of food-plant, the colour resemblance is very generalised, just as the cryptic colour of the infantry soldier is generalised and fits the background only in a general way. Just as the eggs of the Herring Gull have a different colour from that of the young, so the British army puts its faith in khaki while the German army specialised in " Feldgrau," really a bluish green; differences that cannot be accounted for exclusively by differences in background.

Apart from their general resemblance in colour to the background, both eggs and chicks show disruptive coloration, i.e. a pattern of boldly contrasting patches which tend to draw the eye's attention away from the body outline. This type reaches a high degree of perfection in the young. In addition, the young are beautifully countershaded, that is, they are light underneath, which tends to counteract the effect of shadow, the often treacherous companion of light.

As always, cryptic coloration is associated with cryptic behaviour. As I hope to show in later chapters, cryptic behaviour is interesting and highly specialised in the Herring Gull.

On the other hand, the function of the mature Herring Gull's white-and-silvery plumage is quite uncertain. Two suggestions have recently been put forward. Since white has proved to be the most efficient concealing coloration for aircraft on anti-submarine patrol, Craik (1944) considers that the white colour of so many gulls may likewise be cryptic, helping them to approach fish unseen. Whereas, in the case of the submarine, the white colour of the " predator " could be effective only at a long distance, in the case of gulls and fish it might be effective at a much shorter distance, because, first, fish have a very restricted horizon owing to the total reflection of the water's surface, and second, their image of what is in the air is very much blurred owing (1) to the structure of their eyes, which are adapted to short-range vision under water, and (2) to surface rippling.

Craik's view has received criticism from both physicists and ornithologists (Pirenne & Crombie 1944, Armstrong 1944, 1946). In my opinion the criticism is not very convincing and, like Craik's contribution, should be regarded as speculative. Armstrong (1946) has put forward an alternative theory,[1] in which he suggests that the white colour, far from being adapted to inconspicuousness, is an adaptation toward conspicuousness! According to Armstrong, the white colour has value in enabling the gulls to see each other from a great distance, and, since they are dependent on food which has a " patchy " distribution, such as a shoal of fish, and since they usually keep a close watch on each other's movements, their colour would facilitate gathering of large numbers in places where food is momentarily abundant. Armstrong writes that " since formulating this theory I have paid particular attention to the visibility of gulls and have noted that, looking over the sea from a slight eminence corresponding to the height at which gulls commonly fly, and against a distant coast line or sea horizon, they are visible at great distances." (1946, p. 17.)

I do not believe that the Darwin-Armstrong view is correct. While of course we really want to know how gulls react to their comrades' colour, and not how we react to it, in the present state of knowledge our own reactions carry some weight, especially as we know that the visual powers of gulls are very much like our own. The point at issue, however, is not whether gulls are visible from a great distance, but whether such white birds are visible from a greater distance than differently coloured birds. I have spent a considerable time in bird-watching along the

[1] James Fisher calls my attention to the fact that Darwin has formulated the same theory in his *Descent of Man*. Darwin says that by the white colour " males and females could find each other much more easily " and that it might " guide other birds of the same and other species to the prey." (2nd edition, 1890, p. 493.) Darwin applies this to both white and black seabirds though, as distinct from grey birds.

sea shore, and I have the opposite impression to that of Armstrong concerning the relative visibility of white and darker birds, under average conditions. Of course, light conditions vary enormously, and it makes all the difference whether the weather is dull or bright, the position of the bird relative to the sun, and the conditions of the clouds and of the water surface are also of great influence, but I think most bird-watchers of the sea-shore would agree that a crow, a black duck such as a scoter, and even an immature gull, can usually be seen from a much greater distance than white gulls. This, of course, was also the view of the aircraft designer.

As long as it is not settled whether the adult gull's plumage is cryptic or conspicuous, it is rather futile to discuss what function the alleged conspicuousness or inconspicuousness might have. In order to test Craik's hypothesis, which I believe to be correct, experiments will have to be carried out with fish, and the range at which they show escape reactions to objects approaching in the air above them must be studied statistically, for objects of various colours under variable light conditions.

CHAPTER 3

THE SENSE ORGANS

General Remarks

Relatively little is known about the capacities of the sense-organs of the Herring Gull. As in most other birds, its main sense-organs are the eyes and the ears. This, incidentally, is one of the chief reasons why we can understand the behaviour of birds better than that of most other animals, including even our closer relatives the mammals. Our sensory equipment is similar to that of most birds, whereas most other animals have a better developed sense of smell, or of touch, often combined with a poor development of visual or auditory senses. We definitely have great difficulties in understanding animals of the latter type.

Although our knowledge of the sensory capacities of the Herring Gull is slight, we do know something. Also, the apparent general similarity in the sense-organs of most birds justifies us in thinking that much of what applies to birds in general probably applies also to the Herring Gull.

Vision

The capacities of birds' eyes have a bearing upon their behaviour in several respects. First, their visible spectrum interests us. Luckily, they do not seem to be able to see more than we, either on the ultra-violet or on the infra-red side of the spectrum. If they did, we would often be puzzled by their behaviour, as we are in the case of honey-bees, which can react to the ultra-violet colours of flowers, a kind of light which we cannot see at all—let alone distinguish it as a special colour from others. There have been reports that some birds, notably owls, can see infra-red, but later work has shown that this was not true, and in the Little Owl, the sensitivity to the red end of the spectrum is even less than in man (Meyknecht, 1940).

Another problem is the quantitative limitation of vision. What are the lowest light intensities at which a bird can see? Here again, no work has been done on the Herring Gull, but casual observation shows that it has about the same powers of adaptation to low light intensities as man. In this connection, the owls form a true exception as they are able to see and to catch their prey at very low intensities (Dice, 1945).

Apart from these two problems of sensitivity, problems of discrimination interest us. It is clear that birds can distinguish between different shades, but can they distinguish between different colours as well? As we will see later (Chapter 22) we know that a Herring Gull can at least see red as a colour, that is to say, it can distinguish it from any other colour of the same intensity. The power of colour discrimination can easily be tested. The only thing one has to do is to discover a reaction of the bird that is selectively released by a special colour, and then to find out whether the influence of the colour is independent of the intensity. In practice, this is done by presenting the animal with a great number of objects which are identical except for colour and shade, for instance, a finely graded series of grey objects ranging from black to white, and a series of differently coloured objects of the same shape. If the animal reacts selectively to one colour, it is, if certain precautions are taken, proof of colour-discrimination. If the animal does not show an innate reaction to coloured objects, it is often possible to train it to respond to a coloured object, for instance to a food-jar. In this way it has been proved, for instance, that Song Thrush, Sparrow, Jay, and Little Owl can distinguish a number of colours (see Van Eck, 1939; Meyknecht, 1940). The case of the Little Owl is specially interesting, because this species has little need to distinguish colours in nature. Song Thrushes react in nature to brightly coloured berries, and to the orange-coloured mouth of the young. Jays possibly react to the bright blue wing-patch of their species. Many nestlings have a brightly coloured mouth too. In all these species, the bright colour-patterns concerned could not have been developed without the species having a colour sense. But why do Little Owls need a colour sense ? I think the solution is probably that in birds the power of colour-discrimination is a rather old acquisition, of which the species may make use or not. In other words, the colour sense was evolved first, and coloured structures with signal function have developed as adaptations to various needs. If so, we may reasonably expect most birds to be able to distinguish between colours. Yet it would be good to test this point further in the Herring Gull.

The third great problem of sensory capacity of especial interest to the behaviour student is the power of localisation. In the eye, this means the visual acuity, or the smallest angle at which two objects can be seen separately without their fusing into one. Again, no experiments have been done with the Herring Gull, but there is some evidence that most birds have sharper eyesight than man. Thus of the Hobby it has been stated that the distance at which it can see a dragon-fly (on which it preys) is about twice the distance at which we see it. The visual acuity of the Hobby has been calculated as being less than 21 seconds: that is to say it can distinguish two objects provided that they subtend an angle of at least 21 seconds (Schuyl, Tinbergen and Tinbergen, 1936). For the average man, provided he has no real eye defects, this angle is between 35 and 40 seconds. In addition, as every field watcher will agree, birds often show an amazing ability to spot other birds high up in the air. It would be very worth while to study this problem more thoroughly than has so far been done.

The problem of visual acuity involves the analytical cap-acity of the eye. But in the life of an animal such an analytical capacity would be of very little value if not combined with a synthetical capacity. The sense-cells in the retina are the units of vision: each of them provides one local stimulus, one little dot of the visual field. The separate dots are united into systems, and this capacity enables an animal to see forms, and to distinguish between them. This ability to recognise forms is most puzzling;

in fact, it is not merely a function of the eye, but of the visual part of the central nervous system as well. It is in this respect that birds seem to excel, for many observations show that they have astonishing powers of recognition of individuals, which must be based at least in part upon form-discrimination of a very high standard. In Chapters 8, 11 and 24 some evidence will be given for this. That evidence is all based on field observations, which, it is true, are reliable enough, but do not permit of a thorough analysis. A critical study of the form-vision of birds, with special attention to the maximum achievements of which they are capable, is another desideratum of bird ethology.

To conclude, the evidence, though scattered and fragmentary, indicates that in the Herring Gull we have to do with very highly developed eyes, sensitive to a range very similar to our own, capable of distinguishing between colours as well as we do, and having a visual acuity probably surpassing ours, combined with an amazing capacity of distinguishing between forms. As a matter of fact, the bird student investigating a new species has to be prepared for behaviour traits based on a power of visual discrimination well beyond his own. *Un homme avis en vaut deux!*

Hearing

Concerning the other important sense-organ, the ear, much less is known, in spite of the fact that calls and song play a vital part in the community of so many birds. Apart from the owls, which have ears specially adapted for great sensitivity (Räber, 1949) as well as for sound location (Pumphrey, 1948), most birds seem to have about the same auditory capacities as man, although, according to Engelmann's work on the domestic fowl (1928), their location of sound might be poor. During my field studies of the Snow Bunting (1939), I found some striking cases of sound localisation, making me feel rather inferior to the bird, but in Herring Gulls I found no indication of a hearing capacity surpassing my own, which, incidentally, is not exceptionally good. One thing is certain: Herring Gulls hear very well, and even newly hatched chicks react selectively to the parents' calls.

Chemical senses

About the chemical senses of birds little is known. We do know that they can taste; Strong (1914) reports that they have a dislike of highly salted fish. The existence of a sense of smell in birds has been much disputed. Anatomical studies have revealed that most birds have a poorly developed olfactory sensory tissue, although there are some specialised forms, such as the Kiwi, in which it is fairly well developed. The experiments thus far done have given contradictory results. Zahn (1933) using the training method, reported positive results with a number of birds, the best performers, ducks, showing a degree of scent discrimination about equal to that of ourselves—which is admittedly rather poor. On the other hand, Walter (1943) by a variety of methods, succeeded only once in establishing a conditioned reaction to scent. This was in Budgerigars. When, however, as a final control, he severed the olfactory nerves of his birds after the conditioned reaction had been firmly established the birds, much to his surprise, continued to react positively! This showed that their apparent positive reaction must have been due to some secondary clue which the experimenter did not notice. The issue is therefore undecided.

If birds have a sense of smell it cannot be of much significance or else it would certainly be easier to train them to smells. Therefore the problem is, for our present purpose, rather academic. I have never seen any reaction to smell in the Herring Gull. Smell certainly does not help the bird, as it does so many mammals, to detect predators. When an observer, concealed in a hide, takes care not to give visual or auditory stimuli, a gull will never show any response to his presence, even if it is standing down wind at less than a foot's distance, and even if the observer is smoking like a chimney. There is not a single indication that any of the social reactions of the Herring Gull are released or guided by smell.

Touch

Finally, gulls have a sense of touch. This plays a part, for instance, in incubation, for a gull feels whether its eggs are fitting smoothly under it. It may also play a part in fighting, for on the few occasions on which I saw a gull fly in panic from another gull, this was preceded by a thorough beating. Further, tactile stimuli certainly play a part in copulation, but on the whole our knowledge about the sense of touch is exceedingly meagre.

Other senses

Do birds have other sense-organs than such as are known to exist in man or other animals? There is some uncertainty about this. The amazing capacity of migratory birds to orient themselves on both spring and autumn migration routes is still unexplained. Also many birds, and especially the migratory species, show a remarkable homing capacity even when they are transported away from their breeding place over hundreds of miles. The problem is being attacked experimentally now from various angles both in the field and in the laboratory. It would carry me too far to give a review of the many interesting studies which have appeared in the last fifteen, and especially in the last five years. The collected evidence is still insufficient to draw firm conclusions, in spite of the great amount of work involved. In short, it is now known that several migratory species are able to fly home in a relatively short time from territory they have never visited before (Rüppell, 1936–1944 and others). Non-migratory species do not usually show this tendency and capacity (Rüppell, 1940; Creutz, 1949). If migrants caught halfway along their migration route, or right at its start, are transported laterally from their line of flight and released, this often results in migration parallel to the natural route (Rüppell, 1946; Schüz, 1949). Particularly the young, inexperienced birds behave in this way; older birds seem to correct sideways displacement. Caged migrants show a tendency to fly in a constant direction (Kramer, 1949); Starlings could be made to change their direction by changing the direction of the sunlight with mirrors (Kramer, 1951). Attempts to train captive birds to choose a fixed direction when expecting food have failed (Dijkgraaf, 1946), except when the sun or a lamp was offered as a beacon (Kramer, 1952). Explanatory hypotheses have often involved magnetic clues (Yeagley, 1937). An ingenious theory assumes a response of the semicircular canals to the Coriolis force (Ising, 1945). No reliable experimental evidence has thus far supported these theories involving unknown sense-organs. Much can be said in favour of random searching in homing birds (Griffin, 1944; Heinroth & Heinroth, 1941) and the learning of landmarks certainly plays a part in some species in which the young travel with the parents, but it seems doubtful whether all cases of migration can be explained on the bases of known senses. Much new evidence can be expected in the next decade; it is certainly intriguing that recently evidence has been brought forward that birds react to radar beams (Drost, 1949; but see also Schwartzkopff, 1950). Goethe (1937) and Griffin (1943) have reported on homing experiments with Herring Gulls. Goethe reports remarkably fast homing flights by breeding birds taken from Memmert and released as far inland as Berlin (445 km.) and Detmold (240 km.). He points out that Herring Gulls are very good objects for such homing tests because they do not suffer much in transport. Griffin's work is more extensive. Whereas Goethe used 24 birds, Griffin transported 176 gulls. Also, Griffin took them over longer distances, the maximum distance being 872 miles (1403 km.). Further, 25 of his gulls were watched after release and followed in a small airplane. The results are not decisive. Of six birds carried 872 miles inland, to an area which it is extremely improbable they had ever seen before, four returned. But this does not necessarily prove the existence of a " sense of direction", because these birds, breeding on the American coast, may have had considerable experience in areas closer to the sea, teaching them that, in general, the coast lies between south and east of wherever they are when they come inland. The observations of the birds when released showed that they scattered in all directions. Those choosing the right direction at the start were by no means the first to arrive back at the breeding place. Further, several gulls were transported on two occasions to the same release point. Of these nine birds, three were transported over a considerable distance (230 miles = 370 km.); on the first occasion, in 1940, they were quite slow to return, taking 10 days, $4\frac{1}{2}$ days and 6 days respectively, but in 1941 these same individuals came back in 29, 48 and 19 hours respectively. These facts suggest that learning must come into the picture.

The problem appears to be very complicated, even in the Herring Gull, which, being a non-migratory species at least in most parts of its range, may be expected to have less well-developed orientation capacities than migrant birds like the Starling or the Swallow. The question remains open whether birds, or some birds, have organs for the reception of types of energy which we cannot receive, and as long as decisive experimental work is still lacking, it would seem wise to keep an open mind.

CHAPTER 4

NON-REPRODUCTIVE BEHAVIOUR

Foraging

Outside the breeding season, the Herring Gull divides its time among relatively few activities: foraging, preening, sleeping or resting, migration, and, occasionally, escaping from predators. Yet this does not at all mean that its behaviour is monotonous at this time; on the contrary, watching them brings always the excitement of seeing something new. The feeding methods are especially fascinating, because they are so immensely diverse. Not only are there special methods for special types of prey, but the method employed for a particular prey species may be varied according to the general conditions under which it is hunted. Some of these conditions are relatively rare, and thus it occurs that a hunting method, such as, for instance, diving in the manner of a tern, may only be seen occasionally, but when it is observed, great numbers of gulls may be using it. Further, it is remarkable how differently different populations of Herring Gulls behave. The gulls for instance which breed near Wassenaar use earthworms as a staple diet, whereas the gulls of Terschelling rarely if ever eat worms. On the other hand, the gulls of most colonies of the Frisian islands are reported to be terrible predators on eggs and chicks of other birds, including their own species, but in Wassenaar this is only an insignificant, occasional way of finding a living.

The gulls feed most commonly, perhaps, by walking along the edge of the water, their feet only just wetted by it. The gulls feed wherever the sea has washed great quantities of molluscs or starfish ashore, and often collect high up the beach near high tide mark. In Holland, the farmers who cultivate the sandy dune valleys occasionally use starfish as a fertiliser, and carry them by cart-loads to their tiny plots. It is reported that the gulls sometimes follow these carts and liquidate whole loads of starfish in a short time (Verwey, 1928).

Carrion is also to the gulls' taste, though I have the impression that they take to dead seals, whales, porpoises or birds only in an emergency. Their difficulty with the sea-mammals is in getting through the skin. After westerly gales, it is not uncommon to see a group of Herring Gulls and Great Black-backed Gulls gathered round a dead porpoise, noisily quarrelling on priority issues. Usually the Great Black-backs keep the Herring Gulls at a respectful distance, and when they leave, there is much threatening and intimidation among the latter, until one or more new tyrants take possession of the carcase.

During the unusually cold winters of 1928-29, 1939-40, 1940-41 and 1946-47, when the Dutch North Sea shores were sometimes littered with dead and dying Oystercatchers, Curlews, and Ducks, the Herring Gulls were sometimes seen to attack them before they died, and kill them. This same habit is more developed in the Great Black-backed Gull, and many observations concerning it are found scattered in the literature. I saw two particularly striking cases myself which I think are worth putting on record. On one occasion in October my friend G. F. Makkink and I saw a Peregrine Falcon seize a Teal from a flock above the mud flats at the Hook of Holland. When it sailed down with the struggling Teal in its talons, a Great Black-backed Gull appeared and chased it away, immediately attacking the Teal itself by hacking vigorously at it. It was seen to tear the Teal's abdomen open and actually pulled at the viscera while the Teal was still struggling to get away. On another occasion I watched a flock of Sandwich Terns on the beach. Among them was a Great Black-backed Gull, apparently quiet, and not avoided by the terns all around it. All at once the gull gave some violent pecks at a tern close by, whereupon the whole flock flew up except the attacked tern. Before I had reached the gull, the tern was dead, and part of the breast had been eaten. The latter observation is not typical I think, for usually gulls begin with the viscera and not with the muscle, being poorly adapted as predators.

One gets a fair idea of the diversity of prey that a Herring Gull may take by watching the birds bringing food to their young or to their mates at the breeding places. In summer the food consists mainly of fish, at least in Wassenaar and Terschelling, and also, especially during rough weather, of crabs. But they also bring home larger prey: Rats, moles, young rabbits, young birds, and even young cats. Whereas we know that they kill young birds and young rabbits themselves, I am not so sure about how they get rats. I never heard of anyone having actually seen a Herring Gull kill a rat, and I rather suspect that the Wassenaar gulls pick them up dead in the town of Leiden. At least fifty pairs from this colony forage regularly in the Leiden canals, where they pick up all kinds of refuse. I think that this is also the place where they get young cats, which have perhaps been drowned by their owners; it is amazing, when one tries to look at the canals with a Herring Gull's eyes, to see how well supplied they are.

Moles are almost certainly caught alive and killed by the gulls. Once I observed, from a distance, a Herring Gull pecking vigorously at what I thought was a struggling mole; anyhow it was a mammal of that size. After a number of violent pecks it swallowed its prey and flew off, twisting and stretching its neck in a most curious way, as if the mole were still " wriggling and wriggling and wriggling inside her."

Rabbit-hunting is a regular feature in the Dutch North Sea sand dunes. Verwey describes (1928) how he saw a Herring Gull hover above a thornbush, alight and dash into it, wildly pecking at something inside. A young rabbit rushed out into the open, whereupon the gull immediately started pursuing it from the air, swooping down on it again and again, until the rabbit had reached another bush. The gull then stopped in the air, hovering above the rabbit, and gradually descended lower and lower, until the rabbit ran out again, immediately followed by the gull. However, it managed to reach cover again before the gull could get it. The latter then left it alone and continued its hovering inspection flight in another direction, flying systematically from one bush to the next.

I have likewise seen Herring Gulls hover above rabbit holes along a slope facing north, when a north wind caused an updraught which enabled the birds to hang motionless in the air for many minutes with only an occasional wing beat. They were watching the holes and were seen to dive down as soon as a rabbit appeared at the entrance. However, I did not see them actually capture a rabbit, although the Wassenaar gulls regularly carried young rabbits to their nests.

A special habit of the Herring Gull and several of the other gulls is that of preying upon eggs and young of other birds. In some colonies, notably the overpopulated ones of the Frisian Isles, this is so widespread that it has endangered the existence of many other species nesting in the open, such as Common Terns, many waders and some ducks. Ducks are usually preyed upon when they are disturbed by man and leave their nests in a hurry without covering the eggs with down, or, more frequently still, when they are leading their downy young. This habit of the Herring Gulls has created quite a problem and is causing a headache to the bird protection societies. I will return to this problem in Chapter 20, where I will also discuss the repulsive but curious phenomenon of the Herring Gull preying on the young of its own species.

As scavengers, the gulls come to harbours and towns, where they devour refuse, often of the most appalling kind. More rarely the gulls feed in flight. This is done on special occasions, usually when there is a strong wind, which facilitates their hovering in the air over one spot, keeping their balance by treading the water. Also, they follow fishing-boats and pick up whatever small fish are thrown overboard. If the prey is large or hard, they take it back to the beach and, keeping it in the bill, knock it against the ground, or, by hammering upon it, break the skeleton. The function of these movements is not to cut the prey up into smaller pieces, but merely to break its rigidity so that it becomes flexible and can be swallowed more easily.

The Herring Gull has a fascinating reaction to hard shellfish

FIG. 1

Immature bird " shell-smashing "

and other hard objects.   A gull will take a cockle in its bill, fly
up steeply and drop its prey, then dive after it to pick it up immediately after it has touched the ground.   This habit is also known
in vultures and crows, where it must have evolved independently.
It does not work very well on the sandy coasts where I have
studied gulls.   There are various parts of these coasts where
artificial stone dams have been built to keep the tidal current
away from the shore, but the gulls apparently never learn to
drop their shells here, nor do they seem to learn not to drop the
shells above the water.   A gull may be seen to drop a shell again
and again on the soft sand or in the water, only to discover upon
inspection that it is still unbroken, which stimulates the bird to
renewed activity.   Once I observed an immature gull dropping
a shell into shallow water thirty-nine times in succession.

    There are numerous reports about this peculiar behaviour
in the literature.   Oldham (1930) for instance saw Herring Gulls
dive in the shallow coastal water in order to catch hermit crabs,
inhabiting whelk shells of about 8 cm. in length.   The gulls
then flew to the beach, walked three or four yards up the beach,
and then flew up into the air and dropped the shells.   They
exerted some kind of choice, for they never dropped the shells
in the sea, but otherwise, as Oldham states explicitly, they made
no distinction between dropping them on pebbles or soft sandy
soil.   The shells often had to be dropped more than once, up to
ten times.   On another occasion Oldham saw a Herring Gull
capture a shore crab and drop it in shallow water.   This was
repeated twice more, by which time the gull had been passively
drifted by the wind from above the water to above the land,
where it dropped the crab a fourth time and finally succeeded
in crushing it.

    I have observed the same inefficiency in a Carrion Crow,
which, though alongside the pier at the Hook of Holland,
dropped a shellfish a number of times on the mud.   However,
on other occasions I have seen evidence to suggest that Hooded
Crows can learn that shells should be dropped on something
hard.   During the spring-cleaning of the canals in the Dutch
polders, numerous freshwater mussels are usually hauled up

among the water weeds. Once, on a road alongside such a canal, I watched Hooded Crows picking up the mussels and dropping them on the road. As a result of their activities, the road was just littered with broken shells, and from the behaviour of the crows as long as I watched them, I could not but conclude that they had concentrated their " bombing " on the road.

Oldham cites an observation by B. Lloyd, who " has often seen foraging Carrion Crows capture whelks and other molluscs on some tangle-covered rocks in the estuary at Newport, carry them to a patch of shingle 50 yards away, and let them fall there." Oldham mentions a similar observation by Patterson, who observed that crows usually carry hard prey up from the mud flats to a shingle-covered beach; when, however, the flats were covered with ice, the crows dropped the shells there and did not go to the stone-faced beach. It seems therefore that crows show more intelligence in this matter than gulls, which is not surprising in view of what is known about the high level of intelligence displayed by crows and ravens in other respects. The learning process involved is probably not of a very high type. As the crows confined themselves to hard soil in only some of the observed instances, it seems likely that a rather slow conditioning process is involved, and not a flashlike " insight " into the significance of the hardness of the soil.

It is striking that this reaction of dropping shells is nearly always released by prey of a very hard texture. I know of only one instance in which a gull was seen dropping something soft. Harber & Johns (1943) report that they saw a Great Black-backed Gull drop a rat from a height of about 20 feet into a field, and then make several unsuccessful attempts to swallow it. A few minutes later it took the rat up again and in all it let it fall six times, and, after that, was still unable to swallow it. James Fisher writes me that " Greater Black-backed Gulls dropped Pinkfoot-eggs in Iceland. They could not distinguish between bog and hard ground, and sometimes lost their eggs in a bog."

By sheer luck I once observed an unintentional experiment which showed that the gull's response is influenced by the hardness of the prey. In the course of experiments designed to study the reactions of gulls to eggs shortly before the onset of incubation, in which we used wooden imitation eggs, a gull that happened to be uninterested in incubation approached our egg dummy and delivered a vigorous peck at it. It received a considerable shock from the hard egg, jumped up, spreading its wings, then took the egg in its bill, flew up, and dropped it to the ground! Of course it was in this case unsuccessful, for the soil was sandy and covered with vegetation. This, by the way, was one of those wonderful strokes of luck with which most bird-watchers will be familiar. Nature often carries out experiments in front of one, and the only thing one has to do is to be on the alert, to appreciate the significance of what is seen and to cash in on the result.

The significance of hardness as a releasing stimulus in this behaviour is also suggested by the following amusing incident, reported by H. A. Bayliss (1949). I quote his report verbally: " During the autumn and winter of 1947-48 some concern was caused at a certain West London factory by the frequent breaking of windows and skylights. The missiles picked up after these incidents were nuts, bolts and various small pieces of scrap iron, usually weighing about 2 oz. ' Sabotage ' was suspected, and a watch was kept, when the culprits were discovered to be gulls. It appears that a gull would swoop down to the ground, pick up a missile, and then deliberately flew up above the glass roof and dropped it on to a pane of glass. I personally interviewed the safety officer of the factory, who informed me that he himself and various other persons employed in the factory had actually witnessed this behaviour on several occasions. The birds were believed to be Black-headed Gulls, of which many frequent the buildings . . . at least one Common Gull was also seen. The breakage ceased when the gulls left in the spring.

" It seems possible that the birds may have been hopefully treating these indigestible articles as shellfish, which several species of gulls are known to be in the habit of dropping from a height when unable to open them."

Another special reaction, occasionally shown by all Herring

Gulls, and certainly innate, is "paddling." A good description has been given by Walker (1949): "The body remained remarkably still, but the feet and tarsi moved up and down quite quickly—at a guess I should say four beats per second. The head was moved rhythmically from side to side as if the bird was watching for something which might appear on the ground. Nothing, however, was picked up while the bird was being watched." In paddling, the legs are lifted alternately. The birds at the Wassenaar colony, where I did most of my watching, regularly feed in the meadows just inside the coastal dunes and they spend much time there in paddling. In this way they bring earthworms to the surface, and, as I have already mentioned, much of their food consists of worms.

In the literature there has been some confusion about the function of this reaction. Commenting upon Walker's observation, the Editor of *British Birds* remarks: "The habit of course is well known on the shore, where it appears to be effective in bringing worms to the surface." Portielje, in his admirable study of the Herring Gull's behaviour (1928), is even more definite and states that *Arenicola marina* and *Echiurus pallasii* are the worms that are brought to the surface by paddling.

My own observations do not confirm this. Although I saw other species of gulls, viz., Black-headed Gulls and Common Gulls, paddle on (muddy) shores, I never saw the Herring Gull do it anywhere else than in the meadows. This may be just a gap in my observations. What I have seen in other gulls has, however, convinced me that paddling has two different functions. One is the bringing up of earthworms, which seem to have an innate reaction to the quivering of the soil which is of value, enabling them to escape from their arch-enemy, the mole. (As Dr. G. P. Wells informs me, it seems that this reaction is found only in certain species of earthworms, viz. *Allolobophora*, and not in *Lumbricus*.) Secondly, however, when I have observed paddling in Black-headed Gulls on the sea-shore, it was always done in shallow and muddy pools of water. Here the function is, it seems to me, to whirl up the small animals lying on or in the mud, so as to make them visible by making them move. An

H.G.W.

D

analogous type of behaviour is seen of Phalaropes in their northern breeding haunts when the mosquito larvæ upon which they prey are hanging motionless in the water. The Phalaropes do not paddle, but " pirouette " round in a circle centred on one leg, watching the water below, and picking up the black larvæ whirled up by the movement (Tinbergen, 1935). Another analogous case is related by Verwey (1949) of the cuttlefish, *Sepia officinalis*. When it is hunting shrimps, which are not only cryptic but bury themselves in the sand, *Sepia* swims slowly just above the bottom, and through its funnel directs gentle jets of water on to the sand just in front of it. When such a jet hits a shrimp, it is partly exposed because the sand round it is whirled up. The shrimp reacts by covering itself up again with a movement of the antennæ, and this movement is detected and the shrimp is seized.

The paddling of gulls on the sea-shore could not possibly, in my opinion, have the function of forcing worms to the surface because, so far as I know, no marine worm on our coasts has this particular reaction of escaping to the surface upon disturbance. There are no moles in the intertidal zone, and if the earthworms' reaction is really an adaptation to escape the mole, the absence of a similar reaction in animals of the intertidal zone is not surprising. But the possibility remains open that in some other part of the Herring Gull's range there may be shore animals which react as earthworms do on land, and that the paddling behaviour of gulls is adapted to catching these hypothetical animals, but has been retained in that part of the range where they are absent; much as the claws on the toes are also found in Dutch gulls that probably have little use for them. It would be worth while to collect more data on this problem.

The paddling of gulls on grass has an interesting analogy among some other birds. Lapwings, and other plovers force worms up to the surface by making trembling movements with one leg only (Portielje, 1927). This leg is stretched obliquely forward and is rapidly quivered. I have never seen Lapwings perform this action on the mud-flats on the coast, but only on the meadows. This, incidentally, is an example of how the comparative study of animals, usually undertaken only in order to trace out homologies, can also be used for finding analogies and thereby helps in interpreting the biological significance of particular behaviour patterns.

The paddling of gulls is certainly innate and not acquired by experience. Portielje (1928) reports that young gulls often paddle in the Zoo. However, these young gulls paddled even when standing on dry sand. It is possible therefore that this was just a kind of "vacuum activity" due to the accumulation of the urge to paddle, which could not find its normal outlet as no wet soil was available. Another possibility is that paddling is really done by young birds on any type of soil (maybe even on the sea-shore) but that they later learn to do it only where the paddling meets with success, i.e. in meadows.

Portielje has also observed paddling in various other species, not only in the Black-headed Gull but also in Woodcock, Flamingo, Shelduck, Bar-headed Goose (*Anser indicus*), and in several herons. Swans and ducks are known to paddle in shallow water, and an observation by Heinroth (1911) shows how "stupidly" birds sometimes behave when the "correct" stimulus occurs in the "wrong" situation: one of his swans started to paddle in a film of water covering the ice in one of the ponds of the Zoo. Portielje relates an amusing incident suggesting that the reaction is entirely innate in ducks: young Mallard ducklings kept in the Zoo began to paddle immediately when they stepped inadvertently on wet bread in the food cup. Heinroth, again, observed that very young Woodcock raised in isolation from the parents began to paddle on the peat floor of their cage.

It would be interesting to know whether all this paddling of birds is aimed at earthworms. I rather doubt it, for, if it is, earthworms would seem to have many more predators above than below the surface and it would seem strange that the mole should force the worms to escape to a still more dangerous place. One really does not know which creature is the most interesting in this connection, the worm, the bird, or the mole!

Diving for food is seen only occasionally, but whenever I saw it, many gulls were engaged in it simultaneously. Hence the reaction is evidently part of the behaviour pattern of the species but its occurrence depends on special conditions which occur only rarely. The birds fly some feet above the surface of the water and then plunge down into it, often leaving only the extreme tips of the wings visible. Sometimes the gulls may start diving when swimming, and they may then fly up only a foot or so before diving. This occurs only when the quarry is swimming very close to the surface but yet out of reach of the swimming bird. The gulls are, to quote Haviland (1915), " as buoyant as a ping-pong ball," and the whole performance lacks the touch of expertness that characterises the analogous (and doubtless homologous) diving of terns. Yet when the depth at which their prey is swimming necessitates it, they may make quite deep plunges. Knight (cited by Bent, 1921) saw them " plunge with force into the water, quickly rising to the surface as a usual thing, though on at least one occasion a bird was out of sight so long that I had grave fears that it would be carried under the ice by the swift current, but it finally emerged at the edge of the ice and took wing with an unusually large tomcod." Complete submergence has also been observed by other writers, e.g. by Cunnings (1914). Steiniger has observed (1952) that Herring Gulls sometimes dive down from a height of 2 metres and then submerge completely after the manner of terns. He could even see that once under water they made one upstroke with the wings, and could then reach mussels that were two feet below the surface.

Diving is known also of several other species of gulls. I have seen Black-headed and Iceland Gulls do it, and Brown (1940) reports it of the Glaucous Gull. In East Greenland, the Eskimos of Angmagssalik have developed an unique method for capturing Iceland Gulls by releasing this very response. A piece of wood is weighted with a stone at one end so as to keep it floating just below the surface. At the lower end is fastened some seal blubber which acts as bait. At the top end, just below the surface, four snares are attached to

b. The same movement in a half-grown chick

Plate 5a. Preening the plumage of the neck

Plate 6. If the photographer behaves, the birds get used to him

the wood. These snares are ingeniously made of the shafts of a Raven's primaries and are placed in a horizontal position, together covering a circle around the wood. The efficiency of this trap seems to depend on the length of the wood, in other words, on the distance of the bait from the surface, and this confirms the impression one gets from field observations, viz. that the diving of gulls is released by prey swimming at too great a depth to be reached by any other method, and yet not so deep that it is entirely inaccessible.

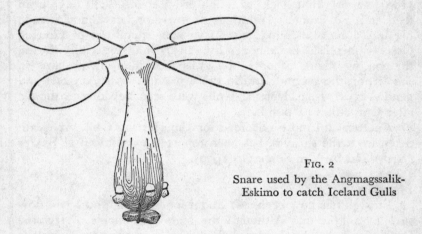

FIG. 2

Snare used by the Angmagssalik-
Eskimo to catch Iceland Gulls

Another side of the Herring Gull's character, developed into a primary method of food-getting by the related skuas, is the chasing of other birds in order to catch the prey which they have taken. The Herring Gull does this on the wing, and chases both other members of its own species and also smaller gulls or terns. I have never seen one consistently parasitising Lapwings or diving ducks, as Black-headed Gulls do. The latter, which are still more generalised feeders than Herring Gulls, often flock together with Lapwings in the meadows, apparently for the sole purpose of robbing them. They walk around among the busy Lapwings like wardens in a Nazi prison camp. They do not try to catch any food for themselves but keep a watchful eye on the

Lapwings. As soon as a Lapwing has caught something which it cannot swallow immediately, the gulls round about fly at it at once, often coming from over twenty yards away. The Lapwing, knowing by bitter experience what this means, flies up as soon as only one gull lifts its wings. If it cannot swallow its prey in the air before the gulls reach it, its chances of keeping it are almost nil.

Occasionally Herring Gulls, like Black-headed and Common Gulls, capture insects on the wing or on the ground. Dutcher (1904) reports that flocks of immature Herring Gulls have been seen eating " immense numbers of grasshoppers and Colorado beetles "; he also found ants in varying quantities in Herring Gulls' stomachs. Lockley reports (1937) that, especially during the mating flights of ants, the gulls feed liberally on ants in the air, on the ground, and in the water (!). Also, on 21st and 22nd August, 1936, Herring Gulls were seen hawking in the air after Crane-flies (Tipulidae).

Another still more odd food for the Herring Gull, viz. grain taken from the sheaves, has been reported by Rintoul & Baxter (1925) and by Van Someren (1930).

Migration

Enough has now been said about food-habits, and I will now turn to migration. Although the mass movements of Herring Gulls along the Dutch coast, which can be observed all through the winter, give the impression of a well-developed migratory tendency, the results of rather extensive ringing show that neither the Dutch, nor the German North Sea population is really migratory. That is to say, there is no shift in the population area from north (east) to south (west) in winter. Yet there is unmistakable movement along the coast. This apparent paradox is due to the fact that the Herring Gull shows a type of migration which has nothing to do with escaping the northern winter but which is related to the need to find a safe habitat. Being coastal scavengers, the Herring Gulls of the Dutch coast are unable to find food on the beach while strong westerly winds are blowing towards the coast. The beach gets completely covered by the sea by the combination of high tide and in-shore wind, and the gulls then begin to migrate. They align themselves on the narrow zone of rising air found above the seaward slope of the coastal dunes, and sail for hours and hours, practically without a single wing-beat. When the wind is between south-west and west, many gulls sail along to the south-west. When the wind is about north-west, which means, in my observation area, that it is at right angles to the coast, a considerable number of gulls travel north-east, and as others are going south-west, one can see the curious phenomenon of two streams of gulls travelling along the dunes in opposite directions. Perhaps owing to the fact that south-westerly winds are on the whole the most frequent, this migration along the sand-dunes is mainly directed south-westward. Yet the Herring Gull population as a whole does not move to the south-west. I think the explanation is that there is a considerable back migration of gulls in calm weather, but this back migration takes place over the sea, sometimes at a considerable distance out from the coast. The concentrated movement along the coast-line is due entirely to the updraught there with a westerly wind. At all seasons, gulls have an amazing capacity of finding the upcurrents, even in quite irregular dune country. On the shore, the influence of the upcurrent on their flight is seen most impressively when, by standing on top of the dunes, one forces the gulls to make a detour out over the beach. As soon as they leave the dune range they begin to flap their wings, and they have to work quite hard to come forward, round the observer, and back to their easy highway.

The function of this migration is not a shift to more southerly regions, but merely a shift to broad beaches where the gulls can safely wait for the gale to subside. On such wide beaches, which are found near the Hook of Holland, near Ijmuiden and on the Frisian Islands, the gulls gather in huge flocks. I am convinced that the only function of this mass movement is to find a safe resting place. During such gales, the sea is so turbulent that gulls cannot alight on it. All other potential resting places, such as the narrow beach, the sand dunes, and the polders, are not really open enough to satisfy the gulls' demands; like geese they require wide, entirely open flats where an approaching predator can be seen in time. We will see later that the gulls have to overcome a considerable inner resistance before settling down on the breeding grounds in spring, just as terns have. In striking contrast to this irregular and non-migratory behaviour of the Herring Gull is the behaviour of its very close relative the Lesser Black-backed Gull. Lesser Blackbacks are genuine migrants. Until about twenty years ago they were considered rare in Holland, but it is now known that they pass along our coasts in considerable numbers each autumn. Whether the numerous reports in recent years are due to an increase in the number of the species or whether it means simply that they were not recognised before, I am not prepared to say, though I cannot believe that the increase has been enough to explain the fact that I have often seen hundreds of them flying south-west in a few hours on favourable days in the middle of September. As the old birds can be recognised much more easily than the first year birds, which in flight and under unfavourable light conditions are difficult to tell apart from Herring Gulls, many of the immature gulls passing in September might be Lesser Black-backs too. Whereas Lesser Blackbacks winter around the Mediterranean and in West Africa (Landsborough Thomson, 1924) the only difference between the winter and summer distribution of the Herring Gulls of NW. Europe is that they are more scattered in winter. The maximum distance which Herring Gulls have been found to travel from their breeding colonies is 550 km. or 339 miles (Drost & Schilling, 1940).

Apart from these migrations, the Herring Gull shows daily movements to and from its social sleeping grounds. Thus the Herring Gull shows clearly how many types of directed flight there are in birds. The most extreme type is usually singled out and called " migration," but this obscures the fact that " migration " is only an extreme case of directed movement, differing in degree only from such phenomena as flight to the sleeping places, return from the shore to the breeding colony, or flight to the feeding grounds.

Care of the body surface

The Herring Gull spends a great amount of time in preening, that is, in ordering the feathers, and in placing on them the fatty secretion of the tail-gland. This is an activity of vital importance to the bird, for its plumage is indispensable both as a protection against low temperature and as an instrument of flight. Considering the amount of use and wear to which this delicate structure is continuously exposed, and considering that it is only renewed at long intervals (the large feathers only once a year) it is not at all surprising that there is an instinct solely for the purpose of keeping the feathers in order. Indeed, it is surprising that these extremely thin, " feather-light " structures can last so long. So far as I can see, the bird's care of its feathers consists mainly of keeping the barbs of the feathers joined, so as to keep the vane intact. This is attained by bringing any protruding feather back into place, and by nibbling individual feathers gently between the tips of the bill. This is done with the utmost care, and often the tiny white feathers of the neck alone take up fifteen minutes of a bird's time, many feathers being worked individually from the base to the tip. I must confess that I have never spent time systematically watching a preening bird, because somehow I seem to have assumed that preening was only a kind of pastime job, filling leisure hours when the bird has, so to say, nothing better to do. It is only recently that I have begun to recognise that preening is a most vital occupation, and that it might well be worth while to study it in detail

The bill is another part of the body receiving constant attention. After feeding, or after regurgitating food to the female or to the young, a gull cleans its bill, either by boring it into the sand, or by scratching it with a foot.

Lastly, I have often noticed a type of behaviour which might have to do with keeping the feet clean. In the breeding colony, gulls can often be seen looking down to their feet quite intently, as if inspecting them. Usually nothing more happens, but occasionally they may gently peck at them. However, I never succeeded in making sure that they picked up anything; if they did, the particles must have been tiny. Yet the deliberate nature of their looking down to the feet suggests that it has some function.

Sleep

I cannot report much on sleeping, except that it seems to be done irregularly, at least during the summer months. On nights that are not too dark a gull colony is far from quiet, and many birds may sleep more during the daytime than they do at night. As an old hand at gull-watching, I might add that I often got the impression that gulls show a special tendency to go to sleep when the observer very much wants them to show some more interesting behaviour, but I know that such impressions are often misleading and I don't really intend that the reader should believe me !

Escape from predators

I never saw a Herring Gull actually attacked by a predator, though I have found the remains of Herring Gulls that were probably killed by a Peregrine Falcon, and I suppose that foxes may have a go at them occasionally. But every bird-watcher has seen reactions of gulls that have to do with their defence against predators. Thus all gulls, instinctively cautious, are disposed to stay in the open, and they will not often trust themselves to alight among high structures like trees or buildings. They will do this occasionally under stress of hunger or when enticed by abundant food, but their natural inclination is to have a wide view all round. In the breeding season, they will settle near large upright structures, such as cliffs, and they are even known to nest on trees and on buildings (usually, but not always, deserted), but this is done only after considerable experience with the locality involved, and it is probable that the presence of predators in such places will disturb them. As I will show later, even the settling down of the gulls on their breeding ground in early spring takes place after considerable hesitation; the birds apparently have to overcome a strong inner resistance before they can feel quite at ease among the vegetation.

Birds of prey are distrusted by gulls, in much the same way as by waders on migration. A hunting Peregrine may cause anxiety, but the gulls' reactions are highly variable. Sometimes they do not pay any attention at all, whereas at other times a flock will fly up at the sight even of a relatively harmless predator like a Harrier.

In the breeding season the situation is different. Not only do the parent gulls show panic and defence reactions to birds of prey, foxes, dogs, man and even herons, but the chicks have their special reactions too. I will return to this point later.

*　　　*　　　*　　　*　　　*

In these chapters I have tried to give a general sketch of the Herring Gull, of its sensory and executive capacities, and of the diverse behaviour-patterns which can be observed outside the breeding season. It has been my aim to show that the Herring Gull is the opposite of a specialised bird. It employs its many capacities in many different directions. The study of each behaviour-pattern reveals special problems, and an all-round picture can only be acquired through study of all the patterns which can be observed. Thus, migration makes us aware of the problem of possible unknown sense-organs, of the nature of mass movements, of differences in behaviour between closely related species; the feeding behaviour brings us in touch with remarkable adaptations such as paddling, and the smashing of shells; it also makes us aware of the peculiar limitations that are to be found in the learning capacities. On the whole, this introductory chapter, however incomplete it may be, may serve to give an impression of the great diversity of action of which a Herring Gull is capable. Yet its capacities are still more fully demonstrated in the breeding season. During the few months which the gulls spend on the breeding grounds, a whole system of the most diverse behaviour-patterns appears. The study of these reproductive activities has brought to light several highly interesting facts which notably enrich our picture of the Herring Gull's nature. Accordingly, the next chapters will be devoted entirely to the behaviour in the breeding season.

PART TWO

Settling Down in the Colony,
Fighting, and Territory

CHAPTER 5

FIRST ARRIVAL

A spring scene

All through the winter the breeding grounds of the gulls are deserted. At that time of year nobody would recognise the site where so many generations of gulls have concentrated in spring year after year, building up a well-organised community. Only an expert botanist might find in the vegetation peculiarities due to the influence of the gulls' excreta which accumulate on the sandy soil each summer. It seems to me at least that Wall Pepper (*Sedum acre*) and Crane's bill (*Erodium cicutarium*) and perhaps other plants occur in abnormally dense growth on those parts of the terrain where flocks of gulls gather throughout the breeding season, the so-called " clubs."

On a warm, sunny day in March we may watch the first revival of the gulls' interest in their traditional breeding haunts. As the tide rises, covering the sandy beach where the Herring Gulls forage, the hazy blue sky above the dry dunes may suddenly become alive with gulls. Their strong and melodious voices can be heard long before one sees the gulls themselves, high up in the air where hundreds of them are soaring and circling. As they come gliding down, we see their wonderful white wings flash up again and again ; like huge snowflakes they whirl around, coming down in what seems to be wild disorder.

This glorious scene may last a quarter of an hour. Now the birds seem on the verge of alighting, now they soar up again. All at once they stop calling as if on command and sweep away

44

Plate 7a. Inspecting the feet

     b. A colour-ringed male

Plate 8. Sand dunes of the Dutch North Sea coast; breeding area of the Herring Gulls

westward, not as a chaotic cloud this time, but " as one man."
And that may be all we see for that day.

The visits will, however, be repeated on subsequent days
when the weather is bright. At each subsequent visit the birds
will come lower, at first without alighting, but one day a single
gull will eventually alight on a dune top, standing for some
seconds or minutes, looking around suspiciously with a long,
stretched neck, clearly feeling anything but safe. Soon it will
join the flying gulls again.

Finally, one day in March, or maybe not before early April,
the whole flock will come down at once, and take possession of
the dunes. It is especially at this first descent that one gets the
impression of enormous snowflakes being hurled down to the
earth. In a few minutes all have alighted, and then the patient
watcher is rewarded by the thrill of discovering perfect order
where there seemed, only just before, to have been chaos. Every-
where around him the gulls are standing in couples. Here and
there, however, dense groups have formed, and disorderly as
they might seem at first, these too show an element of order, for
these groups can be seen to be occupying certain special areas,
where, instead of waving marram grass or irregular bushes on
steep hillocks, a flat green carpet of dense and very short vegetation is found.

It is only natural to consider that the birds standing in twos
are real pairs, although, of course, in the beginning, this is sheer
speculation. But what is the meaning of the groups? For a
long time we did not understand their significance and we used
to call such gatherings " clubs." And, as in the human parallel,
we used the word club not only for the group of individuals, but
also for the patch of ground which they occupied. As we will
see presently, the function of the gulls' club is essentially different
from that of our human clubs, but the word is too useful to be
dropped, and " club " I will call it throughout this book.

Method of study

Anyone who seeks to understand the gulls' community life
must begin his watching at the time of the birds' first arrival.

For although no eggs will be laid for another four to six weeks after this, these first weeks are a period of intense activity and the understanding of what is going on then is important for the true appreciation of social relationships during the rest of the season.

In watching, two things are essential. The first is patience. One must persevere, and never be discouraged when many hours

Fig. 3
A hide

go by without much of interest happening, for Herring Gulls seem to have plenty of leisure time, at least at this time of year, and they spend a great part of the summer day in preening or sleeping. The other essential is a pair of field-glasses. It is not necessary to do all the watching from a hide at a short distance. Indeed, although from a hide much can be seen and heard that is not noticed at a distance, a hide prevents one from having a wide view, and a wide view is necessary for a study of the community as a whole. That is why we will begin our watching from a high viewpoint on a dune top, posting ourselves in full view of the gulls and, therefore, at such a distance that they will not mind our presence. This distance has often to be rather inconveniently long at the start of the season, but with a good pair of 6x or 8x binoculars, much can be seen from 500 yards. However, before long, the gulls will get accustomed to a quiet observer, and will tolerate him as close as 100–150 yards. Of course it is easy to get closer still, but then we may cause some restlessness, which naturally will not do.

We take up our position, then, looking out towards the south-west, so as to have the early morning sun behind us. This has the additional advantage that it enables us, without any obstruction to our view, to build a sand wall as a protection against the N. and NE. winds blowing through our clothing, for although the air temperature may be quite tolerable, our own " microclimate " may be rather unpleasant after some hours of sitting still in the moist, chilly wind. Once we have made this wall, why not make some kind of a roof for it as well, to keep the rain out ? After all, it may be our home for some months to come.

Another useful device is a tripod with a ball-joint support for the field-glasses. The use of this may not be obvious to the mobile bird-watcher who covers a long stretch of country, having a look first at one bird here and then at another there, but to the stationary watcher it is essential. After hours of watching, the elbows and knees will be trembling slightly, and as a result one misses many details, however alert one may try to be. Even when one is not strained the pulsing of the blood causes a slight movement of the field-glasses at every heart-beat, and this renders precise observation impossible.

The first days spent in watching a part of the gull colony do not bring us much farther; on the contrary, the chances are that one becomes confused and bewildered. There are so many gulls within view that it is very difficult to keep our attention focused on a limited number of birds. The result is that new birds arrive and other birds leave without our noticing it, and we do not

know whence they come nor where they go. A hummock
that was occupied early in the morning may be deserted a while
later; did the gulls from it move to that other hummock, where
all at once we discover two birds that were not there before, or
did they leave the area? Now there are twenty birds at the club,
but the next time that we look at them there are only three, and
an hour later there are about seventy. Worse still: after
having on one day apparently tied down some individual gulls
to a particular place and even having given them names, we
find a quite different station occupied on the following day.
Where now are our Peter, our John, and all the others? The
trouble is that there is much more happening than we at first
suspected, and it is extremely annoying that we cannot recognise
particular individuals.

But after these first discouraging days, we begin to see at least
some regularities of behaviour. And it is perhaps as well that
these days of utter confusion come first, because they make us
much more appreciative of our later discoveries; the most
trivial new fact now makes us feel triumphant, even if it adds
only a very little to our understanding of the general rules of
what is going on. What a thrill, for instance, when we find that
one gull with a conspicuous dark ring round the eye is back at the
same hilltop where he was yesterday! And how lucky that his
neighbour has a brown patch on his tail. It does not take long
before we can recognise quite a number of individuals by such
means. One is exceptionally big and clumsy, another one has
a crippled leg, another again has a harsh voice, still another has
an abnormally heavy bill, and so on. Indeed, by the end of the
season, we have come to know many birds individually, not
only by such crude abnormalities, but also by much subtler
properties such as the facial expression, the colour of the bill or
of the eyelids, by special habits, or by slight differences in voice.

It is clearly of paramount importance to have a means of
quick and easy identification of the different individuals, and we
therefore used coloured leg-rings. It took some time and trouble
before we had a sufficient number of colour-ringed birds. We
were unable to catch large numbers of birds early in the season.

Plate 9. A pair returns to its breeding territory

Plate 10a. Lesser Black-backed Gull mated with Herring Gull. Terschelling, 1928

b. A corner of a " club "

The club birds were too wary, and, as we did not want to waste the whole spring in catching birds instead of watching them, we decided to catch them at the nests, hoping that enough of them would return next year—which, in fact, they did.

We used a small net just big enough to catch one bird. It could be snapped over the sitting gull by means of a strong spring, which was released by means of a string, held by an observer in a hide about twenty yards away. As a suspicious gull stretches its neck, and is able to react to the rising net in a flash, various tricks were used in order to catch the gull unawares. The best of these was to disarrange the eggs in the nest. This caused the returning gull to shift them, and in doing so, it bent its neck and buried its bill under the eggs. We soon became experts in disarranging the eggs so thoroughly as to release intense and prolonged shifting, and usually the net was over the bird before it even occurred to it to look up. Indeed some birds were so absorbed that they did not even notice that they had been captured. After all, the very slight touch of a light net is not so very different from the touch of marram grass moved by the wind. It was a ridiculous sight to see a gull sitting contentedly under the net until, on slightly turning its head, it got entangled in the net, when it at once jumped up in alarm.

Reactions to abnormal individuals

A gull struggling in the net promptly causes great commotion among the other gulls. They gather above it in a dense flock, screaming loudly, and swoop down in what seem to be actual attacks. We were always so taken up with getting the captured gull before it could escape, and with ringing and releasing it with the least possible delay, that we never stopped to study the reactions of the other gulls more closely. Yet this would be very worth while, because the phenomenon has interesting sociological aspects. The gulls seem to show a double response. On the one hand, they are alarmed by the disturbance and I think I have heard the alarm call on a number of such occasions. On the other hand, their reaction to the captured gull seems definitely hostile. It is known in other instances too that social animals may attack individuals that behave in an abnormal manner (Goethe, 1939).

One is tempted to compare this with human behaviour. In human society, " primitive " as well as " civilised," a similar instinctive reaction is very strongly developed. It is perhaps possible to distinguish three steps or gradations of rising intensity in the social defence attitude of a crowd. The first is laughing at an individual who behaves in a slightly abnormal way. This reaction serves the function of forcing the individual back into normal, that is to say, into conventional behaviour. The next and higher intensity reaction is withdrawal; the individual has made himself " impossible " and his companions ignore him. This, viewed from the aspect of biological significance, is a still stronger stimulus to the abnormal person to behave normally. The highest intensity reaction is one of definite hostility, resulting in making the individual an outcast, and, in primitive societies, even in killing him. In my opinion, it is of great importance for human sociology to recognise the instinctive basis of such reactions, and to study them comparatively in other social species, and I regret very much that I neglected the opportunity of doing so in my studies on gulls.

Each captured gull was given an aluminium ring of the standard type provided by the Leiden Museum, and a combination of coloured rings which made him recognisable as an individual through field-glasses at a distance. Some of our gulls wore five rings, which jingled happily together when we released the bird. These colour-bands lasted at least three years, and the gulls did not seem to be in the least embarrassed by them, " and lived happily ever afterwards."

Some difficulties

The existence of individually marked birds enabled us to follow at least some of the gulls from day to day throughout the season, and even from year to year. When we first began watching, we expected it to be a relatively simple affair to get a general knowledge of the normal course of events throughout the nesting season. We thought we would merely have to concentrate our study upon a few marked birds. However, affairs did not prove to be quite so simple. First, the most interesting things often happened to unmarked birds. Secondly, there were often interruptions and disturbances, such as robbery of the eggs, by men and by animals. This caused some of the gulls to shift territory, while others gave up altogether for the season. Also, much of interest happened with birds that were breeding for the first time, and these were rarely marked.

There is also a difficulty in such observations of quite another kind: we often did not appreciate what a particular bird was doing. When a bird is sitting on its eggs you know that it is incubating. When it delivers heavy wing-blows at another bird you know that it is fighting. But when two gulls, standing opposite each other, are pecking into the soil, or are tearing at grass tufts, or are walking round each other with the neck drawn in and the bill pointing upward, you have not the slightest idea what they are doing, at least at first. In many cases your understanding of events may not be entirely nil, but may yet be very incomplete. For instance, one bird walks round the other, uttering a peculiar call not unlike the begging call of a half-grown Herring Gull chick. It tosses its head up and down and even touches the other bird's bill. The latter seems to try to get away, but the first one keeps bothering it. Finally, the harassed bird stands still, twists and turns its neck, a huge swelling appears in its neck, moves upward, and suddenly the bird bends its head down, opens the bill widely, and regurgitates an enormous fish. The begging bird begins to eat gluttonously before the food even reaches the ground. The other joins it, and together they finish the meal. It is easy to understand that this behaviour was feeding. But who was feeding whom, and why?

The only way to find out the answer to such questions is to follow individual birds as closely as possible. In this way we could at least hope to get some " case histories " or parts of them, and by adding these together and by fitting in other more fragmentary observations wherever possible, we could hope eventually to build up a general picture. As a result of several years of watching, such a general picture has gradually emerged. However, owing to lack of experience in the beginning, and lack of opportunity later, we have not succeeded in making our picture as complete as we should have liked. There are awkward blanks; and there is an embarrassing lack of balance, and thus, while this book is not the first word on the Herring Gull, it is equally not the last.

I will now attempt to describe what we have found so far, in such a way as to save the reader the phase of confusion and of puzzling which the investigator himself has to go through. I will begin by isolating one part of the whole pattern, viz., fighting, and ignoring other parts such as the formation of pairs.

CHAPTER 6

FIGHTING AND THREAT

The upright threat posture

Fighting in gulls, as in so many other animals, is a very complicated behaviour-pattern. Not only are there various different ways of fighting, but fighting behaviour is often seen in an incomplete form, and it may also be combined with other activities, when it may give rise to what seem at first sight to be quite " new " movements. First, therefore, I will describe fighting in its complete form, as it can occasionally be witnessed during boundary clashes between two neighbouring pairs.

As soon as we are able to distinguish between individual gulls, we see that each pair has its own station. The birds are present there for only part of the time, and as the daily rhythm of different pairs does not exactly coincide, there appears to be less regularity in the occupation of territories than is actually the case. Also, a territory may be temporarily invaded by strangers in the absence of the owners. As soon as the latter return, however, there is trouble. Usually the resident male (males can be distinguished from females by their larger size) walks up to the strangers in a remarkably rigid attitude. Instead of having the neck drawn in, as when at rest, he stretches it upwards and forwards, while at the same time he points his head downward. In this attitude the tension in his neck-muscles can often be seen quite clearly, despite the thick layer of feathers covering the skin. In the highest intensity of this pose his wings are lifted a little, so that they are no longer half concealed in the supporting contour-feathers, but stand out at a little distance from his body (Fig. 4; Plate 11). As we shall presently see, this is the first preparation that the gull makes for actual fighting,

53

FIG. 4

The upright threat posture. (After a film)

i.e. for delivering a blow with the wing. In this posture, the male walks with stiff steps either straight towards the intruder, or, in other cases, by a detour which seems determined by the local situation. This posture I will call the " upright threat posture "; it functions as a threat against other gulls. The human observer is so little impressed by it that he has difficulty in noticing it at all when he sees it for the first time, and he has to learn what it means; but for all Herring Gulls it is full of meaning and their reaction to it seems to be entirely innate. As a rule, the intruders react immediately. Until then, they may have been quietly resting, but as soon as the attacker assumes the threat posture, they begin to sidle away. Usually the attacker is not satisfied by their slow preparations and he then increases the speed of his approach, lifts the wings more and more, and finally charges, half running and half flying. Once such a charge begins, it continues with increasing speed, because the avoiding movements of the intruders act as an extra stimulus to the attacking bird, and the latter's threatening approach induces increased anxiety in the intruders. Few intruders stand up to such a charge; usually they fly away, taking care not to be overtaken. Sometimes, when the intruders are familiar with the local situation, they merely run a few paces, until they are just beyond the territorial boundary, and then stop at a sufficiently safe distance. Both pursuer and pursued may then stand still for some seconds, with their powerful wings raised aloft and their necks still in the rigid threat posture, and this is one of the most wonderful sights to be seen in these fine birds (Plate 12a).

The anxiety posture

The pursued bird usually shows a neck posture that is, objectively considered, only slightly different from the threat posture.

The neck is stretched, but the head is not
pointed downwards but is kept horizontal
or slightly raised (Fig. 5). Further, such a
bird never faces its opponent, but turns
away from it.   However slight the differences may seem to the human watcher at
first sight, the meaning of the posture to
other gulls is quite the opposite of that of
the threat posture. Such a bird is "afraid,"

FIG. 5
The anxiety posture.
(After a photograph)

that is to say it is ready to flee at any moment, and this condition
is at once understood by other gulls. It provokes and encourages
attack.   Further, this "anxiety posture" is a preparatory or
intention movement, the very first beginning of flight itself.
The feathers are pressed against the body, and the wings are
kept ready for action. This stretching of the neck, by the way,
is a general reconnaissance movement, called forth by any kind
of disturbance, and is not necessarily an expression of the intention to escape. For instance, a territory-holder stretches its
neck as soon as a stranger alights in its neighbourhood. In this
attitude it inspects the situation, and decides, on the basis of
what it sees, whether it will attack or tolerate the newcomer.
Coincident with the stretching of the neck, the eye is opened
wide. These details, incidentally, can be fully appreciated by
the observer only at very close quarters. Plates 6, 11 and 16*b*
give a good impression of the differences in expression.

In conclusion, the anxiety posture seems to be composed of
two elements: (1) stretching of the neck and opening of the eyes
as a reconnaissance, and (2) flattening of the plumage and
keeping the wings ready, as a preparation for escape.

The incident described above was only a minor clash. It did
not develop into a fight because the stranger fled right at the
first sign of aggressiveness by the territory owner. This is the
most usual type of hostile encounter. Much more interesting
is a clash between two neighbours at the boundary between
their territories. Each gull has a tendency to claim a territory
of about 30–50 yards in diameter. But in crowded parts of the
colony, there are always pairs which select sites rather too close

to already settled pairs. This seems to be due to the tendency to nest in a community. In the reproductive instinct, there is an interesting conflict between social traits and the tendency to stake out a territory and defend it against intruders. Both tendencies cannot be fully satisfied because they are antagonistic. Each species of bird has evolved a compromise, ensuring sufficient though not optimal expression for each of the two conflicting tendencies separately, but, as so often in life, the compromise is in itself optimal and has survival value as such.

Grass pulling

The " wedging in " of new pairs on already occupied ground, a phenomenon that is especially common around the " clubs," results in fierce encounters. For both pairs are disposed to fight and to defend the same plot. In such an encounter, the fighting rarely begins at once. Usually there is extensive mutual bluffing first. Proceedings begin by both males adopting the upright threat posture and walking slowly towards each other until they are standing about a foot apart, facing each other. Suddenly one of them pecks vigorously at the ground, and tears out a bundle of moss, or grass, or whatever plants may be there (Plate 13). He may keep this in his bill for some seconds, or he may throw it away with a jerky, sideways movement of the head. Either he or the opponent (whichever happens to be the more aggressive at the moment), or both at the same time, may repeat this behaviour. At intervals one bird dashes at the other and tries to get hold of the plants in its bill; if it succeeds, both pull hard at it.

Often the birds do not select moss or light grass but roots, or large tufts of grass that are too firmly rooted to be dislodged, and then they make frantic efforts to tear them out, pulling backwards with their heels on the ground, and even waving their wings. In this posture they may stand for several seconds, exerting the utmost force, so that the observer expects them to get red in the face. Sometimes they succeed in tearing apart whatever they had got hold of, and in a ridiculous tumble they fall backwards, creating quite a panic among the surrounding birds. This grass-tearing may go on for many minutes. The upright threat posture, grass-pulling, introduced by violent hacking into the ground, wing-flashing, darting backwards and forwards, and, in between, long pauses of waiting, make up the main part of this bluff fighting.

A fight

All at once, however, one of the gulls rushes up to the other, and delivers a peck with the bill, at the same time taking hold of any part of the other gull that it can. It may be a wing, the tail, a leg, or, more often, the other gull's bill, because the other wards the attack off with its bill. Once they have come to grips, further developments seem to depend on the strength of the fighting urge. Usually the two birds simply pull back, leaning backwards just as if they were pulling at grass tufts. At the same time, they spread their wings, partly to support themselves better, partly to prevent themselves from being dragged along, and partly in an attempt to deliver blows at the other. These wing-blows are quite

Fig. 6
A fight between two males

fierce, and in the calm still morning air you can hear the impact a hundred yards away.

Pulling may go on for a long time. I once observed a fight in which one bird dragged the other along for a distance of 30 yards. The bird that was dragged then slipped into a small rabbit-hole, which enabled the other to come on top of it. The attacker at once seized the opportunity to deliver a long series of violent wing-blows at the other. In doing this, he lost his grip on the other and began to peck at its head. I never observed such a fierce strafing again. The attacked bird lay helplessly flapping its wings, warding off the pecks as soon as its bill was freed, and finally managed to scramble up. It was in no mood to fight, however, and escaped, calling the alarm-note as it flew away. The alarm call, usually a reaction to predators, is very rarely uttered as a reaction to other gulls; when it is heard, as in this case, it is from a terrified gull after a severe punishment.

Sometimes a fight is unequal right from the beginning. This happens for instance when a territory-holding bird makes a surprise attack on another individual. He may then get on top of the other immediately, and he then does not normally try to pull him backwards, but forces him down, beating him with the wings. In such cases the " under bird " may get a most serious beating, and his neck may become severely twisted, a pitiful but ridiculous sight. Although we often saw the feathers flying, we never observed one bird actually wound another. Yet this happens occasionally, for Dr. David Lack informs me that he once witnessed a fight in which one of the birds got smeared with blood.

The following entries in my diary will give an impression of the more severe type of fighting.

" *16th May, 1936. 6.40 a.m.* The male of nest 3 drives an intruder off and chases it in the air. It succeeds in seizing the stranger's wing with the bill. They tumble down together, the stranger pulls itself free, and is chased over more than 50 yards."

" *18th May, 1936. 7.1 a.m.* Pair R are nest-building on their territory close to territory 4, which is held by an exceptionally pugnacious male. Male 4 arrives back from the shore, and at once attacks ♂ R. The latter withdraws, accompanied by its ♀, giving the choking threat-movement, but not attacking. Male 4 follows them far beyond his usual boundary, until the birds reach the club, ten yards from where the attack first began. Finally the clash develops into a wild fight; R is first punished, then 4 seems to be losing. The males leap up in the air, peck and bite at each other's necks, bills, or heads, and throw each other on the side or on the back. The feathers are flying. Several strange individuals, up to eight in number, come and watch this tremendous fight. Finally the two champions face each other with wings widely spread, then ♂ 4 goes back to his ♀ on the nest and ' chokes,' and pair R return to their territory and ' choke.' (A delightful fight. If the warden had charged us a guilder each we would gladly have paid it.) "

Same day, 8.55 a.m. Male R is again attacked by ♂ 4. For several minutes ♂ 4 had ♂ R by its neck and pressed it against the ground, shaking it now and then as if it were a prey. R is entirely helpless. Eventually ♂ 4 lets go and R seems terribly worn out. Twice 4 gets R again by the wing, R finally lies flat on the ground without even trying to fight back, utters a high-intensity *hahahahaha* with its bill widely open, and

FIG. 7
Choking. (After a film)

finally runs away. Its mate accompanies it, chokes at its side, but R is too much demoralised even to choke. She chases several birds off. During the fight more than ten onlookers were attracted, standing at a respectful distance with stretched necks."

The females, though always interested and excited during the males' fights, do not often fight themselves. They do so occasionally, however, and then usually attack another female. Under special circumstances though they will fight a male, as for instance when they are alone on the territory and a strange male trespasses—either by accident or with the object of love-making. As we will see in the next chapter however, the initiative in love-making is usually taken by the female, not by the male,

FIG. 8

Choking. (After a film)

a very shocking fact to most of my friends when I mention it to them—as I like to do in order to watch their reaction.

Choking

The female not unfrequently joins her mate in defence of the territory, and this gives rise to a form of threat which I have not so far described. At first sight the observer does not get the impression of threat. The pair rush up to an intruding pair, or go instead to a place where they have already made the beginning of a nest. Here they lower the breast, bend the legs, point the head downwards, lower the tongue-bone (which gives them a very peculiar facial expression) and perform rhythmic jerking movements with the head, as if they intended to peck into the ground. They do not reach the ground, however. During this head-jerking they utter a peculiar, deep call, repeated with about the same rhythm as the jerking movements. The call sounds like " huoh-huoh-huoh-huoh . . ." Sometimes the birds also make scraping movements with the legs. The whole performance is rather similar to the actual making of a scrape (a nesting activity found in many birds beside gulls). Usually, however, the actual scraping with the legs is omitted by gulls in a hostile situation.

Noble & Wurm (1943), who have described similar behaviour in the American Laughing Gull, called it " choking," so I will use the same term for the Herring Gull.

The other pair as a rule respond in exactly the same way, and it is a most peculiar sight when two or sometimes three pairs of gulls sit near each other in this way. The funny side of it is that the whole situation is really loaded with hostility, indeed actual fights may occur in between, and yet the sitting together seems such an irrelevant and inadequate way of venting anger. However it is anything but inadequate. The ceremony is understood by other gulls. An intruder usually clears out in a hurry, and aggressive neighbours are irritated and roused to respond by threatening in return. If a real fight ensues, it is usually the males who get to grips, while the females stand by, ready to chase each other, and, especially, other intruders. There always seem to be stragglers about who are attracted to any fight that is going on.

CHAPTER 7

THE ORIGIN OF THE THREAT
POSTURES

ANYONE WHO STUDIES "display" in animals, either threat
display or courtship display, cannot help wondering why the
animals adopt such special, and often grotesque, attitudes. Such
attitudes are usually very typical for the species, and they may
be rather similar in related species, but they are often very
different from one taxonomic group to another. In the last
two decades, much work has been done on this problem, and we
begin now, however dimly, to understand something of the
origin of such displays. In the Herring Gull, I think we have
made a definite step forward, and although the conclusions I here
put forward may not apply to all other types of display, I think
that they may help in understanding many of the types found in
other animals.

The upright threat posture

As I mentioned above, the threat posture figured on Plate 12
seems to be a preparation for actual attack. The main argument
in favour of this view is that a very aggressive bird lifts its wings
out of the supporting feathers and keeps them ready for action.
The posture of neck and head provides another argument.
The neck is stretched and the head pointed downward. This
is exactly the attitude adopted by a gull before it delivers a
peck at its opponent. In a real fight, a gull always tries to jump
on top of its enemy, and then peck at it and/or deliver wing-blows.
It can, therefore, be seen that several elements of this threat
posture are incipient fight-movements. Such incipient movements, also called preparatory or intention movements, are

known to every student of behaviour. They occur especially when a drive is not fully aroused. Before a bird (of any species) decides to fly off, for instance, it flattens its plumage, raises its wings, often bends in the heel-joints and, after that, stretches the body strongly in the direction of flight. With a growing intensity of the urge to fly (for instance when the disturbance which caused the bird's anxiety is approaching), the intention movement develops into real flight. In a very illuminating paper, Daanje has recently (1950) shown how widespread is the occurrence of such intention movements in birds. I myself have studied this type of behaviour more closely in the nest-building behaviour of the male Three-spined Stickleback. When a male stickleback has just settled in its territory, the first signs of nest-building are incipient digging movements. At first, the male merely fixes the sandy bottom with both eyes, bending downwards a little. Nothing more happens on this occasion, and after about a second the male again assumes a horizontal position and swims on. A minute later, however, it may again fixate the bottom, and bend down somewhat farther. On the next occasion, it may bring its head down to the bottom, and may even touch it with its snout. With rising intensity of the drive, it will begin to thrust its snout into the sand, and may even suck some sand into its mouth, only to spit it out immediately. Next, it will bore its snout deep into the soil, take a mouthful of sand, and carry it off a few inches before throwing it out. When digging with complete vigour, it may carry the sand away over a distance of ten inches or more. The increase in intensity is not quite so regular as I describe it; there are irregular ups and downs, but the general trend is an increase of intensity as sketched here. One has only to read Eliot Howard's description (1929) of the beginning of nest-building in birds to recognise the close parallel.

Such intention movements are of great importance for our understanding of an animal's motivation at a particular moment; to the experienced watcher they reveal what drive is activated in the animal, and therefore, what type of activity he can expect to see next. It requires much intensive watching to be able to recognise these rudiments of movements, and the better one knows a species, the more trivial are the clues which one can recognise with certainty. Each time that I study a new species I am amazed to find how much more I see after I have become thoroughly acquainted with it. After more than ten years of close study of the Three-spined Stickleback, for instance, I notice that my ability to recognise intention movements in this species is still improving, thus leading to new discoveries each season, and causing me surprise, and a kind of annoyance about my own previous stupidity. For once you have discovered a new and subtle intention movement, you simply cannot understand how it was possible for you to overlook it before, although it must have been happening dozens of times right under your nose. This experience also works the other way round: it gives one very little confidence in the conclusions drawn by workers who have not spent at least several months in intensive watching of a species. I cannot help thinking that the man who does not have the patience simply to sit and watch for hours, days, and weeks, is not the type of man to undertake a behaviour-study.

Returning, after this confession, to our gulls, there remains one difficulty. Must we assume that a gull that is threatening but no more is only weakly inclined to fight, and is only just beginning to feel the first vestige of anger? The situation rather suggests that the bird ought to be in a very aggressive condition. When it faces an opponent close to or even on its territory, there is every reason to expect that its fighting urge is very strongly activated, and one would expect a wild dash instead of a mere intention movement. However, I have not yet told the whole story ; the upright threat posture is not a pure intention movement. In some cases it may be one, for instance when the opponent is still at a distance. But in most cases I saw evidence of ambivalence, of another urge coming into play at the same time. The most intense threat-posturing is observed in boundary clashes, where an intruder not only evokes aggressiveness but a tendency to flight as well, in the subdued form of just being cautious. I think, therefore, that the threat-posture is in most cases a mixture of aggressive and defensive posturing. This

Plate II. The upright threat posture, high intensity; the wings are kept ready for action

Plate *12a*. After a charge. The male in front has been driven off by the other male

b. Upright threat posture. The bird on the left has the neck withdrawn

can be clearly seen in situations where two neighbours, both equally self-possessed and equally strong, threaten each other over their mutual boundary.   Instead of stretching the neck obliquely towards the opponent, they withdraw it.   This withdrawal cannot be misunderstood: everyone who has seen the real fights recognises it as the intention movement of a defensive attitude.   Its function is a withdrawal of the head from the opponent's powerful bill.   Plate 13 shows the mixed posture in such a situation.

Our conclusion therefore must be that the upright threat posture of the Herring Gull is a mixture of two intention movements,   revealing   an   ambivalent attitude.   The bird is acted upon by two antagonistic drives, which keep each other in check, so that it displays the intention movements of both, united into one posture.

Grass-pulling

No less interesting are the activities of fighting gulls which seem to have to do with nest-building rather than with fighting. Looking at these activities anthropocentrically, one would be inclined to think that, by carrying out nesting activities, the

FIG. 9

A clash between two males. The bird at the left is about to " pull grass"; the other is in extreme defence posture. (After a film)

birds were trying to show intruders that this was the place where they intended to make a nest. Apart from the fact that such an explanation would hardly satisfy us, it seems to be untrue. What knowledge we have of bird behaviour and its underlying causes seems to show that birds usually act without the far-reaching kind of foresight that would be required in this case. Fighting of this type, it should be realised, may occur weeks in advance of true nest-building. Birds do not look into the future to this extent. At least the longer we study their behaviour, the more we become impressed by their dependence on the internal state and the external stimuli operating in the present or in the past, and not on situations to come. That is to say, while the effects of a bird's activities often contribute to some future end, the bird is probably not aware of this, and the causes which motivate it can always be found in the present or in the past. This is a rule which we find confirmed again and again, and, while we must certainly keep an open mind, as long as we have not tested its validity in each new case, it seems unjustified to discard the possibility of a reaction to the present situation and assume, without proof, that birds act with the far future in mind.

The peculiar behaviour of gulls threatening each other becomes more intelligible when threat-behaviour is studied comparatively in a large number of species. It will be seen, then, that many animals occasionally perform activities during and in between actual fights that " don't belong " to the fighting behaviour, but are parts of other behaviour-patterns. Fighting domestic cocks, for instance, peck at the ground now and then as if they were feeding. The same can be seen in fighting male Skylarks. Great Tits and Blue Tits do the same, except that, being tree-feeders, they do not peck at the ground but tear buds apart on the branches where their fighting is done. Alternatively they rise into the air and attack each other in a typical, steep, bouncing flight, and then settle on twigs and peck vigorously at the buds. Fighting Starlings and fighting Cranes preen their feathers in between fights. Fighting Avocets, Oystercatchers and other waders may suddenly turn the head round, put the bill under the scapulars and act as if they were going to sleep! There are many other instances known (Armstrong, 1950; Kortlandt, 1940; Tinbergen, 1939, 1940, 1952). Feeding, preening, nesting behaviour, or even sleep, are suddenly shown when the whole situation seems to dictate nothing but fighting.

Closer study shows, however, that this statement is not quite true. It is not at *any* moment during hostile encounters that these irrelevant movements occur; they are restricted to a very special situation. The typical situation in which such movements occur is a boundary conflict between neighbouring territory-holders. This is significant, for we know that, while a territory-holding male attacks its neighbour when it is intruding, and retreats when it meets this same bird on the latter's territory, it neither attacks nor retreats when they both meet on the boundary, and this gives us the solution of the problem. At the boundary the male is not of course indifferent to its neighbour, but is strongly stimulated by it. The stimulation however, as I have already mentioned before, acts in two ways: it urges him both to fight and to escape. But one cannot fight and escape at the same time; the two behaviour-patterns are antagonistic.

Now it is generally recognised that an animal cannot suspend action once it has been aroused. Man, who keeps himself " under control " (or at any rate prides himself that he does) can suspend action more or less, though only with considerable strain. What little we know of the physiological processes

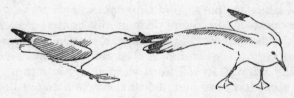

FIG. 10
Pulling at an opponent's wing.   (After a photograph)

underlying instinctive behaviour shows that behaviour (i.e. movement) is dependent on the " firing " of motor impulses by the nervous system. When the motor nerves are cut, no behaviour occurs. Now when an animal's fighting drive is aroused, impulses are sent out by the nervous system which stimulate the muscles employed in the fighting. We still do not know much about the nature of these nervous mechanisms, but we know that they must be there, and we know that there is one of these systems for each " instinct," for feeding, for mating, for nest-building, for incubation, for fighting, for escape, even for sleep (Tinbergen, 1951). What seems to happen when fighting and flight are activated simultaneously, is that the impulses " spark over,"—i.e. they find some other outlet in the nervous mechanisms of another instinct which is not thwarted at the moment and in this way the impulses give rise to a movement belonging to some other and inappropriate instinct. I will return to this principle later, because it is at work in other situations as well. Such irrelevant movements due to " sparking over " are called " displacement activities."

To return now to the Herring Gulls: their handling of moss and grass reminds us of nest-building. However, it is not identical with real nest-building. One difference is that a gull when gathering nest-material picks it up gently, whereas a threatening gull gives violent pecks at the ground. The difference is quite obvious when seen at close quarters. The vigorous and fierce movements of the aggressive gull display a use of force which is quite amazing. Another difference is the tendency of threatening gulls to select objects that offer resistance to their pulling. Lastly, the force exerted in pulling by threatening gulls is very strong, whereas a nest-building gull leaves any material alone that offers too much resistance. The strength exerted by grass-pulling gulls is not very obvious from 100 or 200 yards away, but it is very striking when observed from a hide close at hand. Several times my blind has been situated at a much-disputed boundary. Indeed the gulls often used the guy-ropes of the hide as substitutes for grass, and pulled at them with vigour. The result was rather like an earthquake.

Before we had studied this behaviour closely, we often wondered how another gull knew whether a grass-pulling gull was in an aggressive mood or merely collecting nest-material. For they know this perfectly well! We realise now that the differences mentioned above are responsible, and this is not astonishing when we realise just what the threatening gull is doing. It is collecting nest-material, it is true, but with this material it does what it would do with its opponent if it dared to get hold of it: pecking and pulling. Hence the threat-behaviour is not pure displacement-building but displacement-building with fighting behaviour superimposed on it, and this addition of some of the elements of true attack constitutes the difference between true nest-building and threat.

The conclusion therefore is that the thwarted fighting urge, or the combination of thwarted fighting urge and thwarted flight, find an outlet partly through displacement nest-building and partly through true fighting activities, the latter being super-imposed on the displacement activities, and directed not at the potentially dangerous opponent but at the harmless nest-material.

Thus it seems that both the upward threat-posture and the grass-pulling threat-display are due to the simultaneous activation of two antagonistic drives. I think we also know what determines whether the upright posture or the displacement nest-building will occur. When the activation is weak, the impulses can be vented by a mixture of in-tention movements. When, however, the birds are very strongly stimulated, the impulses cannot be " used up " by mere intention movements, and they break through the barrier normally existing between different instincts, and find anoutlet through displace-ment-nest-building. The difference between the two threat-postures therefore seems to be merely a difference of intensity.

FIG. 11

Threat posture of male Three-spined Stickleback. (After a photograph in Tinbergen, 1951)

Displacement activities in a fish

It is remarkable that behaviour of a very similar nature has been found in fish. The males of the Three-spined Stickleback, like many birds, are strictly territorial in spring.

They fight off other males, and, as men-tioned above, build a nest on their territory. This behaviour can be studied not only in the field but also in the aquarium, and hence the possibilities of experimental work are much better than in most birds.

The male stickleback shows threat-behaviour during boun-dary disputes. A threatening male adopts a vertical position, head pointing downward. It turns its side towards the opponent, and erects the ventral spine of this side. When very much stimulated, both ventral spines are raised. In this position, jerky movements down and up are made, as if the fish were going to push its head on the bottom. However, it rarely touches the bottom. Now and then a fish resumes its horizontal position and dashes towards its opponent, but it withdraws immediately afterwards, then makes another forward dash, retreats again, and so on. This incipient attack and retreat in quick alternation indicates the ambivalence of the male's condition: it is stimulated to fight but gets intimidated as soon as it leaves its territory, and withdraws. Back on its own territory, or rather, when it comes a little closer to the centre of its territory, its fighting urge overwhelms it again, and it again charges.

The vertical posture of the stickleback seems to occur in a situation essential for a displacement activity. As is often the case with displacement activities, it seems to be an incomplete movement. This incompleteness might be due to a low intensity of activation, and we therefore decided to increase the intensity of the boundary fights by bringing the territories closer together. This can be done by crowding several males into a relatively small aquarium, provided that they are given a dense vegetation. As in other territorial animals, the fighting drive increases the closer the defending individual is to the centre of the territory, in this case to the nest site. Huxley has expressed this very vividly (1934) by comparing territories with rubber discs, which resist compression with more force the more they are compressed.

The result of our crowding experiment was that the vertical posture was much more often shown by the sticklebacks and that it developed into complete digging behaviour. Now digging is the first part of nest-building, as described above. The male carries mouthfuls of sand away until a pit 2–3 inches wide and $\frac{1}{2}$–1 inch deep is formed. The threat-posture therefore is a low-intensity form of sand-digging, a nest-building activity. As long as we knew only the low-intensity form, in which the fish rarely touched the bottom at all, we had been in doubt whether we had to do with displacement-feeding or with displacement-digging. As a matter of fact, our first conclusion was that it was displacement-feeding, the possibility of digging not occurring

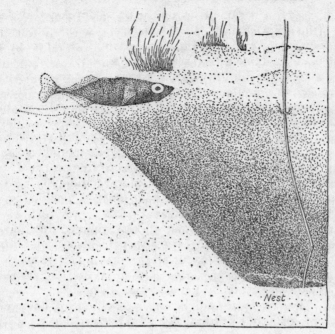

FIG. 12

Male stickleback with nest in deep pit made by " displacement-sand-digging." (After Tinbergen & Van Iersel, 1947)

to us at all, and in my first paper on the subject (1940) I actually wrote of it as displacement-feeding.

A second experiment was designed to test our supposition that the threat posture was the outcome of a conflict between the fighting drive and the drive to escape. Previous experience had taught us that a crude model of a male stickleback in full spring colours (red underneath, greenish blue on the back), when presented in a male's territory, released attack. We now lowered such a dummy into an occupied territory, and when the male attacked it, we did not withdraw the model, but made it hit back as hard as we could. At first this caused the male to attack furiously, but after a while the model " won," and the male fled, that is to say, it became dark on the back, developed dark cross-bars (the stickleback's disruptive camouflage pattern) and withdrew into the vegetation. Our dummy had beaten a male stickleback in its own territory—quite a feat!

We kept the dummy where it was. The result was that it continued to stimulate the male's fighting drive. But as its urge to escape was not reinforced by renewed beatings, this urge gradually died down, and after a while the male came out again and attacked anew. But just before it attacked it adopted the vertical threat-posture! Exactly at the moment therefore when flight and attack were in equilibrium, the vertical posture appeared. This shows that our interpretation of the vertical posture as a displacement activity due to conflicting urges, finding an outlet over an irrelevant pattern, was correct.

Now here again the displacement activity differs in various respects from real digging. First, the stickleback turns the side of its body towards the opponent and erects its ventral spine. This is part of the defence pattern. Both male and female roll over on the side when attacked and cornered, and erect the ventral spine. Females do not adopt the vertical posture, however; this is characteristic of territorial fights between males.

Further, the threatening males may, as I pointed out above, perform forward jerking and thrusting movements with the whole body. These movements seem to me to belong to the actual fighting; it is as if the animal is hitting an opponent, but the peculiar thing is that it is not aimed at the opponent itself but at the bottom, which is the object of the sand-digging. The parallel with the grass-pulling Herring Gulls is striking. In the stickleback, therefore, we have to do with displacement-digging, combined with an element of defence, and with an element of attack.

I hope the ornithological reader will not be annoyed by this rather lengthy narrative of the behaviour of a mere fish. I cannot promise that I will not deviate from the ornithological path in this book again. In ethology, comparison is too powerful a tool to be neglected. The bird student may acquire a better insight in his birds by studying a fish or even an insect; conversely, the study of bird behaviour may help us in understanding the behaviour of other creatures, man included. As a matter of fact, the student of animal behaviour finds himself continuously applying his findings to his own species, and, without entering into details, I must confess that much of what little understanding I have of human nature has been derived not only from man-watching, but from bird-watching and fish-watching as well. It is as if the animals are continuously holding a mirror in front of the observer, and it must be said that the reflection, if properly understood, is often rather embarrassing. . . .

Choking

The other threat activity, choking, is indistinguishable from an activity we see during real nesting. The two birds of a pair may be seen to go through exactly the same behaviour together at the site of their future nest when there is no stranger to be seen. In such cases it is sometimes accompanied by the scraping leg movement. This scraping and shovelling is, I think, less rare in this situation than in hostile encounters, though I have seen it done by threatening birds on several occasions. I am inclined to believe that this is mainly a matter of intensity. As will be clear from what has been said on the grass-pulling behaviour, and on displacement-digging in sticklebacks, it is one of the characteristics of displacement activities that they are usually incomplete. Unless the thwarted drive is exceptionally strong, only the beginning of the activity is shown. The grass-pulling gulls merely peck at the grass, but do not carry it to the nest. The stickleback merely inclines its body forward and downward, and rarely digs at all. This is only done under conditions of the highest hostile tension. It is therefore not surprising that aggressive choking should be less complete than the real scraping and shovelling.

The environmental situation also points to the conclusion that the aggressive choking is a displacement activity. It is always performed under the same conditions which call forth grass-pulling. It seems to depend on the presence of the mate whether a gull will indulge in grass-pulling or in choking; possibly there is also a difference in intensity, choking indicating a still stronger activation than grass-pulling. This may in turn be caused by the mate's presence and interest.

Some authors give an interpretation of the aggressive choking which differs from the one given here. Goethe seems to have failed to recognise that choking, which he calls a nesting move-ment (" Nisttrieb ") may represent two entirely different condi-tions of the bird. Steinbacher (1938) did recognise the aggressive character of displacement-choking, but he does not consider it a nest-building movement. He says: it is as if the gull is going to sit in the nest and vomit food. Portielje (1928) interprets choking as premature nest building-behaviour, and further reports that he has seen choking gulls, in what seems to have been a hostile encounter, peck into the ground and scrape with the legs. Recently (1944) he has changed his views, and agrees that choking may be a form of aggressive display, but he thinks it is derived from the movements of feeding the chicks. He has observed a choking gull bring up food, swallowing it, however, before it was dropped. Both Steinbacher and Portielje therefore appear to consider the movement similar to the movements of feeding the chicks. Kirkman (1937) says that in the Black-headed Gull the movement which I think may be homologous to choking reminds him of the movements of feeding the young.

While I cannot claim the right to judge in the case of the Black-headed Gull, I disagree with Steinbacher and Portielje about the nature of choking in the Herring Gull. It certainly is interesting that Portielje actually saw incipient regurgitation, but this was observed only once and might have been a case of ambivalent behaviour. After a discussion with Dr. Portielje, I have again studied the aggressive choking very carefully during a whole season, with the special intention of trying to find any connection with feeding behaviour, but I think there cannot be the least doubt that aggressive choking is identical with nest-choking. As I will describe in Chapter 21, and as can be seen in a detailed film of the Herring Gull's behaviour which G. Paris, B. van Noordwijk and I have made in the course of several years, the movements of feeding the young are different; they have only a very superficial resemblance to choking. In feeding, for instance, the choking call, with the accompanying unmistakable movements of the tongue-bone and the breast, is never uttered. The only resemblance between choking and feeding the young is the downward position of the head. This, however, occurs in other patterns of behaviour as well, such as wiping the bill, turning the eggs, eating, uttering the mew call, uttering the first phase of the trumpeting call, the copulation attitude of the male, and looking at the feet.[1]

In conclusion, I should like to point out that these objective analyses of threat behaviour, based on an accurate description of the behaviour and a consideration of the prevailing conditions, has made the whole aggressive behaviour-pattern more intelligible. Varied and differentiated as it is, it can be shown to be always an expression of two fundamental drives or instincts: the fighting drive and the drive to escape. Through simultaneous activation of these two drives various activities arise. Part of them are relatively pure fighting activities, part are pure flight, and between these two extremes are various results of a mingling of the two drives. Mixed intention movements and displacement activities are the results of this mingling of drives: while they seem at first sight to be quite " new " movements, our analysis shows that they are " derived movements." I believe that this type of approach, which has proved so fertile in those species which have been closely studied, offers unique opportunities for the study of other species as well.

The results seem interesting from another angle too. There are psychologists who are mainly interested in the subjective phenomena experienced by animals. These colleagues sometimes display—to put it mildly—a lack of appreciation for the type of study applied in this chapter. To quote Bierens de Haan (1947), an outspoken representative of this group of psychologists, we ethologists are like a man, who, viewing an oil painting, first

[1] Since the above was written (1950) the Black-headed Gull has been studied in detail by Mrs. R. M. Weidmann and Mr. M. Moynihan. Their (as yet unpublished) results, while generally supporting my views, show that choking offers more problems than indicated in my discussion.

puts a monochromatic colour-screen in front of his eyes, and thus deliberately misses the essential quality of the painting, colour. Without entering into a discussion of this statement, I should like to point out that in the case of the Herring Gull our accurate and painstaking objective study has enabled us to see that the various movements used as threat are " fed " by two fundamental drives of fighting and escape. It is only thanks to this objective analysis that the subjective psychologist will be

FIG. 13

Hostile choking (above) and friendly choking of the Laughing Gull. (After Noble & Wurm, 1943)

able to conclude that a gull displaying the upright threat-posture, grass-pulling, or choking, feels emotions like anger and fear simultaneously. I do not think it probable that the subjective psychologist would have been able to draw this conclusion about the " essentials " of the gulls' life without taking the trouble of carrying out such a detailed objective study. The comparison with the man ignoring the painting's colour does not hold—and may well be a boomerang.

The various forms of threat behaviour described here for the Herring Gull have been reported for several other *Larus* species. The Great Black-backed Gull shows both the upright threat posture and the two forms of displacement-nesting, and so do, according to my own observations, the Glaucous Gull, the Iceland Gull, and the Lesser Black-backed Gull. Wachs (1933) reports the choking in the Common Gull. The Black-headed Gull is different.[1] Kirkman (1937) describes an upright display and a forward display, but it seems doubtful whether either one has to do with the upright threat posture of the Herring Gull. Further, Kirkman describes an activity which seems to me the

[1] See the footnote on p. 75.

same as choking.   Not knowing it from my own observations, I must leave this problem open.   The related Laughing Gull from North America does show choking, and even in a more specialised form than the Herring Gull, for, according to the description and illustrations in Noble & Wurm's paper (1943) the displacement-choking in a boundary conflict is different from the real nest-choking in that the body and neck feathers are ruffled.

CHAPTER 8

INDIVIDUAL RECOGNITION

Selective responses to provoking individuals

Continuous study of the situations provoking fight, and, simultaneously, of the situations that do not, reveals some highly interesting aspects of gull community life.

First, numerous observations showed us that a territory owner rarely attacks all strangers indiscriminately. It depends on how a stranger is behaving whether it will be attacked or not. By comparing cases of selective attack, it is possible to find out what behaviour traits are especially fight-provoking. Quiet birds are often tolerated at places on or near the territory, where nesting or calling birds were chased. The following observations give an idea of how a male may ignore some birds and attack such offensive birds often much farther away.

The first three entries show the fight-provoking influence of choking.

" *14th May, 1936. 6.18 a.m.* A young male on the club is approached by a mewing female. They walk in the direction of territory 4, where ♀ 4 is incubating and ♂ 4 is on its station. Still at considerable distance from the 4-territory, the strangers begin to choke together. Male 4, who has tolerated them and three other pairs till now, flies immediately towards them when the choking begins, and chases them away. In order to reach them he has to pass three other strangers which have been sitting quietly at the club. His aggressive response is aimed selectively at the choking birds. The three quiet birds seemed to understand that the attack was not directed at them, for they remained where they were."

" *15th May, 1936. 7.6 a.m.* Male 4 is on its station. It runs suddenly to the club, where, 16 yards away, two birds are choking and nest-building together. On his way ♂ 4 passes and ignores several quiet birds."

" *15th May, 1936. 8.55 a.m.* Male 4 again chases a choking pair while leaving quiet birds close by alone."

The next entry shows that the trumpeting call is also provocative.

" *15th May, 1936. 6.13 a.m.* Male 4 is on station, ten birds on club not far away. Some birds begin to utter the mew call and the trumpeting call. Male 4 promptly attacks the trumpeting birds."

Even purely sexual behaviour causes offence, as the following observation shows:

' *2nd June, 1936. 7.30 a.m.* An immature ♂ and an adult ♀ are mutually head-tossing at the club (this is the introduction to coition). Male K comes running from his station and drives them off; while the ♀ chokes in response, the immature ♂ is afraid. Male K returns to its station, and then the head tossing begins anew; the male regurgitates, whereupon K again attacks them, passing many other quiet birds but disregarding them."

Such observations show that it is the reproductive activities that release attack in the territory-holders. Fighting is directed mainly at other gulls in reproductive condition, in other words, at potential reproductive rivals or competitors.

Genuine personal ties

However, apart from this, which is doubtlessly a matter of innate reactivity, there is a selectiveness which seems to be dependent on previous experience of the territory owner. Not all neighbours are attacked with equal vigour. On the one hand, there are cases in which special individuals are left alone and tolerated on places where no others are admitted, on the other hand some individuals may be singled out for attack wherever they may be.

First, it is a striking fact that a male Herring Gull does not attack its own mate, nor do females attack their husbands. Somehow they must " know " each other, that is to say, distinguish them from all other gulls by some characteristics; and on the basis of these characteristics their fighting, which would be immediately elicited by another gull on the territory, must be suppressed. This is indeed the case, and it is worth while to study this faculty more closely. I will, however, not dwell upon it here, but will return to it in the next chapter when the relations between members of a pair are discussed.

More amazing still is the fact that gulls seem to know their neighbours. This must be concluded from numerous observations we made, of which I will describe one. Two pairs, A and B, which I kept under observation during several weeks, had their nests exceptionally close together, indeed, no more than five yards apart. The boundary between the two territories had long been disputed, and as a consequence was very sharp. During a gale, the B-nest was entirely covered by sand, and the B-birds deserted it and disappeared from the scene. Immediately the A-birds occupied the old territory. About a week later, a new pair, distinguishable from the B-pair (the new male for instance had brown on the wing-coverts, remnants of the immature plumage) settled on the old B-territory, and these B_2-birds were soon tolerated by the A-pair. However, the B_2-birds were very lax in their territorial defence and often tolerated trespassers. Such trespassers into the B-territory were, however, always driven off by the A-birds. Trespassing males were chased by the A-male, while the A-female took charge of the females. Now in all these fights we never saw one of the A-birds charge the B_2-birds. This proves that they were able to distinguish them from other strangers. The discrimination was not dependent on the behaviour, nor on the presence of the B_2-birds. When the latter were preening or sleeping—both situations in which recognition may be extremely difficult—nest-building, or just walking around, they were not attacked. The promptness with which a stranger was perceived as such was highly remarkable. Often, during the absence of the B_2-birds, we were unable to decide whether a bird alighting on the B-territory was a stranger or not. Sometimes we knew, because they were behaving in a rather shy way. But other strangers seemed to be quite at ease, and then we were, at first, quite at a loss. The A-birds, however, never hesitated. In several cases we could check the identity of an attacked bird afterwards, for instance by tracing it to its own nest some hundreds of yards away, or by seeing the B_2-birds return while we knew where the stranger was, etc. Always the A-birds were proved to have been right.

Of course, this individual recognition must be based upon a learning process, and a very remarkable learning process at that.

The opposite may also occur: some neighbours are much more attacked than most others. As here again the intensive attack is independent of the behaviour of the attacked bird at the moment, we must assume that personal likings and dislikes play a prominent part. Such personal " hatred " must also be based upon individual recognition.

Similar relationships have been described by Kirkman in colonies of Black-headed Gulls. Here the nests are not evenly distributed but arranged in groups, often clustered around a bush or a tree. The birds of a group show a different attitude to birds belonging to the group (" inside birds ") than to those belonging elsewhere (" outside birds "); the inside birds are tolerated to a degree, the outside birds are much more readily attacked. Apart from this, Kirkman describes incidents which may be based on personal " hatred."

The fact that gulls know their mates, and, at any rate, some of their neighbours personally, raises the question as to how they do recognise them. What little we know about this will be discussed in Chapter 11, p. 99.

CHAPTER 9

SITE TENACITY

Return to same territory

Many of our colour-ringed gulls returned to the colony for several seasons in succession, and they enabled us to state that, as a rule, a Herring Gull returns to the same colony, and often even to the same territory, year after year. In some cases we even found that the nest was made at exactly the same site in two, once in three successive years. This did not mean simply repairing the remnants of the old nests, for there were no such remnants; in the sand-dunes the winter gales completely destroy the nests.

Our evidence on return to the same territory does not concern many ringed gulls, but together with circumstantial evidence based upon gulls which were recognisable in some other way it is quite convincing. In 1934, we caught 14 gulls at the nest and gave them coloured and aluminium rings. Next year nine of them returned, and all of them occupied the same territories as in 1934. The five missing individuals could not be found in spite of intensive search throughout the colony. As neither we nor any of our colleagues has ever seen a colour-ringed gull in the other Dutch colonies we assume that they had died. In 1936, five of the nine gulls were found again. Of these, four were again nesting in their old territories, while the fifth had settled at a new site about 120 yards north of the old territory. Again, no trace was found of the four missing birds, nor of the five individuals missed the year before.

The conclusion that return to the same territory is rather the rule is confirmed by numerous observations about the annual return of otherwise known gulls. Some individuals can be

recognised by the type of their eggs, others by behaviour characteristics like excessive nest-building, or a harsh voice, or by a
crippled leg, or by an exceptionally strong or an exceptionally
weak fighting drive, etc. We often knew such individuals quite
intimately and found them returning year after year.

Return to colony of birth

In a slightly different way evidence was procured showing
that Herring Gulls do not as a rule move from one colony to another. Ringing of Herring Gull chicks has gone on for many
years in the Dutch gulleries, especially during the 1920's. Chicks
are easily found in large numbers and provide nice long banding
lists. During the time we were carrying out our studies, a ringed
breeding gull was not a rare sight in the Wassenaar colony. We
decided to catch a number of them at the nests in order to read
the numbers of their rings and so to find out where they had been
born. Of eleven ringed gulls we captured on their nests at
Wassenaar, ten had been ringed as chicks in the Wassenaar
colony, whereas one was hatched near Bergen in the province
of North Holland, a colony about 45 miles north of Wassenaar.

Before interpreting this, we had to bear in mind that these
data did not mean anything as long as we did not know how
extensive ringing had been in other colonies. If there had been
much more extensive ringing at Wassenaar than in any other
colony our find would not amount to much. Another colony
where many chicks had been ringed throughout the 1920's and
early 1930's was the next northerly colony beyond Bergen, viz.,
the gullery at the island of Texel, 25 miles farther north. In
1938 we spent some days in this large colony, catching 15 ringed
individuals on the nest. Of these, 14 had been born in the
Texel colony, the 15th was from Bergen! The Bergen colony
in those days was the only one of the three, and I think the
only one in the Netherlands, that was not protected and was
often disturbed.

In North America, where the Herring Gull breeds in many
places along the east coast and even on the Great Lakes, a study
of this type has been carried out on a large scale. During 1937,

1938 and 1939 more than 22,000 chicks were ringed in 11 colonies, and a great number of recoveries have been reported. The data were used for studies on migration, longevity, plumage sequences and also on return to the nesting colonies. The paper by Gross (1940) on the Herring Gulls of the large Kent Island colony, inhabited by 25,000 birds, gives evidence pointing in the same direction as my own data. Ringed birds found in the colony in the breeding season (actual breeding was reported in only a few cases), numbering 64 individuals in all, were all ringed either as chicks or as adults on Kent Island or on islands nearby. No birds ringed elsewhere were found on Kent Island in summer, nor were Kent Island birds reported in summer from any other colony.

This American work has the advantage of large numbers. Our work, although concerning relatively few gulls, provides more accurate information about the individuals studied. We do actually know that our birds had nests; an interpretation of the status of a bird sighted or shot near a gullery, even if it is in the breeding season, is always uncertain, for numerous gulls straggle far from their home colony. It now seems unlikely that many Herring Gulls *breed* far from their home colony. The Bergen gulls show however that birds from a severely disturbed colony may join existing colonies as far as 45 miles away.

The facts obtained thus far show how strongly the Herring Gulls are attached to their home. Whereas in winter they may wander over an area covering many breeding colonies they are extremely conservative as regards their actual breeding place.

Although, considering what was already known about other birds, this was not a very remarkable or in any way unexpected result, the accumulation of these data gave us immense satisfaction. It is quite a thrill to discover that the birds you are studying are not simply specimens of the species *Larus argentatus* but that they are personal acquaintances. Somehow, the colony becomes much more interesting when you realise that it is composed of individuals that you know personally. Somehow, you feel, you are at home, you are taking part in their lives, and their adventures become part of your own life. It is difficult to explain this more fully, but I think everybody who has studied animal communities will understand how we felt.

Site tenacity in other birds

The same strong attachment to birth-place, and, more emphatically still, to the place where the bird has once bred successfully, is found among many other birds. The evidence for Common Terns (Austin, 1949), English Robins (Lack, 1943), European Redstarts (Ruiter, 1941), Song Sparrows (Nice, 1937), American Robins (Farner, 1945), American House Wrens (Kendeigh, 1941), Pied Flycatchers (von Haartman, 1949), Swallows (Boyd and Thomson, 1937), to mention some of the best-studied species, is much more extensive than our data on the Herring Gull. On the whole, as the studies of von Haartman, Richdale (1951) and Fisher (1952) show, the tendency to return is stronger in old birds than in young birds, but in some species even the attachment of young birds to their birth-place is very strong: Nice (1937) showed that of the Song Sparrow population of Interpont, Columbus, Ohio, 63 per cent of the young that survived the winter returned to the area studied, which measured about 1400 x 600 m. This site-tenacity is especially amazing in creatures like birds which have such extremely well-developed powers of travel, and indeed do travel over such enormous distances. Mayr has characterised the situation wittily by saying that birds have got their wings not so much for the purpose of getting away to places but rather for the purpose of getting back to their territories—which, of course, is only part of the truth, but is, I believe, meant as such.

Not all species of birds show this site-tenacity. For instance, the Rose-coloured Pastor, a bird which breeds in enormous colonies and feeds in the breeding season, entirely on migratory locusts, follows the locust swarms and settles down to breed at the place where the locust swarm happens to settle down for the same purpose. This site may change from year to year (Serebrennikov, 1931).

Another factor counteracting site-tenacity has been reported of ducks. As Landsborough Thomson has pointed out (1931) ducks may associate or perhaps even mate in their winter quarters with birds from northern countries, and in spring migrate back with them (" abmigration ").

Attachment to locality and evolution

The tendency found in these site-tenacious birds to return to the place where they were born, and to stick to that place in all subsequent breeding seasons, has an important bearing on problems of speciation, because it means that a species may be composed of many populations, which, though they are often mixing outside the breeding season, interbreed scarcely if at all. In other words, they may be reproductively isolated from each other, and if any genetic change happens to occur within one population, the chances that the change will spread to other populations are much smaller than they would be if there were completely irregular interbreeding. It depends of course on the degree of reproductive isolation whether such local genetic changes will have a chance of becoming typical of a larger group. Given a fair frequency of genetic changes, reproductive isolation is the condition allowing them to lead to differences between populations. Such differentiation is of course a very well-known phenomenon on the plane of the formation of subspecies. And as a matter of fact, the Herring Gull and its relatives are known to be involved in evolutionary differentiation of this kind. Systematists distinguish between several subspecies of Herring Gulls, and in some cases subspeciation has even gone so far as to lead to forms that are generally considered to be different species. Stegmann (1934) even considers the various races of Herring Gulls as conspecific both with the Iceland Gull and the Lesser Black-backed Gull. Concerning the Iceland Gull, commonly considered a separate species, I can add that according to my own observations in East Greenland in 1933 the behaviour is identical with that of the Herring Gulls I studied, so much so that I was unable to see any differences in posture, nor even hear any difference in calls, which is very remarkable in view of the fact that the Lesser Black-backed Gull, although closely related to the Herring Gull, yet has a very different voice.

Stegmann distinguishes only five species of large gulls, of which especially the *argentatus*-group is a veritable superspecies, a border-line case between a species and a group of species. His five species are *Larus hyperboreus*, the Glaucous Gull; *Larus marinus*, the Great Black-backed Gull; *L. argentatus*, the Herring Gull; the isolated Mediterranean *L. audouini*; and *L. canus*, the Common Gull, to which the Ring-billed Gull, *L. delawarensis*, is also reckoned. His work has received criticism (Geyr von Schweppenburg, 1938; Goethe, 1937) but, in my opinion, the different views presented differ mainly in degree.

Our results, indicating the possibility of reproductive isolation of a high order even between separate colonies, might mean that the genetic make-up of two such colonies may even be slightly different, and that each subspecies would consist of micro-subspecies.

CHAPTER 10

SOME ASPECTS OF FIGHTING AND TERRITORY

Why threat instead of fighting ?

Returning now to the problems of fighting, it is remarkable that real fights are so relatively rare. Whereas during half a day's watching one sees clashes every quarter of an hour or so, many days may pass before one sees a real man-to-man fight in which the birds touch each other. The fighting urge is strong enough, as anyone who watches the fights closely enough will agree, but it is nearly always vented through displacement nest-building and incipient attacks, alternating with much calling.

This is the general rule throughout the animal kingdom. In mammals, birds, reptiles, fish, insects, crustaceans, even in molluscs, species are known in which the reproductive season brings much intraspecific strife. Yet it is usually bluff rather than fighting. The bluff may consist of showing incipient attack, or of giving the opponent an exaggerated picture of one's body-size, or of showing off conspicuously coloured structures, or of performing displacement activities. It always has the function of threat, that is, of intimidating the opponent who ventures too close to the defender's centre of " reproductive interest."

This raises an interesting evolutionary problem. Fighting seems to have two effects: inflicting damage, and effecting withdrawal. Whereas most naturalists will agree that the second effect is somehow of advantage to the individual and through it to the species—a problem to which I will presently return—the inflicting of injuries certainly is not of any advantage to the individual. Somehow the evolutionary development has favoured a form of intraspecific antagonism with a minimum risk of actual damage. The interest of the problem lies in the difficulty to see how selection—as the most probable agent—can have suppressed the development of fierce, ruthless fighting. At first sight it seems that ruthless fighters, mutants in which the fighting urge is exceptionally strong, would be at an enormous advantage. There are, however, several possible reasons why this may not be true. The most probable reason seems to me the following. In many species, pair-formation takes place in the following way. The males become aggressive towards other males of the same species. The aggressive behaviour, like so many if not all other types of instinctive behaviour, is released by special " sign stimuli " from the opponent. Because of this dependence on sign stimuli given by the opponent the male directs its fighting mainly to its own species, or, in psychological terms, it recognises its own species. Now in many species (especially, though not exclusively, those in which sexual dimorphism is relatively slight) the sign stimuli which release the male's first reaction to an approaching newcomer are so generalised that both male and female may provide them. The result is that the male's very first reaction to any newcomer, either male or female, is a hostile one. This however, lasts only a very short time. Immediately after this first reaction, the newcomer will react to it, and these reciprocal reactions are different in females and males. According to these responses of the newcomer, the male's next reaction may be either a continuation of the hostile behaviour, or a shift to courtship behaviour. While a strange male will either try to escape as a response to the hostile first reaction, or will threaten in return, or sing—all signs of his masculinity—a female in sexual condition usually does neither of these things, but shows a typically female reaction in return. The male cannot resist the female's behaviour, which acts as a social releaser by sending out sign stimuli which suppress his hostile behaviour and elicit his courtship as well. This has been worked out experimentally in the Three-spined Stickleback, but there is also evidence in a number of other species. This type of pair-formation has been found in such widely different species as, for instance, the Snow Bunting, the Robin, Storks, Gulls, Lizards, Sticklebacks, Bitterlings, and Cuttlefish. The male's first reaction is always a type of hostile behaviour, and it bifurcates into two possible further lines of behaviour, viz., either fight or courtship, dependent on the newcomer's response.

The bearing this has on our problem is as follows. I think it highly probable that a ruthless fighter, an individual with an unusually strong fighting urge, would reduce its own chances of reproduction by not responding readily enough to the female's releasers, and attacking instead of courting her. As a matter of fact, such individuals are known to bird fanciers. Especially among song-birds there are some males that become so extremely pugnacious that it is impossible to pair them; they invariably attack any other bird that comes in their vicinity.

Now one might object that, if an increased fighting urge is a disadvantage, a change from mere threat behaviour to attack could be effected by a decrease in the intensity of the escape drive. Threat, as we have seen, is always the outcome of a balance between the fighting urge and the urge to escape. This, however, would possibly have the consequence of reducing escape from predators too, which of course is disadvantageous in another way.

Concluding, it would seem that it is impossible to consider intensities of drives separately. There are always interrelations between the various drives; they are, in each species, well balanced. This, of course, is the result of selection. Selection always results, in surviving species, in compromise, in balance between the numerous mechanisms serving maintenance, and no mechanism can be developed to the extreme when a balanced relationship to other mechanisms is vital. The study of instinct, practised from this angle, reveals this principle of balance and compromise as clearly as morphological study. The only prerequisite necessary for understanding this, is the recognition that instincts are physiological mechanisms and that they are units, or " organs," however complicated they may be as systems.

Territory

The existence of a territorial system in the Herring Gull raises still another problem. The territory system is such a widespread one in the animal kingdom that it is only natural to expect it to be of value to the species possessing it. The problem could even be phrased in a more general form: what is the use of all this fighting in the reproductive season?

Not all fighting is connected with territory. There are species in which the males defend—that is, fight in the vicinity of—something that is not restricted to a special place, but is moving about. For instance, a male of the Bitterling, a little fish that lays its eggs in the mantle-cavity of fresh-water mussels (*Anodonta*) fights off other males from the particular mussel it has selected. In a sense this could be called a territory, but this " territory " is not always in the same place, but moves about with the slowly wandering mussel. Many deer and related species, and also some birds, as for instance the Avocet, do not at all confine their fighting to a territory, but restrict it to the vicinity of the female wherever the latter may be. In the Herring Gull, as I hope to show in the next chapter, both " free fighting " and fighting restricted to a territory occur. Before mating-up, the males fight on the clubs but not on a particular part of them. After pair-formation has taken place, the pair select a territory and restrict their fighting to this territory, which of course results in its defence.

It is a matter of taste whether one describes such cases of " free " fighting as defence of a mobile territory or as the defence of a mussel or a mate. Apart from this nomenclatorial question, so much is certain that fighting, confined to the vicinity of something, and directed against reproductive rivals, results in the defence of that " something " against interference by rivals. Now comparison of all known cases of reproductive fighting shows that this " something " is always an object or a situation indispensable for reproduction, and the rigorous warding off of intruders tends to prevent the concentration of many individuals upon one of these objects, while others might be available but not used. Too many Bitterlings with one mussel might well cause an excessive crowding of parasitic eggs in the mussel, which might have a harmful effect on the offspring of the Bitterlings involved. Too many males mating or trying to mate with one female might well be a waste of sex-cells. Fighting in such cases, while possibly it does not absolutely prevent more than one male from sharing the " indispensable object", certainly tends to space out the males, forcing them to make better use of the available objects.

It seems natural to conclude that territory is also a situation that is indispensable for reproduction, and that defence of territory helps in spreading males out more evenly and more widely than they would otherwise be, and, consequently, that defence of territory is a help in ensuring maximum efficiency of germ-cells.

In some cases, the use of a territory is evident. In many hole-breeding birds, for instance, fighting is defence of a nesting hole. That is, the presence of a suitable nesting hole is a condition for the full activation of the fighting urge in the defending individuals, the attention of trespassers is aimed at the hole, and they are the more intensely attacked by the owner the closer they are to the hole. This state of affairs is found, for instance, in the Jackdaw (Lorenz, 1931), in the Kestrel (L. Tinbergen, 1935), and in the House Sparrow (Daanje, 1941), to mention only a few cases.

In many cases the use of a territory is still uncertain. Personally I believe that in many song-birds its use is to be found in the ensurance of a food-supply for the young. Although this interpretation is not generally accepted and is even opposed by some workers, among them Lack, the following facts seem to me to be decisive. First, the time available for collecting food for the young is limited, especially when the young are still very small. Howard (1935) has shown experimentally that young Whitethroats have to be brooded regularly with short intervals as long as they are very young. When the parents leave the nest exposed too long, the young, upon their return with food, will not gape, and gaping is necessary for feeding. The colder the weather, the shorter is the maximum tolerated time of absence of the parents. This means that the foraging trips of the parents must be short, and that it is of advantage when there is an adequate supply of food in the immediate vicinity of the nest.

Second, this function of territory may become obvious and critical only under adverse conditions. A striking demonstration of this was given by a pair of Snow Buntings I was once watching (Tinbergen, 1939). This pair was nesting on a small island in an East Greenland fjord. When the weather was warm and sunny, the parents collected all the food on their island. During cold and rainy weather, however, they left the island to forage on the mainland, which necessitated long trips. Of course, the island situation made the difference between good and bad weather much more impressive than it would be in other situations, but the observation proves that foraging trips will take more time the worse the weather is, at least in birds feeding the young with insects.

These observations show that the importance of territory as a food-supply may be evident only during the first days after hatching, and only in very adverse weather conditions. A territory might be of enormous importance in this respect, saving masses of individuals on some occasions, and yet this function might escape attention even in accurate ecological studies if the observer happened to miss one of the rare critical days.

However this may be, enough has been said to show that it is worth while to try and find the use of any case of territory we meet with, and this brings me back to the Herring Gull. Is, in the Herring Gull, territory indispensable for reproduction? An answer in the affirmative could only be given if we could point to a harmful effect of a decrease in the size of territories. So far as I can see, there is only one harmful effect. This is not connected with any of the possible functions of territory advanced thus far for other species, and it seems to me worth while to put my hypothesis forward in some detail, as I think it could apply to a number of other species as well.

Food is of no importance. Although both adults and chicks will occasionally snap up a fly or a beetle I cannot believe this to be of any consequence. The main bulk of food is collected outside the breeding grounds. There are cases known of starving colonies, it is true, but these cases had probably nothing to do with territory, but with an absolute growth in numbers, upon which territory had no influence, since the colony simply spread out.

Territory in the Herring Gull most certainly has nothing to do with the reservation of a nesting site either, as it has in hole-nesting birds. The number of nest-sites available is practically unlimited. It is only tradition that keeps a colony at its locality, and a growing colony expands into territory that was unoccupied before, simply because it was too far away from other resident gulls.

Neither is a territory necessary to prevent interference in copulation, a function that has been suggested for the territories of Blackcocks and Ruffs (Lack, 1939). Many copulations occur in the group at the " clubs," and I rarely saw them interfered with, except when they were attempted at or very near an occupied territory.

I believe that the territorial system in the Herring Gull is connected with the defence of the brood against predators. By " defence " I do not mean active defence but passive defence by the use of cryptic coloration. Of course there is active defence, the adult gulls joining in a social attack upon predators, but this active defence is not sufficient and is only part of the defence system. A man, a dog, a heron, a buzzard are fiercely attacked. The attack, however, is not very efficient. The gulls swoop down on the predator, and occasionally hit him. I have seen a heron forced down by such a social attack, and a " hell of a time " he had before he got out. A buzzard does not mind the gulls much, but I must say I never saw one actually try to come down and take chicks. Dogs occasionally visit colonies and cannot be warded off by the gulls. When a dog happens to roam through the colony when there are chicks, it kills whatever chicks it finds, and leaves the bodies where they are. Once I saw the results of repeated raids by a fox in the egg-season. Judging from its tracks, it found several nests. It took one egg at a time, carried it to a spot some 12 yards away, buried it, then returned to the nest, took a second egg, which it buried at another place about the same distance away, then returned again to take and bury the last egg. This happened with a couple of nests every day until the fox was shot. It was still early enough in the season for the gulls to start a new brood. A great part of those gulls which had lost their eggs deserted their territory and I am sure they started anew at the border of the colony. The result was an extension of the colony and an appreciable decrease in the number of nests per surface unit. As I said already, the result in such a case is an actual increase in size of the remaining territories, the deserted territories being immediately incorporated into the remaining territories.

Exactly the same phenomenon of spreading is effected by intensive egg-collecting by man, as I have often observed.

This spreading-out therefore is the reaction to egg-predation; and it is important that it is shown by colonies which, because of the complete protection, were more densely populated than they are under more normal conditions when a certain amount of predation is going on. Judging from the enormous increase after protection has begun, the normal clutch of three is large enough to allow for a high mortality through predation.

Now from what I have seen I am sure that egg predation either by dog, fox, or man, is less serious the farther the nests are apart. This, no doubt, is due to passive defence through the cryptic coloration of eggs and chicks. Finding a nest with its cryptically coloured eggs takes some time and some attention. In this connection the active attacks by the parent gulls, while not absolutely preventing the larger predators from taking eggs, may well have the function of at least diverting their attention to a certain extent. As in all similar cases, no absolute hundred-per-cent results can ever be expected, the function of cryptic coloration—as of all other adaptations—is always relative, partial.

The conclusion that a certain extent of spacing out is an essential element of cryptic adaptation receives considerable support from a comparative study of the behaviour of cryptically coloured animals. In caterpillars, for instance, a group where, owing to their food value and lack of devices for active defence, visual adaptations are highly developed, there is a very close correlation between gregariousness and conspicuous coloration (usually functioning as warning coloration) on the one hand, and between cryptic coloration and spacing out on the other hand.

It seems therefore that the territorial system in the Herring Gull has primarily the function of " passive " defence of eggs and young. As I will show in the next chapters, the Herring Gull possesses other behaviour characteristics connected with the concealing colour of eggs and young.

Plate 13a. (*Left*) male in upright threat posture, medium intensity; (*right*) male grass pulling

    b. (*Left*) male in upright threat posture, medium intensity

    c. (*Left*) male grass pulling. Compare his posture with text Fig. 10

Plate *14a.* A bird in immature plumage on the " club "

b. On guard on the territory

PART THREE

Pair Formation and Pairing

CHAPTER II

THE OLD PAIRS

Status of birds on arrival

As we have seen, many, though not all, Herring Gulls are already mated when they arrive at the gullery in early spring. For several reasons I believe that these mated birds are old birds that have bred before and have returned to their old territories. The reasons are the following—they seem convincing to me. First, most of our colour-ringed birds behaved in this way in the season or seasons after they were marked. Second, quite a number of relatively young birds, wearing spotted secondaries and tail feathers, settled down in the colony each year, and we followed their behaviour in a number of cases. Such birds are often fertile; they mate and produce offspring. These young birds, of which we can be certain that they are breeding for the first time, are never paired when they arrive, and they never take up a territory right at the beginning. They always settle down first on the " clubs."

I will discuss the old pairs first. We have several observations pointing to the conclusion that Herring Gulls, as a rule, pair for life. Of the fourteen colour-ringed birds mentioned before, twelve had an unringed mate. The two others formed a pair, and this pair could be observed on the same territory, nesting at exactly the same place, in three successive seasons. We have also known pairs of which the male and female could be easily identified, and which we found breeding at the same spot in successive seasons. The decrease in the numbers of our ringed birds in the course of years suggests a relatively high mortality, and although we cannot be absolutely sure, we think that a widowed bird usually takes a new mate in the next season. Apart from death, or from other causes which will be treated later, Herring Gulls seem to pair for life.

Do they remain together during the winter? Probably not. In any case, if two mates join the same winter flocks, they never show any behaviour indicating personal attachment; a winter flock seems to be made up of individuals, not of pairs. The behaviour during the winter is, in this respect, entirely different from that during the breeding season, when birds of a pair show their attachment in many ways. Also, the winter behaviour of gulls is quite different from that of social birds that live in pairs all through the winter, such as, for instance, Jackdaws (Lorenz, 1931). In this species it requires only a few minutes' watching in winter to single out the pairs, for they keep very closely together. It seems probable therefore, that the Herring Gull pairs break up in autumn.

How, then, do they find each other in spring? It has often been suggested that the mates in such cases do not really recognise each other, but that a bird mates with the individual that presents itself on its territory. Such birds would not recognise their mate but their territory, or, to say it in another way, they would " recognise " each other by their being on the same territory. This, however, does not apply to the Herring Gulls, for they find their old mates again outside the territory, often even outside the colony. When, in February, the gulls develop their wonderful white breeding plumage, they begin to concentrate around their old breeding places. Weeks before their first visit to the dunes they begin to form pairs, and from then on one sees them in pairs on the feeding grounds, in the polders, along the beaches, in the towns. Once I have been so lucky as to observe the colour-ringed pair mentioned above, well before the first visit of the gulls at the breeding stations. They kept strictly together, and when they moved from one meadow to the other they were attached to each other as if by a string. Nothing else in their behaviour indicated that they were a pair, but their known history and subsequent developments proved it.

Individual recognition

These observations seem to show that both partners find and recognise each other in spring when they return to the wider environment of their own breeding colony. This shows an amazing faculty, not only of recognising individuals, but also of memory.

The ability to recognise individuals has been studied somewhat more closely during the breeding season. We did not tackle the problem by systematic experimentation but by collecting incidental evidence, which is not too difficult provided one has the problem continuously in mind during watching. As a rule, Nature makes numerous experiments for us and it is amazing how much evidence one can collect if one is continuously on the alert and appreciative of the possibilities.

It often happens, for instance, that a gull falls asleep when resting on the territory, or while incubating. Passing birds, as long as they do not come too near, usually do not wake up such a sleeping bird, even if they are calling loudly. We have observed several times, however, that the voice of the approaching mate instantly woke up the sleeping bird. Such observations are by no means rare and it is a matter of attention and of time only to collect quite conclusive evidence of this kind, proving that mates may recognise each other by voice. This does not mean that the mate has to utter a special call. A bird returning to its territory usually utters the long-drawn mew call, but the same call uttered by any other bird leaves the sleeping bird unconcerned.

Visual stimuli are also sufficient, however. We have seen clear evidence of personal recognition in entirely silent birds. Some of these data show that a Herring Gull can recognise its mate in flight at 30 yards' distance. To illustrate the type of evidence that proves individual recognition I will quote one entry of 22nd May, 1935.

" I am observing a group of about 35 birds on a " club." In the environment are various occupied territories. Some of the birds on the club are evidently single, others are standing in pairs. Some of these pairs are very active, and we decide to concentrate on one of these. The female begs food from her mate, now and then it chases other females; it entices the male to join it in nesting activities, and he chases other males. This goes on for about half an hour; then their activity wanes. After a while the female flies off, travels just above the ground to the north-west, till she is about 500 yards away, then makes a wide turn and comes back from the north-east. During this time she disappears now and then behind hills and trees, and she must have been unable to see the club for about half of her trip. In the meantime, another observer has kept an eye on the male. We are very fortunate this time because the male, right after the female's departure, started a fight with two other males, which caused some commotion, and resulted in a drastic change of position, not only of this male but also of that of the surrounding birds. When the female returns, therefore, the male is at least 20 yards away from where she left him, and several birds have taken up entirely new positions. Nevertheless the female, apparently without any hesitation, alights at the side of her mate."

This was one of the first indications we got about individual recognition. Later we saw many more proofs of this amazing power of recognition. Mates recognise each other instantly, in various positions, and from great distances : in fact they were infinitely better at it than we. It is true that, after a season of close watching, we knew most of the gulls in the neighbourhood, partly by the expression of their faces, but we never reached the degree of promptness with which the gulls reacted.

Apart from recognising each other outside and on the territory the gulls instantly identify a stranger on their territory. When we saw this for the first time, we thought that recognition of the stranger might be due to its uncertain behaviour, for as a rule a bird, while behaving in a rather self-possessed way on his own territory, is ill-at-ease when on strange territory. However, this is not always the case. Especially when a pair is temporarily absent, or when one bird is incubating, which ties him to the nest, strangers may trespass and make themselves quite at ease, behaving " as if they were at home." Yet as soon as the owner(s) return or an incubating bird is relieved, the strangers will be chased.

Individual recognition has been found in several other species. It seems to be highly developed in social birds. Interesting accounts are given by Lorenz (1931), who has studied a breeding colony of tame Jackdaws. The members of such a colony know each other individually and recognise each other instantly. This is indicated, amongst other things, by the existence of a rigid dominance order. The situation is much like that in a school form or a boys' soccer team. There is a recognised " leader," that is an individual for whom all the others have respect and who is obeyed whenever he exerts his power. There is an individual who, while not daring to revolt against the leader, yet is recognised by the others as superior to them. Next lower in the scale is one who is regarded as relatively superior by all but the leader and the next, and so on. In birds, such a dominance order is only seen when two individuals happen to compete for the same thing, e.g. for food, or for a perch. Continuous watching reveals that a clash between two individuals always results in the withdrawal of the same individual. The clashes, however, are not very spectacular, fierce fighting is rare, and the inferior bird usually withdraws at the slightest indication of the superior bird's intentions.

Jackdaws remember each other for a long time. Lorenz once observed the return of one of his Jackdaws after it had been away for seven months. From the way in which the other Jackdaws reacted it was obvious that they recognised it at once.

It would be of the greatest interest to find out how birds recognise each other in such cases. We have only very fragmentary knowledge of this problem. All that is known thus far indicates that recognition may be visual but that it may also be auditory, just as in the Herring Gull. Brückner (1933) found that chicks of the domestic fowl recognise the mother by her voice. Heinroth (1911) relates a fascinating little incident with swans. A male in the Berlin Zoo once attacked his own wife while she was feeding with the head under the surface of the water. When she raised her head, he stopped at once, which indicates that he recognised her by her face. It is very well possible that facial expression is an important help in recognition in other birds as well, for every bird-watcher who is really familiar with a species can detect numerous differences in proportions between the individual faces.

Monogamy

From all these facts it is evident that the Herring Gulls are monogamous. This monogamy is very strict indeed. We have observed several times how stray birds (for reasons usually unknown to us) tried to " seduce " already mated birds. In no case was such a bird accepted. Usually it was chased away by the bird it had approached. In the majority of cases their advances were not answered at all: sometimes the mated bird would show some friendliness, but even then this response would not go beyond occasional feeding or some other sign of relatively weak sexual arousal, and in the end such a bird would suddenly charge at the stranger and drive it off. I will return to these observations later; it is first necessary to describe the general procedure of pair-formation.

CHAPTER 12

THE FORMATION OF NEW PAIRS

TILL NOW I have been speaking exclusively of the birds that are already mated when they arrive at the breeding places. We saw that these were always birds that had already been breeding in at least one previous season.

It took us rather a long time to find out where and how the initial formation of these pairs takes place. We had to build up our picture from many partial case-histories, but we think we have now got a fair idea of how mating-up usually occurs.

As we soon suspected, this takes place at the clubs, and we have spent a considerable amount of time in watching club life. This is a job that unites all the peculiar aspects, pleasant and unpleasant, of bird watching. The unpleasant sides are: irregular mobility of the birds, which increases the difficulties of following special individuals on the one hand; and the long spells of non-reproductive activity such as sleeping and preening, which interrupt quite promising series of observations, on the other hand.

Sexing the birds

The first prerequisite is, in such a case, to recognise the sex of a bird. In species where no conspicuous sexual dimorphism exists, the surest criterion is the laying of the eggs. A slightly less reliable criterion is copulation, in which, in all the birds known, the male mounts the female. However, in pigeons, grebes and other monomorphic birds the females are known to mount the males at least occasionally, and the possibility of such a reversal of roles could not be excluded right at the beginning. However, from our study of marked birds we know that in Herring Gulls the male always mounts the female. Using this behavioural difference as a check, we soon found many other differences between males and females. The chief of these is that, on the average, the males are larger than the females, and have a more sturdy head. The female has a higher forehead than the male, giving her face a somewhat more rounded and milder appearance than that of the male, whose forehead is flatter, more a continuation of the upper margin of the bill. Of course these differences are much clearer at some times than at others, owing not only to individual differences but also to flattening or ruffling of the head feathers. An interesting feature to which I must return later has been pointed out by Goethe (1937) and fully confirmed by us. While there is considerable overlapping in size between males and females, exceptionally large females being larger than exceptionally small males, in every pair the male is larger than the female. Pairs in which the female is larger than the male have never been observed.

As said before, life at the club may be very dull for hours continuously. This, incidentally, shows how well chosen is the name club. The birds are either dozing, or preening themselves. The arrival of a newcomer, or any other displacement however begun, may cause one bird to adopt the upright threat posture and approach other birds. This threat gesture is instantly reacted to, and all the birds in the neighbourhood wake up, stretch their necks, and walk away, leaving a vacuum around the threatening bird. Such an aggressive bird is always a male. In most cases the matter does not develop into anything like a fight, for usually there is no other male intending to resist; everybody just fades away, and the aggressiveness dies down. If one bird fails to move in time, and then flies in panic when it sees a threatening bird immediately in front of him, this may release a sudden attack, and if the bird is unfortunate enough to get caught, a thorough thrashing and general aggressive commotion may result.

Initiative of the females

Now in many cases such outbursts of aggressiveness are provoked by the females. Females usually take the initiative in pair-formation. This happens in the following way. A female walks towards a male, her neck drawn in, body and head pointing

FIG. 14

Female (right) proposing to male. (This and the two subsequent pictures have been drawn from a film)

horizontally forward. Now and then she will make a tossing movement with the head, uttering a subdued, very melodious " klioo " at each tossing of the head. In this way she walks round the male, describing one or several circles around him.

The male's reactions

The male may react in one of two ways. He may stretch himself to the extreme, making himself as large and broad as possible. Looking around, he seems to be in search of potential opponents. His whole attitude suggests force, and also readiness to use this force. If, on such occasions, other males are in the neighbourhood, he will approach them, gradually adopting the upright threat posture, and if opportunity arises, he will charge. If other males happen to be accompanied by interested females too, bitter fights may ensue. These fights are independent of territory; the male may show some attachment to the part of the club it happens to find itself on, but the attachment is very loose and real settling upon a territory will not occur until after pairing-up, and the final territory may be far from the club. The loose attachment at the club is no more than just incipient territoriality.

The second type of reaction to the female's approach is quite different. The male stretches his neck forward, and utters the mew call. He then walks with the female to a place, usually not more than 10 yards away, and makes incomplete nest-building movements in which the female joins. These movements are not distinguishable from the aggressive " choking " (p. 59). It is possible that it is more often accompanied by real scraping than is the aggressive choking.

Sometimes the male reacts in still another way. At the approach of the female, he stretches his neck incompletely and turns and twists it in various directions. The female immediately reacts to this by intensifying and speeding up her head-tossing. She walks back and forth in front of him, even occasionally holds his bill for a moment. The male seems to try to avoid her solicitations by hurried head-movements, yet he does not walk away. After a while, the male's neck swells, the swelling travels upwards, then he opens his beak widely, at the same time pointing it downward, and, evidently with some exertion, regurgitates an enormous quantity of half-digested food. As soon as the male opens his bill, the female frantically pecks into his mouth, and begins to swallow the food with incredible greediness.

I do not quite understand the part played by these three ceremonies. Our general impression is that fighting is the most probable reaction of the male when the tie between him and the female is still loose, and that nest-building and feeding increase in frequency as the birds become more and more attached to each other. At the same time it is certain that there are individual

differences, some males being primarily fighters, while others are much less aggressive and more inclined to court a female. In favour of the interpretation that fighting is the first reaction of un-mated males is the fact that young males, recognisable by the brown mottling of wing-coverts and secondaries and by a

Fig. 15

Female (above) proposing to male, 2

remnant of the brown tail bar, are the most fierce fighters on the club, and are rarely seen to feed the females or to build with them, although they are often approached by head-tossing females.

However this may be, fighting, nest-building and feeding belong to the period of pair-formation. They are not confined to that period, and extend well into the period of mated life, but they occur very frequently before the birds are paired.

I believe that pairing-up is a relatively slow affair. We have many observations indicating that an unmated bird may begin by courting a number of other birds rather promiscuously. With unmated females the evidence is quite unmistakable. We have often seen a female making advances towards a number of males in succession and walking straight from one discouraging male to the next. In 1949 we watched a female approach four different males within two minutes. With males, the evidence is less clear, because what seems to be his very first reaction is not aimed at the female, but is aggressiveness towards other males. It is not always easy to see what female he is trying to impress. Yet we have known males that changed from one female to another rather early in the season, and especially at the clubs there seem to be many males that show low-intensity courting such as uttering the mew call, making half-hearted nesting movements, and coming to the verge of regurgitation as reactions to apparently unmated females.

CHAPTER 13

THE BEHAVIOUR OF MATED BIRDS

Copulation

Gradually, and maybe in some cases suddenly, pairs are formed. At this stage several new behaviour-patterns appear. Copulation is one of these. Although I am not sure whether some birds may occasionally copulate before they are paired, I think this is an exception. Coition is preceded by a long and very remarkable ceremony. The head-tossing movements and the accompanying begging call uttered by a female enticing a male to feed her is the pre-coition ceremony for both sexes. In general one can predict copulation or at least an attempt at it when the male, instead of regurgitating food, begins to toss his head and to utter the begging call himself. The pre-coition display therefore is entirely mutual, male and female making the food-begging movement a great number of times. The male, therefore, may react to the female's begging by either feeding or head-tossing. In relatively rare cases do these two reactions of the male more or less merge. He may, for instance, make some initial regurgitating movements, and then switch to head-tossing, but this is rare : the two reactions seem to be relatively independent.

The initiative may be taken by either sex. A normal copulation runs as follows. Both birds toss their heads, each in its own rhythm. Now and then they take a few steps, turning around each other. After a while the male begins to stretch his neck upward, still tossing his head, and takes a position obliquely behind the female. He begins to lift his wings a little, then stops head-tossing but lowers his tongue bone and begins to utter a rhythmic, hoarse call. Immediately afterwards he jumps on to his mate's back, waving his wings and settling down on his tarsi on her shoulders. His feet rest on the female's upper arm, which the toes are holding in their grip. The female continues and intensifies the head-tossing, touching the male's breast every time, and even rubbing her bill against his breast. The male, uttering the copulation call all the while, lowers his tail till it touches her tail, then makes a series of sideways rubbing movements and finally brings his tail down at the side of the raised tail of the female, and, waving his wings to keep his balance, brings his cloaca into contact with hers. This is repeated a number of times (up to seven). Thereupon the male stops calling, folds his wings, and jumps down at the side of the female. There is no post-coition display, but usually the birds begin to preen after a while.

Low-intensity forms

Copulation provides a very interesting behaviour-pattern for a study of the results of varying intensities of the underlying drive. Low-intensity copulations can be seen early in the season. The first copulation may be seen several weeks before the first eggs are laid. Sometimes the male's reaction is too low in intensity, sometimes the female's, sometimes both.

If the female's drive is too weak, she objects to the mounting of the male by stretching her neck, walking away until she has thrown him off, and sometimes pecking at him. When the female refuses the male repeatedly, he may be led to explosive copulatory behaviour. In the weakest form, this consists of a few seconds' undirected tail-wagging after being thrown off. Continuous frustration may cause males to approach other females, and even to desert their mates and re-mate, but this seems to be rare, for although we have repeatedly studied pairs in which the male could not copulate, for instance because the female was limping and fell down when he mounted, or because he was limping and could not settle into the right position for copulation, we have only observed two cases of re-mating, both after a number of unsuccessful copulations extending over a number of days. In these cases, the bond of the pair to the territory began to slacken first, they began to roam around the clubs, and only after some days did they abandon each other and the male pair with another female.

Among other social-nesting birds, for instance the Grey-Heron (Verwey, 1930), the Rook (Yeates, 1934) and the Cormorant (Kortlandt, 1940) it has been observed that some males assault females of neighbouring nests and " steal " matings. Although I have repeatedly observed both mated males and females making half-hearted sexual approaches to strangers, I never saw attempts at forced matings. The observed approaches were always according to Herring Gull etiquette, that is, through either mew-call, nest-choking, or head-tossing. It is possible that I have insufficient experience because I have spent less time in watching incubating birds than in observing the behaviour at the clubs (where identification is often difficult) and in experimenting with individual gulls. Yet I find it difficult to believe that I would have missed, in all these seasons, such events if they were as common as in the said species, especially since the opportunity to survey and watch a great number of pairs is better with Herring Gulls than with Herons or Rooks.

Returning to the phenomenon of low-intensity copulations, we may now consider the cases of failure due to the male. If a male's sexual urge is very low, he may simply not respond to the female's head-tossing, but avoid her, or even peck at her. In less extreme cases he may perform some half-hearted head-tossings, or he may even mount. The half-hearted head-tossings are interesting, because, although their frequency may be very

FIG. 17

Incomplete copulation due to the female failing to co-operate. (After a film) low indeed, each separate toss is complete and of full intensity. It is as if, when the urge reaches threshold value, the head-tossing can only go off in full. It is "all-or-none"; a phenomenon that is common in simple elements of a behaviour pattern, but not in most more complicated instinctive actions.

When the male mounts in spite of a low urge, he often fails to complete coition. Instead of bringing his tail down, he will fold his wings, and, in spite of the female's head-tossing, remain standing on

FIG. 18

Incomplete copulation due to the male failing to continue after mounting.
(After a film)

her back, looking alternately down as if not " understanding " what to do, or looking unconcernedly, a very silly spectacle. Sometimes he will spread his wings again after a while and bend his legs. This suggests that in this condition it is the head-tossing of the female that, by summation of repeated stimulation, brings him beyond the threshold. Still more interesting are those cases, in which even a male that has lowered into the sitting position does not proceed to copulate. If, in such cases, the female raises her tail, giving him a tactile stimulus, the male responds immediately by tail-wagging and copulating, thereby showing the releasing value of stimuli given by the female.

A close study of these phenomena, therefore, shows very clearly the interplay of the internal drive and the external stimuli.

CHAPTER 14

THE ORIGIN OF COURTSHIP DISPLAYS

Head-tossing

A few words must be said on the head-tossing as a pre-coition display. It is indistinguishable from the head-tossing shown by the female begging for food. It is not identical with, but very similar to, the food-begging of full-grown young. The differences are mainly a matter of voice; whereas the young Herring Gull emits a not very loud, harsh squeaking, the begging call of the adult has the beautiful clear timbre characteristic of most Herring Gull calls. In the begging call it has a certain sweetness not to be heard in the sturdy trumpeting call or in the mew call. Further, the young adopt a horizontal posture with the neck drawn in just like the adults, but they toss their heads only occasionally. More often they quickly stretch their neck vertically and immediately withdraw it, while the head is not tossed up but is kept horizontal. The begging movement of the adult therefore differs from that of the young gull in that it does not have the " pumping " element, and that the tossing is much more frequent than in the young. The starting posture is the same in both cases, although it is usually more horizontal in the young.

The same flat posture, now in the extremely horizontal position of the young, is adopted by the unmated adult female, and occasionally by males, when " proposing " as described above.

Courtship-feeding

The begging for food, therefore, is part of the sexual behaviour pattern. In this, the Herring Gull does not stand alone; feeding, and the reciprocal part, begging for food, is part of the courtship

Plate 15a. Male (right) about to feed the female

b. Herring Gulls copulating

Plate 16a. The mew call

    b. Expression of alarm (this bird is a hybrid between a Lesser Black-backed Gull and a Herring Gull)

or of the pre-coition behaviour of many birds, and even of other animals. A valuable review of " courtship-feeding " by birds has been given by Lack (1940); similar phenomena in other groups have been reviewed by Meisenheimer (1921).

Here again, the problem of the origin of this queer connection between two behaviour-patterns, here that of the feeding drive with that of the sexual drive, may be considered. Feeding another individual is of course part of the parental behaviour-pattern, which is another pattern belonging to the reproductive drive as a whole, a pattern usually appearing long after the strictly sexual activities have waned. Parental behaviour is dependent on the activity of the reproductive drive, as is the sexual drive; the tendency to employ the nervous mechanisms responsible for the feeding movement normally appear in the last phase of the breeding cycle, much later than the sexual behaviour. The appearance of feeding movements *as part* of the sexual behaviour therefore is entirely irrelevant.

Now the occurrence of " irrelevant " movements is just as common in sexual behaviour as it is in aggressive behaviour, a fact known for a long time and becoming more evident as more and more species are being studied and compared. As usual, comparison, by showing that certain phenomena that may seem to be isolated oddities at first are in fact of widespread occurrence, focuses attention on problems that might otherwise seem unimportant.

In 1914 Huxley had already described what he called " habit-preening " in courting Great Crested Grebes. Preening as part of the courtship is also found in many pigeons, in ducks, and in Avocets. Jays and some Birds of Paradise wipe their bills in a ceremonial way during courtship. The females of several gallinaceous birds make feeding movements when the male is courting in front of them. In popular accounts of the display of the Peacock and the Turkey it is often stated that the female is " entirely unconcerned " and is feeding as if the male did not interest her at all. I believe that the feeding reactions of the female are a sure sign that she is interested, just as the preening in pigeons is an indication of a strongly activated sexual drive.

H.G.W.   I

Again, as in the study of fighting behaviour, it is useful to extend our comparison beyond the group of birds. Once more the Three-spined Stickleback shows behaviour that is entirely comparable. In a sexually strongly activated male Stickleback we observe a type of parental behaviour well known from a later phase in his reproductive cycle: the movements of " fanning," of ventilating the eggs. This is as essential a part of the parental behaviour as incubation is in birds.

Now this " fanning " is shown again and again by a male when a female enters his territory. Again and again the male swims away from the female which he has been courting intensely, and goes to the nest for a series of fanning movements. Yet there are no eggs in the nest that might need ventilation.

In trying to find an explanation of these instances of irrelevant behaviour we are naturally inclined to compare them with those other types of irrelevant behaviour I have discussed above. As I argued there, the irrelevant behaviour during aggressive encounters provided an outlet for strong impulses that were blocked because actual fighting was inhibited by the urge to escape. The irrelevant behaviour was shown to be a displacement activity due to a conflict of motor impulses. Is it possible that irrelevant movements during courtship are also due to a thwarted urge? Could the sexual urge, somehow prevented from discharging itself into the adequate movements, find an outlet through some of the other central nervous mechanisms? This is indeed the most plausible conclusion. The arguments are briefly as follows. One of the functions of courtship is the release of the partner's sexual responses by giving specific signals. The sexual responses may be immediate overt acts, or " latent " internal changes, resulting in a gradual increase in sexual responsiveness. The specificity of the signals and of the partner's response to the signals prevents the animals from mating with other species. Usually, this courtship is reciprocal, that is, the female has to stimulate the male just as much as the male the female. The male's signals may be quite different from those given by the female, or, in other species, they may be the same (" mutual courtship ").

Now in many cases irrelevant movements are made in situations when the animal is under the influence of strong sexual impulses, yet cannot actually mate because the mate has not yet given the final signal necessary to release the mating act. Birds, and many other animals, are dependent on such releasing stimuli to such an extent that, unless their inner urge is quite exceptionally strong, they will not make an attempt to mate when the releasing stimulus from the partner has not been delivered. Both the internal urge and the releasing stimuli given by the partner are necessary for the mating act. Now the courtship situation, and more especially the pre-coition situation, is characterised by a strong inner mating urge, but, as long as the partner's final signal has not been given, its impulses cannot find an outlet through the mating act. Just as in the aggressive situation therefore there is frustration, although the cause of this frustration is different in the two cases. As in the aggressive situation, the irrelevant movements seem to be displacement activities.

Parallel behaviour in sticklebacks

This hypothesis about the nature of " irrelevant " elements in courtship or pre-coition behaviour has, so far as I know, not been tested experimentally in birds. But in fish there is some quite interesting experimental evidence. Also, a comparative study of alleged displacement activities in bird courtship shows that they really occur at the moments in which there are indications of a very strong but unsatisfied sexual urge. A further study of these phenomena would be very worth while for several reasons. I should like to point out that such a study can only yield results of value if the behaviour itself is closely and continuously watched and the conditions under which irrelevant movements occur are critically analysed. A mere study of fragmentary descriptions in the literature, or occasional observations, are entirely insufficient as a basis for conclusions.

Now it is a very remarkable fact that such displacement activities, being outlets of a strong sexual or aggressive urge, and used by the ethologists as indications of such a strong urge, have

an influence upon the partner too. The partner somehow
" understands " their meaning. When the displacement act is
due to a blocked fighting urge, the opponent is intimidated.
When the displacement activity is due to a strong sexual urge,
the partner is sexually stimulated by it. How is it possible that,
for instance, displacement nest-building of a Herring Gull is not
reacted to as nest-building but as a threat?

In the case of the threat movements, we have seen that their
distinctness as threat display is often due to the superposition of
incipient fighting movements. In the case of sexual displacement
activities we do not know how the function of social releaser
originated; the only thing we do know is that many displacement
activities really act as releasers.

Ritualisation

Not all of them do, however, and this has led to an interesting
discovery. Displacement activities which form part of courtship
and influence the partner, and displacement activities which
play a part in threat behaviour and have an intimidating influence
on the opponent are, in many cases, slightly different from the
activities from which they are derived. When preening is done
by ducks for its own sake, it is different from the displacement
preening forming part of the courtship. The latter usually has
a certain rigidity, it has the character of a mere formality.
Accordingly, this type of movement was called " formalised " by
Selous (1933). Huxley (1923) has proposed the term " ritualised," which I will use here. Because, so far as we know at present,
this ritualisation seems to be characteristic of such derived
movements as have a releasing influence on another individual's
behaviour, it is natural to conclude that ritualisation is the
result of a secondary evolutionary process which is closely linked
to the releaser-function. This is even more obvious when, by
comparison of a number of such ritualised displacement activities,
it is discovered that ritualisation always results in making the
movement more conspicuous. In many cases this is brought
about by " exaggeration " of the movement. The displacement
activity serving as releaser often has a kind of exaggerated, em-

FIG. 19

Displacement preening of courting male ducks. From top to bottom: Shelduck (after Makkink, 1931); Garganey; Mandarin; Mallard (all after Lorenz, 1941)

phatic character. Another way in which conspicuousness is attained is the development of brightly coloured structures which are located in such a way that they are apt to be shown off by the displacement activity. Very fine examples are found among the ducks. During displacement-preening, a male Mallard lifts it wing so that the beautiful blue wing-speculum becomes visible. In the Mandarin Duck, displacement-preening confines itself to one ritualised stroke with the bill along one of the secondaries. This special feather is entirely different from the other secondaries; the outer vane, instead of being narrow and dark greenish, is extremely broadened and bright orange.

By the ritualised preening movement the male seems to call attention to this feather. The displacement-preening of the male Garganey is again different. This species does not bring the bill beyond the wing, but touches the outer side exactly at the field of bluish hand-coverts. The Sheldrake has added an auditory component to the ritualisation of the displacement preening movement: by just one rapid stroke of the bill along the shafts off the wing-quills it produces a low, rumbling sound.

Ritualisation not only results in making the movement more conspicuous: it also makes it more specific, in the sense of characteristic of the species. As I remarked before, this enhances reproductive isolation because it renders interspecific mating less liable to occur.

The process of ritualisation, making the derived movement more conspicuous and more specific as a signal, therefore tends to obscure the origin of the movement. It is probable that this tendency is encouraged in evolution because it must be of survival value when a derived movement cannot be easily confused with its original. As I mentioned in Chapter 6 the type of threat-display called choking is very similar to, if not identical with, the original movement from which it is derived. In the Herring Gull, this movement is not (yet?) ritualised. As I pointed out, it is ritualised in the Laughing Gull, which ruffles its feathers during displacement-choking. It seems to me of considerable interest that I have once seen a " mistake " in a Herring Gull male, which failed to recognise the threat character of the aggressive choking and reacted to it as if it were friendly choking. This male approached a mated female on her territory in the absence of her mate. The female responded with choking, and, in view of the fact that she did not first walk over to him, and also in view of the further development, we were sure that her choking was aggressive. The male, however, immediately ran towards her and was going to join her, as mated birds do, when she rose and attacked him. I think that such a failure of the system of social signals would have been less liable to occur had the displacement-choking been ritualised as it is by the Laughing Gull.

We know that closely related species often have the same displacement-activities in the same situations. We saw this in ducks, in gulls, and it is also known, for instance, in sticklebacks and in cranes. In the various species of such a group, ritualisation has gone in different directions, resulting in increased specificity. Also, ritualisation has gone farther in some species than in others. It may have gone so far that it is at present impossible to recognise the origin of a strongly ritualised displacement-activity. In such cases we would be entirely at a loss if we could not compare the various species. Lorenz has pointed out (1935) that the origin of the threat behaviour of the Manchurian Crane would be entirely obscure if comparison did not enable us to see that it was only an extreme case of ritualised displacement preening. Similarly, it is quite possible that most observers would fail to recognise the Mandarin's wing-tipping as displacement-preening, if they were not familiar with other species showing the displacement-preening in a less ritualised form.

Ritualisation has still another highly interesting aspect, which can only be briefly mentioned here. By ritualisation the movement becomes more and more different from its original. This means that the underlying central nervous structure changes. In other words, the ritualised displacement-activity becomes more independent than it originally was, and it becomes increasingly difficult to decide to which drive it belongs: to the instinct from which it is " borrowed " or to the instinct by which it is used. With progressing ritualisation, the displacement-activity loses its displacement character and becomes incorporated into the pattern of its " new boss."

Owing to the relative paucity of data, these considerations are still relatively tentative. It will be clear that it would be highly promising to study various threat and courtship displays from this point of view. By making detailed comparative studies of closely related species and trying, in each case, whether it is possible to find the origin of display movements by applying the hypotheses outlined above, we might acquire a better insight into how and why display activities have evolved into what they are now.

Let us now return to the Herring Gull's head-tossing movements and see whether the ideas outlined above can also be applied here. As the head-tossing is the main part of the pre-coition behaviour, and is easily recognised as the food-begging behaviour of the young, it must be considered a displacement-activity serving as an outlet of the sexual drive. Further, it can easily be stated that it has releaser function: head-tossing usually produces a sexual response in the mate. Comparison with the original food-begging of the young shows that it is but little ritualised, though I said above there are some differences in the form of the movement and this might be due to some degree of ritualisation. The begging call is different in young and adult, but this seems to be merely the consequence of the general change in timbre found in all the vocal utterances during individual development. The alarm call, the trumpeting call, and the begging call are all produced by juveniles, and in all three cases their calls are harsh and squeaky, those of the adults clear and melodious. The change in voice therefore is not typical of the begging call. There is no morphological structure comparable to, for instance, the Mandarin's vane. Ritualisation, therefore, seems to be absent.

This fits in with the fact that when the female is begging for food it shows exactly the same behaviour as when it tries to rouse the male to copulate. And it is an unsolved mystery to me how the male knows whether the female wants food or is willing to copulate. There seem to be two possibilities: (1) either the female is in exactly the same condition in the two cases, and being fed satisfies the same drive as copulation, with only a possible intensity-difference, or (2) the male reacts to slight differences which we have been unable to detect.

As regards the first possibility, it is not unthinkable that the female's head-tossing is always an expression of the mating urge, and that being fed gives sexual satisfaction, but of a lower intensity than actual copulation. A fact pointing in this direction is that copulation may occur after feeding but that we never observed the reverse. Concerning the second possibility it may be recalled that we have actual proof of the fact that the gulls' visual capacities surpass ours, and that we must not too soon discard the possibility that they may react to clues too subtle for us to observe with the relatively crude method of field observation, however trained we may be.

Sex recognition

While it seems beyond doubt that the head-tossing is an expression of an activated sexual urge and is derived from the food-begging, it remains to be explained why it is exactly this juvenile pattern that is used as an outlet of sexual impulses. As I pointed out above, this connection is found in many birds. I think that the Herring Gull may give us the clue to this problem. We have seen that the first sign of aroused sexual activation in the male is aggressiveness towards other individuals. This aggressiveness is especially directed against males. It is important to realise that this offers a problem. How is this selectivity of the male's fighting brought about? Why does not the male attack females as well? In other words, how do the gulls recognise the sex of another individual? Here again, comparison with other species helps us. It shows that in such species where sexual dimorphism is obvious, males are able to recognise the sex of another bird by plumage alone. Thus a male Golden Pheasant will try to copulate with a mounted female, but it will attack a mounted male (Noble & Vogt, 1935). In species where male and female have the same plumage, the male recognises the sex of another bird mainly by its behaviour.

In the Herring Gull this seems to be the rule. The reaction to a male's initial aggressiveness is very different in a female and in a male. Whereas a male either tries to escape or to threaten in return, a receptive female adopts the flat posture described above.

This flat posture is in all details the opposite of the upright threat posture. The neck is drawn in instead of stretched and this brings the bird into a disadvantageous position in case of a fight. Also, the wings are not lifted: in other words, the female does not prepare to fight. Her attitude is exactly the same as that of full-grown juvenile birds. It is the submissive attitude, and both the larger young and the female have the same "reasons" for adopting it; they both have to suppress the potential aggressiveness inherent in the male in reproductive condition. It is very interesting that the young develop this posture only when they change from chicks into gulls. A downy chick apparently is different enough from an adult gull not to elicit any hostile reactions whatsoever, but as the chicks grow up and acquire the adult posture, a need for protective behaviour seems to develop. Soon after the breeding season, when the young become entirely independent, the tendency to hostility between individuals overrides the tendency to be tolerant towards young.

Submissiveness in the female

The fact that the female's posture is identical with the submissive posture which the species has developed for other kinds of inter-individual conflict, throws light upon the curious fact reported above that although males and females overlap in size, it has never been reported that a male pairs with a female which is larger than himself, and vice versa. This is another indication that submissiveness of the female is an essential condition for pair-formation.

The circumstance that the male's first reaction to other individuals is in so many cases aggressive seem to me to be the basic reason for the close relationship that exists between pair-formation and social dominance. Because the male is primarily aggressive, the female has to evolve a means to ward off the male's attack and elicit his sexual responses instead. For this purpose, it makes use of a behaviour-pattern which already exists: it adopts the attitude of submissiveness already in use in social conflicts. Because of the male's aggressiveness, pairs in which the female is not submissive are simply impossible. Of course, this applies only to such species as have this type of pair-formation. In saying that the female makes use of an already existing behaviour pattern, I do not mean to imply that phylogenetically the social conflict is older that the sexual conflict. Both have evolved together, and it would perhaps be more proper to say that the species has evolved the same behavioural social releaser for the suppression of attack in these two types of conflict.

From this submissiveness of the female, necessary to make sexual contact with the male, the food-begging may well have evolved as a continuation of this type of attitude. When the female, in sexual encounters, has to fall back into an infantile attitude, it is plausible that other parts of the infantile pattern appear along with it. Two circumstances may have helped to fix the begging reaction into the pairing pattern. First, the male's parental drive, although not appearing in full force until there are young, may, like all reproductive drives, be slightly active a long time before it is actually needed. This would make him ready to respond to the submissive attitude by feeding behaviour. Second, extra food might be useful to the female in the time when she has to develop the eggs, and selection may therefore have favoured conjugal feeding once it started in incipient form.

The male's head-tossing

However, there still remains one difficulty: why does the male show the begging behaviour before coition? He has no reason to develop submissiveness, and he is never fed by the female. The two alleged factors favourable to the development of begging in the female therefore cannot have contributed to the development of his behaviour. So far as I can see, various explanations are possible, but none can be sufficiently documented. Therefore, it seems best to leave the issue open.

Leaving the problem of the origin of the pre-coition pattern alone and returning to the mechanism of the behaviour in its present form, we may ask: what are the factors that stop the head-tossing and allow it to change into copulation itself? For the female, it is the actual performance of the copulatory act by the male. She goes on tossing her head until the cloacas are in contact. In between two contacts, she resumes the head-tossing. This is according to expectation, for if the head-tossing is a displacement activity fed by the sexual drive, it must stop as soon as the sexual drive can express itself in coition.

In the male, the situation is different. In mating behaviour of many species, as for instance in the sticklebacks, a displacement activity goes on until a stimulus provided by the partner releases the next step in the sexual behaviour-chain. In the male Herring Gull, the male changes head-tossing into mounting without any new stimulus from the female. The latter just tosses the head again and again, no change in her behaviour is visible ; the male gradually stretches his neck (the intention movement of mounting) while still tossing his head, and then he mounts rather suddenly, at the same time stopping the head-tossing and beginning to utter his rhythmic copulation-note. About the cause of this change in the male only one conclusion seems possible: the stimuli provided by the female add their influence on the male until the threshold of the next link in the chain of his copulatory behaviour, mounting, is reached. Because we see that the female's head-tossing is so important as a means of starting the male's sexual behaviour, this conclusion seems to be more plausible than assuming that the male stimulates himself by his own head-tossing.

It seems to me that this analysis gives us an idea as to how such a relatively complicated co-operative behaviour-pattern may have arisen. Its main spring seems to be the ambivalence of the male's behaviour. Fighting is necessary in spring, as we have seen, in order to secure space for the pair and for its offspring. This fighting urge of the male has to be suppressed by the female or mating would be impossible. The only effective way to do this is by adopting a submissive attitude. But suppressing the male's aggressiveness is not sufficient; his sexual drive must be activated.

This is done by displacement activities, which appear anyhow, as a consequence of the female's unsatisfied sexual urge. This urge is not satisfied because of the male's initial lack of sexual co-operation. The displacement activities become engraved in the pattern because the male reacts to them by sexual responses, which means that the displacement-begging of the female leads to success. It would seem, therefore, that the complicated reciprocal behaviour-pattern is again primarily caused by the existence of more than one drive, each of which must be ready for action in the reproductive season. A secondary function of such patterns is that they serve as sexual isolating mechanisms, preventing the animals, because of their innate selective responsiveness to the releasers of their own species, from mating with other species. The existence of the two drives is responsible for the complex nature of the pairing behaviour; the fact that species which have identical mating behaviour would merge into one has led to the situation that the mating patterns in existing species are different and act as reproductive isolating mechanisms.

Interbreeding with Larus fuscus

In this connection it is interesting to see that one of the closest relatives of the Western European Herring Gull, the Lesser Black-backed Gull, although so different in colour and rather different in voice, occasionally mates with Herring Gulls. This means that the mating behaviour-patterns have not yet been sufficiently differentiated to prevent interbreeding in nature. Especially on the Dutch island of Terschelling mixed pairs have been known to breed since 1928 (Plate 10a). The offspring of such pairs is fertile, and since the spreading of the Lesser Black-backed Gull into other Dutch Herring Gull colonies, quite a number of breeding birds have been seen which were clearly hybrids between the two. In 1949 I filmed a male hybrid, which was mated with a pure Herring Gull, with its downy chicks. It was planned to collect this pair and to rear their young in captivity in 1950 but the hybrid was not seen in that year.

There is, however, no complete interbreeding between the two forms. Even in the colonies where interbreeding occurs, there is usually not more than one mixed pair. In 1928 there were 4 pure *fuscus*-pairs, and one mixed pair on Terschelling. In the years after the war, there were usually over twenty pure pairs, and again only one, or in some years no mixed pair. At Wassenaar there were five *fuscus*-pairs in 1949 plus the curious pair mentioned above. It seems therefore that mixed pairs are only formed when a Lesser Black-backed Gull attaches itself to a colony where there is no conspecific mate available. If this were true, the hybridisation would be a phenomenon typical of pioneer populations, and its importance must decrease with an increase of the total number of Lesser Black-backs breeding in the newly colonised area.

NEST-BUILDING

" Selection " of nest-site

We have no exact data about the period elapsing between the formation of new pairs on the club and their settling on to a territory. Many of the newly formed pairs try to establish themselves on the ground adjacent to the club. This causes a considerable pressure between pairs in this area, and a crowding of nests around the clubs. But other newly-formed pairs settle far from the club. Whether they always try to settle near the club first, I am unable to say.

The general procedure seems to be about as follows: when two birds become more or less firmly attached to each other, conjugal feeding becomes relatively less important, and copulations occur more and more, often on the club, where it does not give offence to other club birds. At the same time, the birds intensify their nest-building activities. At first this consists of much choking. In this period, a great part of the choking has nothing to do with hostility against other birds but is part of the friendly behaviour of the partners. Then there comes a phase in which the birds begin to search for a nesting place. They select a territory and from time to time they walk around on this territory, frequently calling the mew call, and choking at various places. Such places are usually near some plants or bushes. This is the only instinct in which the adult gull reacts positively to such vertical elements. Gulls want flat open country, except when looking for a nesting place. The choking now gradually develops into scraping, and several scrapes may appear in the course of one or a few days.

This is exactly comparable to what can be observed in other

birds, and in nest-building fish. It has probably nothing to do with purposeful selection after comparison of various sites, but in the beginning a number of equally attractive sites stimulate the birds with equal strength, and it seems to be conditioning dependent on accident that makes them decide in favour of one place. By " accident " I mean the following. During this time there is irregular waxing and waning of the building drive. When a nest-building wave overtakes the birds, they go to one of the many suitable sites on the territory. In the beginning of the season, they will just forget about such a site as soon as the building wave is over. With each new wave, they select a suitable site in a rather haphazard way, independent of previous experience. Gradually the waves become stronger, and then one half-hour of very intensive building may result in tying the birds down to one of the sites, which now sticks in their memories as the site that gave satisfaction to the building drive. Of course I cannot prove this, but it is the impression one gets.

I watched a similar accidental decision as to nest-place by Red-necked Phalaropes. Here the female does all the courting, she defends the territory, and she also selects the nesting site. During the pre-egg stage, male and female go about together in the territory, and make scrapes at many places. None of these places, as far as I could see, was better than the others. About an hour before the female is going to lay her first egg, she begins to visit the various scrapes. She suddenly stops feeding, and flies off to one scrape, uttering her song, which had stopped since she had attracted and secured a mate. The male immediately reacts to the song by following her, and together they visit one of the scrapes. Their interest will subside again, and they go back to the pond to forage. After a while, the female again starts with a sudden outburst of song, the male follows her, and she leads him to another scrape. This irregular visiting of the various scrapes goes on, until in one of them the female lays the egg. This decides the place of the nest, and from now on she goes to this particular scrape when she is about to lay another egg. When the clutch of four is completed she loses interest and leaves the nest to the male (Tinbergen, 1935).

Again, while I am unable to provide proof, my impression was that the scrape where the female happened to be when the egg appeared was the one promoted to the status of nest.

Actual Building

Once the Herring Gulls have selected the nest-site, they show more perseverance in building. Both male and female collect material, but each without reference to the other. The male definitely does more of the collecting than the female. Time after time he starts on a collecting trip, gently picking up straws and beakfuls of moss, and carries them to the nest, uttering the mew call as he approaches it. This makes him lose much of it before he reaches the nest, because he cannot keep his bill closed when a really strong inclination to mew overtakes him.

Both male and female sit in the nest, and there is much choking when they are together, and in turns each of them sits in the cup, scrapes, picks up material that has been deposited round the nest, and lays it on the rim with the peculiar sideways movements of the head shown by so many species.

In this haphazard way the well-shaped nest emerges. The picking up of material; carrying it to the nest-site; scraping while sitting in the nest-cup; turning in all directions (which gives the cup its circular shape); and putting straws in it or on the rim with the sideways movement: these are all the elements of nest-building. The contrast between the happy-go-lucky way in which these activities are carried out, in irregular order, now intensive, now a mere vestige, and the neat result in the shape of a well-rounded and well-lined nest-cup, is very striking and impressive and gives one a very good idea of the relative efficiency of " blind " instinctive action.

Monogamy

All through this period of mated life, and until there are eggs, the mates adapt their daily rhythms to each other. They leave together for the feeding grounds, and return together. From the status of club-bachelors they have changed into the status

H.G.W.   K of mated birds, and unless the marriage breaks down owing to a deficiency in one of them, or death takes one of them away, they will not fall back into the state of bachelordom. They may return to the club now and then, and each of them may begin an occasional flirtation with unmated club birds, but I never saw such a flirtation develop into a bond of any significance. No triangle relationships have been observed by us, and it seems to me that monogamy is very strict in this species.

First awakening of the brooding drive

At the end of this period, the first signs of the awakening of the incubation drive appear. The female especially may sit, as if she is incubating, days in advance of the appearance of the first egg. We have occasionally given such birds another gull's egg in order to see whether their normal reaction to eggs, which is to eat them, would give place to incubation even before the first egg was laid. When an egg is presented to a bird that is already occasionally sitting in the nest, the bird usually sits on it when it is given in the nest, but when it is presented outside the nest it will be eaten.

We have begun a more systematic study of the awakening of the incubation drive by presenting the standard stimulus of one egg in the nest-cup in a number of cases. Of course we could not know in advance when the first egg would be laid, and that made it necessary to begin as early as possible, that is to say as soon as there was a real nest, and then repeat the test at regular intervals until the first egg was laid. We soon discovered that the incubation drive did not appear very long in advance of the egg, and we paid the fee for this lesson in the form of a number of other gulls' eggs. This forced us to change our tactics. Knowing from previous years that the gulls will accept wooden imitation eggs readily, we changed to wooden eggs. This yielded us the surprising and wholly accidental experiment I mentioned in Chapter 4: our first gull approached the wooden egg as it would do a real egg in this phase: with gastronomic intents. It delivered a powerful peck at it, and got the surprise of its life when the egg did not break. It then took the whole egg into its bill, flew up, and dropped it on the soft sand bottom. When it did not crack, it repeated this another time, and then left the egg alone.

This was the outstanding success of the experiments; for lack of opportunity we did not continue them, and I have nothing to report about the awakening of the brooding drive.

PART FOUR

Incubation

CHAPTER 16

BROODING BEHAVIOUR

Division of labour

The appearance of the first egg brings an abrupt change in the daily rhythm of the pair. Whereas till then both birds were continuously together, leaving for the feeding grounds and returning to the colony together, now the eggs are never left unguarded; while one of the mates is absent the other remains near the nest. The return of the former does not instantly induce the other to leave; the birds may be on the territory together for hours continuously; the duration of the foraging trips varies according to the weather. On the whole, it seems to be very easy for the gulls to get their daily ration during this season. In winter, it is sometimes different; severe frost which covers the beach with a heavy layer of ice, and long north-westerly gales (especially at spring tide when the shore may be covered with tremendous cushions of foam) seem to be the most dangerous conditions. In the summer these conditions do not occur along the Dutch coast; in winter they promptly stimulate the gulls to migrate.

The new division of labour is typical for the whole period of incubation and for the greater part of the time when there are chicks. Only when the chicks are nearly fledged do the adults occasionally leave the territory unprotected. For protection really is the function of the new system. During the first days, the egg or eggs are not at all consistently brooded; especially in the one-egg phase the bird often stands a few feet away from the nest. It is however continuously on the watch and reacts immediately to potential egg-robbers. In the protected colonies in Holland, where both man and fox are ruled out as predators, the most common egg-predators are other gulls. The most successful method of egging I saw used by gulls was to fly low over the colony and swoop down immediately upon a nest when they sighted one. Usually such a raider is warded off before it can get at the eggs, but sometimes one manages to peck at an egg and to break it—to be chased away, however, before it can eat its contents. Very rarely has it time to take the egg into its bill and fly away with it. Goethe reports that Herring Gulls sometimes swallow each other's eggs whole, and regurgitate them undamaged in front of their female!

The intervals during which the eggs are left uncovered, which may be as long as one or two hours in fair weather during the one-egg phase, become considerably shorter during the next days. Goethe has also noticed this, and Elliott & Moreau (1947) stated that of 200 single eggs only ten per cent were warm; in " over a score " of pairs of eggs about half of them were warm and half were cold. The *Handbook of British Birds* therefore is right in stating that incubation starts with the first egg, but brooding is incomplete at the beginning.

The eggs are laid at varying, usually long intervals. I never collected systematic evidence on the interval, but the occasional notes we made indicate that there is usually a lapse of about 48 hours between two successive eggs. Goethe (1937) says: " The interval is mostly two days, often three days (this may happen especially between the first and the second egg), in rare cases 24 hours " (p. 51).

The Herring Gull a determinate layer

The normal clutch is three, and although I have repeatedly seen clutches of four that presumably could not be accounted for by human interference, I very much doubt whether in any of these cases the four eggs were from one female.

We have had ample opportunity to study the effect of egg-robbing and of the addition of eggs on the number of eggs laid.

The general result is that neither the taking nor the addition of eggs, at whatever stage and in whatever way or sequence it is done, changes in any way the fixed number of three in a clutch. For instance, when we consistently took every egg as soon as possible after laying, the bird involved would still lay three eggs with normal intervals, and then stop laying, until, a week or longer after this, it started a new clutch. We could study this in quite a number of cases in the Terschelling colony, where egg-collecting in the periphery of the gullery (as well as shaking in the centre : p. 173) was an essential element in the control scheme (as it was in our foraging scheme).

A systematic study of this problem was made by Davis (1942), who came to the same conclusion. Davis tried to influence the number of eggs laid by either robbing the nest or adding eggs to it. Whenever this was done, the bird could in no case be prevented from laying three eggs with normal intervals. The Herring Gull is therefore a " determinate " layer; the stimuli from the eggs present in the nest do not influence the number of eggs laid. This is not so in all birds; there are species which react to robbing by compensatory production of eggs. An American woodpecker, the Flicker (*Colaptes auratus*) for instance, is known to have laid 71 eggs when an egg was taken daily from the nest. It is supposed that such species will continue to lay until the nest contains a definite number of eggs. The activity of the ovary of such species can obviously be influenced by stimuli from the clutch, an interesting—though by no means unique—instance of sensory stimuli influencing " somatic " processes.

The period of incubation, which has now begun, is a rather monotonous phase in the reproductive cycle, monotonous at least for the observer who, missing any incubation instinct himself, has some difficulty in understanding the satisfaction which a bird presumably feels when just sitting on eggs. Both birds take part in incubation, the female being on the average a slightly more devoted brooder than the male. There is however considerable variation, and there are pairs where the male takes the major part of the burden. We once observed a male that left the task of incubation entirely to the female; at least we never saw him on the nest during a period of 21 days when we watched these birds daily for from 2 to 8 hours. Instead this male spent much of his time in fighting other gulls. The female left the nest only rarely, until at the 21st day, when, after some hours of restlessness, she suddenly abandoned the nest altogether.

Usually, however, male and female take more or less regular turns, relieving each other every two to five hours.

Nest-relief

Nest-relief is always an interesting event. First, it is a break in the monotony of watching. Second, it may take place in various ways, and it is worth while to try to understand the different types of behaviour shown by both the relieving and the relieved bird.

Sometimes the sitting bird gets up from the nest at the least indication of broodiness in the partner. Only if the partner fails to take the initiative for a very long time, will the sitting bird leave the nest spontaneously, though rarely for longer than about fifteen minutes. As I mentioned already, we once had a pair under observation the male of which never relieved its mate. The female spontaneously took some short offs each day, but it was not until the 21st day after the completion of the clutch that her incubation urge was extinguished.

At the other extreme is a mate which tries to relieve the sitting bird before the sitter is prepared to go. The mate may first approach the sitter, uttering the mew call. When the sitting partner does not rise, the other bird stops by the nest and just waits, uttering some mews, maybe. It then may go and fetch some nest-material and come back mewing, often losing half of it or more because when giving the mew call with emphasis it opens its bill. If this does not work, the relieving bird may show another building activity, viz., choking. These activities seem to stimulate the sitting bird to rise; at least it often does so after some time. But sometimes even all these signals fail entirely, and the sitter simply will not go. If, in this extreme case, the relieving mate is really trying to take his turn, he may force his way on to the eggs and we may watch the curious spectacle of male and female trying to push each other from the nest in a struggle which may last for several seconds and during which wings may occasionally flash.

It seems to me that the variation in the behaviour of the birds at nest-relief is primarily due to variations in the intensity of the incubation urge. When a sitting bird has been brooding for a long time, the urge has weakened, and a weak stimulus from the partner is sufficient to induce it to take its turn off. But when the mate comes too early, it must give much stronger signals. The external stimulus is important; as I mentioned already, a gull will only very rarely leave the nest spontaneously. This is an adaptation safeguarding the continuity of incubation; it prevents the eggs from being left alone before the partner arrives, even if he might be exceptionally late. Sometimes the brooding urge of a bird is tried very severely, viz., when an incubating male sees his territory invaded by other males. Although such a male becomes very restless, he will not leave its nest until relieved. But even if the relief arrives abnormally early, he will promptly leave the nest and attack the strangers at once. In such cases the fighting drive, being stimulated by the intruders, evidently suppressed the incubating drive to some extent so that the least signal from the female causes him to rise; yet he did not desert the nest too early.

It is not only the reaction to the other's signals that is dependent on the intensity of the brooding urge. The signals of the relieving bird too are expressions of its brooding urge. The stronger that urge, the more persistent it is in its attempts to get at the nest. In case of prompt reaction by the sitting bird the reliever can at once satisfy its urge by actual brooding. In case of frustration, however, nesting activities appear, and it seems quite plausible to consider them as displacement activities through which the thwarted drive finds an outlet. So here again there seems to be a connection between irrelevant movements and an internal urge forcing the animal to act.

When a gull is about to settle down on to the eggs, it raises

Plate 17a. A typical Herring Gull's nest

    b. Herring Gulls' eggs, a perfect food

Plate 18. A female alights at the nest after driving off a stranger which pecked at one of her eggs

Plate 19a. The female of Plate 18 one second later: the broken egg no longer releases incubation, but is eaten

    b. A few seconds later still: she is sitting on the two intact eggs while finishing her meal

Plate 20. Models used in the tests on egg-recognition
(photographed by P. van Kempen)

all its ventral feathers. In then withdraws its neck, and, gradually bending its legs, it steps into the nest-cup. Very slowly and carefully it brings the breast down, at the same time bending its head down a little. Supporting itself on its feet and wings it lowers the breast in front of the eggs. This is the first phase; it now proceeds to bring the eggs in contact with the naked skin of the brooding patches. This is done by working the ventral feathers around the eggs during a long series of waggling movements of the body. The legs make scraping movements, the function of which is, in part, to keep the nest-cup in shape, as can be easily seen in nests on more or less bare sand. Every time a gull sits down in such a nest, some sand is shovelled out by the feet. During these waggling movements the bird also brings the feet farther and farther forward until, when it is finally sitting quietly the feet are presumably somewhere under the eggs. In this last phase, the bird makes some curious motions with the bill, without producing any sound, however. I do not know what these movements mean.

Shifting of the eggs

An incubating bird may sit quietly for one or more hours, but now and then it will suddenly get up, bring down the head under the breast, and move the eggs with the bill. This shifting of the eggs can also be released by abnormal touch-stimuli from the eggs. For instance, eggs of abnormal shape (as many of our egg dummies were—on which I will report below) and an abnormal arrangement of the eggs will invariably invoke it, usually, however, only after the bird has settled down on them, and can feel, though not see, the eggs. After a varying amount of time spent in shifting and reshifting the eggs, the bird may sit quietly upon them for hours, but finally it will get up " spontaneously," that is without there having been any change in the eggs' position or any other noticeable external stimulus, and then it will shift the eggs again. Shifting, therefore, is done (1) at the arrival at the nest, (2) after settling on the eggs, if the tactile stimulus is abnormal, (3) after a long spell of quiet brooding.

When we first became interested in shifting we began to realise that we did not really know whether it really turned the eggs about, or whether the eggs remained with about the same side up all the time. We therefore marked a number of eggs

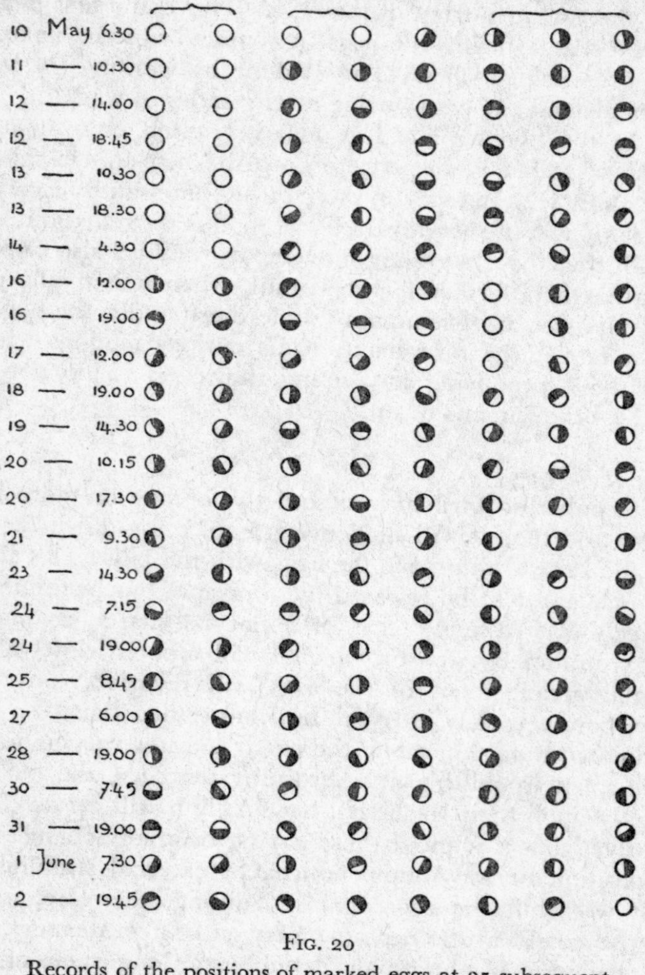

FIG. 20

Records of the positions of marked eggs at 25 subsequent checks

and noted their positions daily during several weeks. The egg
positions are given in Fig. 20 and united in a graph in Fig. 21,
and it will be seen that the eggs are really turned round quite
irregularly.

The observations on the irregular turning of the eggs, though
in themselves perhaps not of much interest, deserve attention in
relation to what happens at the end of the incubation period, as
we will see later.

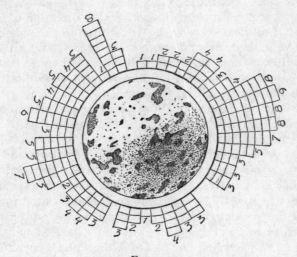

FIG. 21

Diagram based on Fig. 20, showing random position
of egg during incubation

Another part of the behaviour-pattern of incubation is the
inhibition of defecation in the brooding bird. I have never
observed a gull defecating while sitting on the eggs. Usually it
will wait until it is relieved. Occasionally, however, this seems to
be too high a demand, and then the bird gets up quietly, walks
about ten yards away from the nest, and unloads, mostly with
a tremendous explosion—one of the few definitely unattractive
features of the gullery. The fact is interesting because it shows
to what an extent incubation inhibits defecation.

Egg-retrieving

Finally, the act of egg-retrieving must be mentioned, as it is another highly interesting part of the brooding pattern. Although rarely, it happens sometimes that a gull is so suddenly disturbed at the nest that one of the eggs is kicked out when the bird flies up from the nest. A Herring Gull, like many other birds, has a special reaction reserved for this occasion. Upon returning, it will sit down on the eggs, and sooner or later it will react to the egg outside. First, it looks at it, again and again. After some time it will stretch its neck in the direction of the egg, at first in a half-hearted way, but this intention movement will be repeated with more and more completness, and all at once the gull will stand up, bring the bill beyond the egg, and then, carefully balancing it against the narrow ventral side of the bill, it will roll the egg back into the nest.

The whole act is a very clumsy and apparently ill-adapted performance. First, it makes a poor impression that the stimulation by the egg has to go on for such a long time before the gull reacts—sometimes it involves an hour or even more. Further, the balancing movement is far from efficient. Especially when the nest has a high rim, the egg may escape sideways and roll back four, five times. In watching such clumsy attempts one is struck by the restrictedness of instinctive behaviour. It would be so easy to roll the egg back with an extended wing, or by using one of the webbed feet! Yet it does not " occur " to the gull to try it; it is rigidly confined to this one type of action. The executive organs are there, but the central nervous mechanisms to use them in these circumstances are absent.

This limitation of the central nervous system happens to have struck us in this particular case because it is so obvious here, but is not this remarkable restrictedness a character of all instinctive behaviour? Both on the motor side and on the sensory side an animal could often do much more with its instruments (muscles and sense-organs respectively) if only the central nervous system would enable it to. As we will see later, a gull will ignore its eggs when they are placed a foot away from the nest, and will sit in the empty nest. It will take a shellfish with a hard shell up in the air and drop it where it happens to be, above the rock, the soft beach, or the water. Although its ability to recognise other individuals reveals a perceptual (visual and auditory) acuity of extremely high standard, it will contentedly brood for days and even weeks on a wooden cylinder with rounded edges.

These " stupidities " are rarely noticeable under normal conditions. They become, however, at once obvious in abnormal situations, and therefore the experimenter happens to be confronted with them again and again. They prove to him that the central nervous mechanisms, complicated as they may be, yet have their very strict limitations. They seem only to be developed to a degree of efficiency that is just enough for letting the species survive. As long as a Herring Gull can handle the rare emergencies of this type in his own clumsy way it will do. In birds of the bare sandy seashore, where eggs are often blown away or half covered by sand, as can be often observed with Little Terns, Ringed Plovers, or Oystercatchers, the movement is much more easily released; here the situation " egg outside the nest " occurs much more frequently, and there is a premium on quick and reliable response.

The conclusion to be drawn from these, and hundreds and thousands of similar facts, is that the animal could do much more with its sense-organs and its executive organs if it had only the central nervous mechanisms to use them in more ways. Most animals may have, as E. S. Russell says (1934), more than one way to attain a biologically useful end, yet there are many more possible modes of behaviour which they do not employ. The central nervous system, while having an amazing number of action patterns at its disposal, yet misses even many more patterns. In other words, behaviour is dependent on something like definite mechanisms or systems in the central nervous system, and the number of these mechanisms is limited.

Evolution of egg-retrieving

The act of egg-retrieving is also a very interesting one from the viewpoint of the evolution of adaptive behaviour patterns from apparently unimportant beginnings.

By terns, an egg outside the nest is retrieved in a rather accidental way. The bird walks over from the nest until it is almost but not entirely above the egg. It will then sit down, at the same time making the normal egg-shifting movement: that is, reaching with the bill beyond the egg, and shovelling it under the breast, thereby moving the egg a little distance towards the nest. It remains sitting on this single egg only a short time, and walks back to the nest as soon as this catches its eye. Back on the nest, the sight of the exposed egg will again stimulate the bird to go over towards it and to shovel it under the breast as soon as it can reach it. But again the bird will see the nest and walk back towards it. Thus it is torn back and forth between nest and egg. When walking towards the single egg, it leaves the accustomed nest-site only reluctantly, and goes only just as far as is absolutely necessary, that is to say it does not go beyond the place where it can incubate the egg after having rolled it under its breast. In other words, it employs the normal shifting reaction, and its attachment to the nest-site causes it to do this as soon as it can reach the egg. In coming back to the nest, there is nothing compelling it to draw the eggs towards it. In this way, the unequal competition between nest-plus-two-eggs, and one-egg-outside-the-nest, combined with the egg-shifting movements, results, after some time, in the egg being rolled back into the nest. This procedure was described for various terns (Watson & Lashley, 1915; Tinbergen, 1934) and it led these authors to describe egg-retrieving as the accidental outcome of this competition and normal egg-shifting.

In the Black-headed Gull, egg-retrieving is more than this. Kirkman, in his book on the Black-headed Gull (1937), describes egg-rolling in this species and emphasises the fact that eggs may be retrieved a considerable distance from the nest. Several of his birds rolled an egg in even when it was placed 1½ feet away. Kirkman comments: ". . . there is nothing accidental about the rolling by the Black-headed Gull. It seemed a specific retrieving reaction directed to the goal of restoring the egg to the nest. To what extent the egg is rolled, to what extent dragged, I am uncertain. The essential feature is the *walking backwards*, which is not part of an incipient brooding reaction; in the performance of the latter the bird is stationary " (p. 216). Kirkman therefore concludes that egg-retrieving is an independent, adaptive behaviour element. The same is undoubtedly true of the egg-rolling of the Grey Lag Goose, which may also occasionally step right out of the nest and walk backward, balancing the egg on the bill all the while.

Still much more developed is the reaction of the Nightjar. After disturbance, the Nightjar may move its eggs for many yards. This is done in the same way as the " incipient " egg rolling of other birds, viz., by walking backwards with the egg balancing against the ventral side of the bill.

It seems to me that the very existence of the controversy about egg-retrieving behaviour being either an independent, adaptive reaction, or an accidental by-product, shows us the way along which the highly adaptive types of egg-rolling may have evolved. The origin is obviously the egg-shifting movement. Interaction between the nest and an outside egg, inducing the bird to reach or walk towards the egg after it has settled on the nest, may account for the accidental shifting of the egg towards the nest, which may bring the egg back in steps. Increase of the distance at which an egg is reacted to, and walking back, are possibly two later additions, which have made an adaptive act out of what may previously have been an accidental by-product.

CHAPTER 17

EXPERIMENTS ON EGG-RECOGNITION

THE REACTIONS of birds towards their eggs offer a fine opportunity for a study of the external stimuli to which the bird is responding, for eggs are easily handled, and because they cannot move, as chicks or adult birds do, one can easily present perfect substitutes. Starting with such substitutes one can study the influence of various properties of the eggs, such as colour, or shape, by comparing the birds' reactions to these perfect substitutes with those to various other substitutes deficient in such properties. Moreover, an analysis of the stimulus-situation controlling the brooding behaviour is one of the first tasks presenting itself to a bird watcher—because the gulls' ability to find their own nest among so many other nests is one of the striking phenomena of colony life. It is especially striking to the city-dwelling sightseer visiting a gullery, because his own miserably poor power of orientation in the dune scenery, where there are no streets with conspicuous name-plates, leads him to have an undue admiration for the birds' powers of orientation.

The first problem occurring to the bird student therefore is: how do the birds find and recognise their own nest?

Nest-site

One simple experiment is sufficient to show how different the gull's reaction is from ours. When we take the three eggs out of the nest and put them at about a foot's distance in plain view, the returning gull usually goes to the empty nest, and, often after some hesitation, sits down in it. It may look at the eggs outside, it may occasionally roll one of them into the nest, but at this distance it often ignores them.

This shows that, against our expectations, it is not primarily the eggs the bird is reacting to. The nest at the accustomed site is a much more important element than the eggs.

Nest-cup

Now to what extent is it the nest, and to what extent the site that stimulates the bird? When the empty nest is removed and the pit filled up with sand, the bird, although hesitating, usually sits down at the spot where the nest was, thus showing the nest-site to be the prominent element in the stimulus situation.

FIG. 22
Gull sitting on empty nest in full view of displaced eggs.
(After Tinbergen, 1951)

But when in this same situation we make an artificial nest under the displaced eggs, the gull's choice is in favour of the eggs. The nest itself, therefore, is also of influence, for it strikes the balance in favour of the eggs.

These tests do not always give exactly the same results. Most gulls do not choose rigidly either the nest-site or the eggs, but they hesitate, looking from one to the other, and even sitting down on each alternately. Also, one bird may be more attracted by the nest-site, while another may be more inclined to choose the eggs. This may depend on innate differences between the individuals, or on differences in the external situation in which the tests are taken in the different cases, or in different histories of the birds involved. For instance, we have strong indications that in a monotonous environment, such as a grass plain, it is much easier to lure a bird away from the nest-site to the displaced eggs than in a situation with conspicuous field marks like shrubbery, or strong relief in the ground. The history of a bird may play a part when a bird that has been sitting for three weeks might be more strongly attached to the nest-site than a bird that has only just started incubation. However this may be, it would certainly be wrong to conclude that the variability of the responses proves innate variability in the birds. Such a conclusion is only warranted when both the differences in individual history and the differences in environmental conditions have been studied.

These experiments, which we have done a number of times, clearly indicate that both the nest-site and the nest itself form part of the stimulus situation. From occasional reactions to the eggs in the first experiment, as well as from other tests to be described below, we know further that the eggs are also part of the stimulus situation.

We scarcely studied nest-site recognition. The type of country is rarely suited for the experiments needed for such a study. Displacement of alleged landmarks is often difficult. However, we did some tests with gulls nesting on the bare shore, when there happened to be one conspicuous landmark in the neighbourhood, such as a box or a barrel washed ashore during winter gales. In such cases displacement of the landmark caused a corresponding disorientation in the gull. When nest and eggs were not displaced at the same time, the gull's disorientation was always of short duration, however; after some hesitation it always found the nest. In the dunes where the vegetation offers a multitude of landmarks the gulls really use many of them. This is obvious from the fact that a small change in the surroundings of the nest is evidently perceived, causing minor disturbances in the gull's orientation, but, presumably because so many parts are left intact, the gull always finds the nest. Such reactions to a very complex and detailed situation are always very impressive, and the difference from other reactions, in which only very few

Plate 21a. The setup of a choice experiment: the owner of a clutch of blue eggs has to choose between two of its own eggs and two more normal eggs

    b. Another choice test: an egg of normal size versus an egg of double dimensions

a
Mew call

b
Bringing nest material

Plate 22. Three types of nest relief

c
" *Chocking* "

" sign stimuli " play a part, is striking. As Lorenz (1943) has pointed out, reactiveness to a highly complicated and detailed situation might well be typical of conditioned responses, while reactiveness to few sign stimuli seems to be the rule in innate behaviour. The facts found in the Herring Gull support this. Knowledge of the individual nest surroundings must of course be the result of conditioning. We will see that the reactions to eggs show much less evidence of learning, and that they are really dependent on a few simple stimuli. Chapter 22 will provide another, still more striking example of an innate reaction to sign stimuli.

" Blue " eggs

While we did not penetrate further into the problem of how the nest-site is found, we spent some time in analysing " egg recognition." Even if, as we had found, nest recognition was primarily a matter of nest-site recognition, the great variability of clutches, especially of their coloration, naturally led us to suppose that the birds would at least know their own eggs. This seemed probable anyway in the cases of birds with very abnormal eggs. As is well known, some eggs are deficient in the outer olive brown layer of pigment and appear light greenish blue, without or with only very few dark dots. By colour-marking the birds of a nest containing such eggs we had found that in subsequent years the same birds were responsible for the blue eggs, a conclusion we were already prepared to draw because we knew that blue clutches are usually found at the same place in the colony year after year. Sometimes we found clutches in which one egg was blue, one was " normal," and one was intermediate. In 1936 one of our colour-ringed females that had laid a normally coloured clutch in 1934 and 1935, laid such a clutch of three different eggs, of which the blue egg was laid first, the intermediate second, and the normal egg last.

To return to our problem, we next decided to try whether the birds of the blue clutch would recognise their own eggs when they were given the choice between their eggs and another clutch. If the birds had learned to know their own eggs they

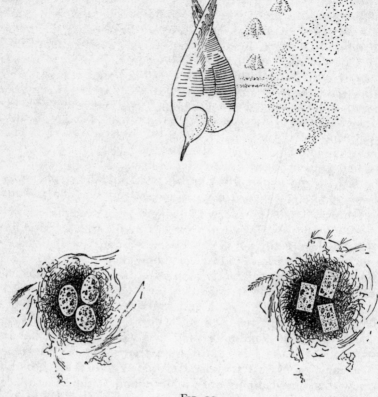

FIG. 23
A preference test as discussed in text

would certainly prefer them. It seemed also possible that they would prefer the " normal " eggs, because, if they had not learned the colour of their own eggs and if they had an innate responsiveness to the " ideal " gull's egg, it was conceivable that they would prefer the normal eggs above their own pathological eggs.

The preference test was carried out in the following way. Two artificial nests (usually no more than shallow depressions) were made at about a foot distance from the nest. In the beginning we left one egg in the original nest, put the remaining two in one of the artificial nests and two more normal eggs in the other artificial nest (Plate 21). We then watched from a blind which of the outside eggs would be rolled in. Later we left no egg in the nest, and put all three in the artificial nest. The other artificial nest of course got also a full but normal clutch. Usually the gull, upon finding the nest empty, would after some time go to one of the two artificial nests, a decision which we encouraged by covering the old nest with sand. Of course the two clutches were often interchanged; sometimes the place of the artificial nests had to be changed. We watched from a blind the reactions of both male and female in a number of tests. The results of the tests of the latter type were measured in number of reactions. Three types of reaction were distinguished: (1) approach (a), (2) the intention movement, in which the bird raised its ventral feathers and bent its legs as if going to sit upon them (i), and (3) incubation (s).

Here follow the results:

CHOICES OF THE MALE						CHOICES OF THE FEMALE					
"Normal" eggs			Blue eggs			"Normal" eggs			Blue eggs		
a	i	s	a	i	s	a	i	s	a	i	s
2	3	8	7	–	9	3	4	4	5	5	3
13			18			11			13		

These tests were carried out during three days, on 25th and 29th May, and 2nd June, 1936. Shortly after 2nd June the eggs hatched, but the exact date is not known. The male spent more time on the eggs than the female, and that is why we have a higher total from him.

The figures indicate that the birds did not make much difference between the two types of eggs, although there might have been a slight preference in favour of the blue eggs. The absence of an outspoken preference was already indicated by the hesitating behaviour of the birds in each test. Not only would they stand for many seconds in front of the two nests, looking from one to the other, but even after having walked over to one of them, a bird would often look at the other nest, and step over into it, or sometimes even sit down in it, only to go back again to its first choice after some time. This changing back and forth was often observed, and it seemed to depend on accident, or at least not on the colour of the eggs, at which nest the bird would finally settle down.

This was a rather unexpected result. It showed not only that the gulls, even in this extreme case, were not (or scarcely) conditioned to the exceptional colour of their eggs, but it seemed also to indicate that the normal colour did not play a part in whatever innate " knowledge " of the eggs there might be.

Wooden egg-dummies

We decided to follow this up, and to investigate what characters of colour, if any, of size, and of shape might play a part in the release of the incubation behaviour. We applied the same method as before, allowing the birds to choose between two sets of eggs which differed only in the character to be studied. This made a slight change in technique necessary. In the experiment described above we had been lucky, since the different colour-types used were really found in natural eggs. But when we wanted to study other colours, or even different sizes and shapes, we could no longer expect the birds to supply us with all the abnormal eggs we would like to put before them, such as bright red eggs, or eggs of double size, or cubical eggs. So we made substitutes of wood.

Our first concern was to find out whether a wooden egg of normal size and shape, and painted in the best possible way so as to resemble as closely as possible a real Herring Gull's egg, would be accepted by the gulls as readily as a real egg. The eggs were presented to three gulls, and we noted their reactions to the dummies and to the eggs of the gull concerned. The total result was:

WOODEN EGGS				OWN EGGS		
approach	*intention*	*sitting*		*approach*	*intention*	*sitting*
5	4	4		7	2	12
	13				21	

This points to a certain preference in favour of the real eggs, although this preference was not strong. The inequality of the figures is due to one of the three birds, which did not choose the wooden dummies in one single case, but reacted to its own eggs 8 times. This means that the two other birds did not show preference at all. There was, however, a qualitative difference: the reactions to the wooden eggs were more often confined to intention movements than were the reactions to the genuine eggs, which elicited more sitting. The total numbers are small, however, and more tests will have to be carried out. Yet it seems clear that our wooden eggs, though probably slightly inferior to the real eggs, were quite good substitutes. In all the subsequent tests we eliminated the possible differences between wooden eggs and real eggs by letting the birds choose between two sets of wooden eggs.

Influence of colour

The tests on colour were made with eggs of normal colours and, compared with these in separate tests, bright blue, bright yellow and bright red eggs. The coloured eggs were dotted in as natural a manner as possible with dots of various sizes and darkness of shade, but all of the same colour as the background.

The following results were obtained with blue; five individual birds were involved.

BLUE				NATURAL		
approach	*intention*	*sitting*		*approach*	*intention*	*sitting*
10	—	14		6	1	15
	24				22	

This result was of course not unexpected. Yet we could not help being astonished each time we were watching the birds settling perfectly at ease on these funny Easter eggs, as if they had done so their whole life.

In these tests, as well as in other tests in which we offered two types which differed little in releasing value, after a few tests, or even sometimes after one, the birds usually developed a clear preference in favour of one of the two nests, independently of its contents; a site-preference. If this happened we always moved the two artificial nests to the right and left of the preferred site, and this was usually sufficient to break the site-preference and to force the birds to choose between eggs and not between sites. Site-choices occurred so regularly in cases of " no preference," that gradually we began to consider it as a sure sign of the relative equality of the two types of egg dummies used. On the other hand, when no site-preference developed or when even an incipient site-preference could be broken by merely inter-changing the egg dummies, this was a certain indication of inequality in the dummies.

With yellow eggs we got essentially the same result as with the blues; two individuals took part.

YELLOW				NATURAL		
a	i	s		a	i	s
5	9	4		1	2	12
	18				15	

Here again the real incubation-responses were more numerous with the naturally-coloured eggs than with the yellow ones, and this might mean that the birds made some distinction.

With the red eggs we got a different story. Seven animals were tested, with the following result:

RED				NATURAL		
a	i	s		a	i	s
3	6	5		16	6	21
	14				43	

This, we think, shows that red eggs are really less attractive than eggs in natural colours. Site-preference did not often develop and incipient site-preferences could be broken by putting the red eggs on the preferred site. In addition, we observed four times that a bird, after having approached the red eggs and even showing the beginning of a response, suddenly pecked at the eggs! This is in accordance with observations reported by Culemann (1928) and by Goethe (1937) who both reported that Herring Gulls remove red objects found in the nest. Dircksen (1932) mentions a similar reaction to red objects in Sandwich Terns. It seems not impossible that this is a reaction to injured chicks. It is especially interesting that a red egg does not always and invariably release pecking, but that a bird may rapidly change from pecking to the intention-movement of brooding. It is clearly torn between two entirely different responses. We think we know the cause of this ambivalent behaviour. As we will see later, the shape of an egg is a very important stimulus. Now the red eggs had an optimal shape, but a repellent colour. The red colour released pecking, the rounded shape released brooding. The result was a curious mixture of the two responses. This demonstrates the typically instinctive type of reaction. A human being in such a situation would think about the conflicting properties of the egg, would make up his mind whether it had to be considered an egg or not, and would then show a consistent response. I would not claim that humans behave so intelligently in all situations, but they often do. Instinctive behaviour is different; it is an immediate reaction to present stimuli, based on a much more rigid mechanism in which stimulus and response are very intimately linked.

Concluding, we may say that genuine eggs are slightly more stimulating than our best wooden models, and that various colours have about equal releasing value, although there are indications that the natural colours are somewhat more stimulating than blue and yellow. Red, however, is definitely less stimulating, and even releases another response.

It is interesting to compare these results with those obtained by others. Goethe (1937) and Steinbacher (1937) have studied reactions to abnormally coloured eggs. Their method differed from ours, however. Whereas we offered a bird a choice, both Goethe and Steinbacher studied the gulls' response to one set of eggs, which were left in the nest. Steinbacher merely reports that eggs coloured " brownish red " or black were accepted. Goethe replaced the real eggs by eggs of the Shelduck (white), light blue Herring Gulls' eggs, and bright yellow, green, blue or red egg-dummies, made of gypsum. He reports that, although all the eggs except red eggs were usually accepted, the birds showed by their behaviour that they perceived the change. He also mentions pecking responses to the red eggs, and in one case to a white egg. Goethe's reports give the impression that his type of test is less suited for a comparison of the releasive value of different egg-substitutes than is our choice test.

Influence of Spotting

Our next step concerned the patterning of the eggs rather than the colour. Would it make much difference whether the many dark spots found on all Herring Gulls' eggs were present or absent? We made five series of eggs of a smooth unpatterned coloration. One was white, one was black, and three had intermediate shades of grey: light, medium and dark.

The results were:

	WHITE				NATURAL	
a	i	s		a	i	s
4	1	9		10	5	12
	14				27	

	LIGHT				NATURAL	
a	i	s		a	i	s
6	3	15		5	6	13
	24				24	

	MEDIUM				NATURAL	
a	i	s		a	i	s
4	5	11		10	5	22
	20				37	

	DARK			NATURAL	
a	i	s	a	i	s
4	5	5	3	3	5
	14			11	

	BLACK			NATURAL	
a	i	s	a	i	s
5	1	7	8	5	11
	13			24	

The results are not very consistent. Whereas white, medium and black received definitely less attention than the eggs in natural colours, light and dark did not seem to be less stimulating than eggs in normal colours. Clearly the experiments should be continued. However, it seems likely that the different results can be explained by assuming that a bird with a strong brooding drive is less selective than one with a relatively weak brooding urge. We got the impression that, on the whole, the gulls were more selective at the beginning of the breeding season than at the end, when the brooding urge is high. Goethe is of the same opinion. Also, after our tests were done, Prof. Baerends from Groningen took up this work again, using the same models as we did, and, although his results till now involve relatively few tests, all his birds were more selective than ours. Now his work was done in a colony where eggs had been taken continuously, and it is likely that his birds, by being robbed so often, had on the average a lower incubation-drive than our birds. The inconsistency of our results might be due to the fact that our experiments were done with birds of varying degrees of broodiness.

I think we are justified in concluding that the spotting of the eggs is not, as I originally believed (Tinbergen & Booy, 1937) of no importance, but that it does play a part, though a minor one, and that this is especially evident when the incubation drive is low.

Influence of shape

The influence of shape was next studied. Here again the number of experiments is insufficient, but the first results do at least give some indications. Some of our models were based on the assumption that the roundness of the egg might perhaps be an important character. We therefore made a series of models of varying degrees of roundness. One type was rectangular, of roughly the same dimensions as a Herring Gull's egg (Plate 20, p. 137), another type was a cylinder of about the same size, another again was a prism. These three types were made with sharp edges and with rounded edges. I will not present the results in detail, but only give the general outcome. It was shown that the rectangular models were less attractive than the egg-shaped models, especially when the edges of the rectangulars were sharp (sharp versus egg-shape: 5–17; rounded versus egg-shape: 9–18). The cylinders were inferior when sharp-edged (8–18) but less so when rounded (8–11). The prisms were not inferior even when sharp-edged (18–12; rounded versus egg-shaped: 22–20).

The experiments with the sharp-edged eggs yielded another and quite interesting result: although they were relatively often selected, the birds did not brood them. If they sat down on them, they usually kept shifting them, and then either went over to the other eggs, or tried again and again to find a comfortable position. This restlessness was only shown after the bird had actually touched the egg with the body, and it was clearly determined not visually but by touch stimuli. This made us once more realise how incorrect it was to interpret our choice-tests as indicators of " egg-recognition." For when the birds made their choice and went to the rectangular blocks, they could truly be said to " recognise " them as eggs. But when, after touching them, they left them, one could with as much justification say that now they did not " recognise " them as eggs. The trouble is that we have used a terminology fit to describe human reactions, but unfit to describe those of birds. We humans " recognise " an egg and then, after rational thinking, decide to treat it as such, but the bird reacts differently. This is one reason why it often brings us farther when we avoid anthropomorphic terms and describe the bird's behaviour in objective terms of reactions to stimuli received from the egg. The reactions involved are clearly of a serial character; incubation consists of a chain of activities. When a foraging Herring Gull begins to obey its incubation urge, the first thing it does is to fly back to its territory. In doing so it is directed by landmarks to which it has learned to react. Within the territory, the way from its look-out post to the nest is again directed by landmarks to which it has also learned to react. Coming closer to the nest, it begins to react to the nest itself; and only after the mate has stood up and leaves the eggs uncovered do the eggs themselves begin to stimulate the bird and to release its reaction of settling down on them. This reaction, as our experiments tell us, is a visual one, in which the nest-site, the nest-pit and the eggs play a part. The stimuli from the egg have not much to do with their colour, something with spotting, and much with their rounded shape. After that, touch stimuli begin to play a part. If the eggs do not fit nicely, the birds react by shifting them. If shifting does not help, even after repetition, the bird deserts the nest.

Although our tests on the part played by the shape of the eggs were not very complete, we know really more about the influence of shape than they could tell us, thanks to occasional observations. First, small irregularities of the rounded surface invariably release a kind of exploratory pecking. Both outcrops and holes are nibbled with the bill. This is the more remarkable, as later in the season, when the chick pips the egg and makes a hole in it, the parent bird does not nibble at it. This is a matter of internal change, of maturation, for when we give pipped eggs to a gull which has been incubating only for a week or so, it will peck at the hole, and by tearing small bits of shell away it may kill the chick.

Another indication of the importance of shape is the following. When an egg is broken, for instance when a strange gull has managed to peck at it, the parent no longer broods it, but instead eats it (Plate 19 p. 136). We can now understand why a broken egg does not release incubation: it has lost its main stimulus, its rounded shape. The contents of the egg probably provide extra stimuli releasing eating, and thus the behaviour changes suddenly from incubation to eating.

When we changed the proportions of the eggs without creating sharp edges, we got other results. Egg models with half the length of normal eggs but of normal width were not appreciably less attractive than dummies of normal shape (20–24). Eggs of normal length and half the width, however, were definitely inferior (15–34).

Influence of size

Finally, we did a few experiments with eggs of normal shape but of abnormal size. Eggs smaller than normal eggs are inferior: those half the normal linear dimensions were not chosen at all (0–13). Very peculiar results were obtained with eggs double the (linear) size, which had, therefore, a volume eight times the normal.

When one of the eggs was put in one of the artificial nests, and a normal egg in the other, the giant egg was chosen 6 times whereas the normal egg was never taken. Our general impression was that such a large egg stimulated the bird much more than a normal egg did. All birds which were given the large egg became very excited and made frantic attempts to cover it. In doing so, they invariably lost their balance, and their evolutions were, I must confess, most amusing to watch.

It will certainly be worth while to extend this work. The results obtained thus far are fragmentary and often inconsistent. This is due partly to the fact that we did not stick long enough to one type of test, and shifted to a new experiment before we had got entirely clear results. We had some excuse, incidentally, because only half-way through did it become clear that our series ought to be longer. Also, we had to avoid using the same models with the same birds too often, and as it was efficient to stick to individual birds with favourably situated nests, or with obligingly low escape-drives, we had to change our models often.

Our results thus far obtained show that it will pay to measure or assess in some way the strength of the incubation-drive in each bird and with each experiment, further to make an attempt to trace learning processes which might occur during the advance

Plate *23a*. On hot days the chick moves into the shade of the parent bird

b. A pipped egg. The chick's bill with its egg tooth can be seen

Plate 24a. On cool days the chicks enjoy the sunshine

      b. Feeding a chick

of the season.   Also, the tests with the giant eggs should be continued, for it may well be that they really offer stronger stimuli than the natural eggs.   This was actually found in Oystercatchers.   An Oystercatcher must be a frustrated bird, for not only do our experiments prove that it loves to sit on giant eggs rather than on its own modest products, but it would also sit on 5 eggs rather than on just 3, the most common clutch-size. As I will show later, such " supernormal " stimuli have been found in other cases as well.

CHAPTER 18

THE HATCHING OF THE CHICKS

The hole in the top half

The incubation period is about four weeks, but its length varies considerably. We followed the fate of 13 eggs closely, which we had individually marked as soon as they were laid, and found that the time between laying and hatching varied between 28 and 33 days, with an average of 30.5 days.

The hatching of the young is a lengthy process. One, two or sometimes three days before the chick finally breaks the egg-shell in two, the first crack appears. In the course of the next few hours more cracks show, and after some time the chick makes a real hole in the shell. It struck us that in heavily pipped eggs the hole was often visible from above. This of course might be only apparent, because when the hole is not visible from above how would we know that an egg was pipped? The only way to make sure whether as a rule the hole was in the upper half of the egg, was to examine a large number of eggs at about the time of hatching, and note the position of the hole in pipped eggs. The practice of egg-shaking on Terschelling did not allow us to collect many data, but we have 43 observations, from which we obtained the graph of Fig. 24.

Each rectangle indicates one observation of the position of the hole in a pipped egg as seen from the sharp pole. It shows that in the majority of cases the hole was in the upper half of the egg, and in about half of the cases it was even exactly in the middle, at the highest possible spot.

This could mean one of two things. Either the parent turned the egg with the hole up as soon as it was pipped, or the chick itself selected the site for the hole. But the latter possibility would imply that the parents would stop shifting and turning an egg when it is pipped. This made us realise that as a matter of fact we did not really know whether or not a gull normally turns the eggs around when it shifts them, and this was the reason why we collected the evidence represented in Figs. 20 and 21. A glance at the two graphs shows at once that a pipped egg is treated differently from a non-pipped one.

We must conclude that an egg is, as a rule, no longer turned once it is pipped. The observations did not tell us, however, who is responsible, chick or parent, for the hole being on top or at least in the upper half of the egg. Some facts suggest that it is the chick. In most of the pipped eggs there is a line of cracks around the obtuse pole. This line may be long, and cover, for instance, almost 180 degrees; often it is much shorter, and it may even be absent. In the majority of our observations the crack-line ended at the hole. This indicates that the chick turns round in the egg, making the cracks, until its head is in the highest possible place. In this position the chick's head is horizontal, that is, neither inclined to the left nor to the right. If the parent bird does not turn the egg, the chick remains in this position and makes the hole.

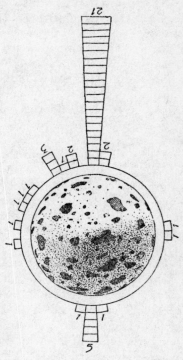

FIG. 24

Position of hole in pipped eggs

(See pp. 160-2)

Gravity reaction of the chick

In this connection it is remarkable that in seven of our

observations we found the hole exactly in the lowest part of the egg. As in the top position the chick's head is horizontal, in the reversed position it must be exactly upside down. This suggests that a sense of gravity must play a part. This sense is located in a symmetrical set of sense organs, which are stimulated by little stones, the statoliths, which exert a pressure in the direction of gravity. In the horizontal and the reversed attitude pressure is at right angles to the organ; in the first case the stones exert a " positive " pressure, in the second they hang down from the sense epithelium, and, being embedded in a gelatinous substance which connects them with the sensory cells, it exerts a pull, or a negative pressure. Whenever the head is held at an angle, the stones of left and right side exert oblique pressures on the sensory cells. The seven observations of reversed chicks can be understood if we assume that in this position their gravity receptors do not tell them that their head is upside down. This is exactly in accordance with the newest views of the functioning of gravity receptors in vertebrates, as based on highly specialised experimental work. According to these views, the sensory cells do not distinguish between pull or pressure, but react to oblique or sideways pull. Whenever the chick's head is held at an angle with the vertical, the pull on right and left sensory patches is oblique and the chick is able to work itself into a horizontal position. Only when the chick's head lies exactly upside down at the moment when it begins to crack the shell, its gravity receptors cannot tell it that it is not in the correct position, because there is no oblique pressure. If this is what happens, our next problem is: why does the parent stop turning the eggs when they are pipped? The first supposition would be that it perceives the crack in the shell. This could easily be tested by presenting a gull at the end of its incubation period with a wooden egg with an artificial crack or even a hole in it. We have done this a few times, always with the result that the gull was much interested in the hole. Its interest was misguided, however, for it nibbled at the hole, which it never does when the eggs are really pipped, at least not in this late phase of the incubation period. Also, the few gulls which we tested in this way went happily on turning the "pipped" egg. We think now that perhaps the parent reacts to the call notes of the chick, for the chick begins to squeak at about the time it begins to crack the egg. The parent's reaction is not very prompt, however. We often saw an incubating gull turning eggs even when one of them was already pipped. It is possible that the reaction is gradual and not abrupt. When the squeaking of the chick begins, it may effect a gradual change in the parent which in the course of one or even a few days changes its disposition from incubation to care of the young. This change, however, does not take longer than it takes a chick to hatch, for we have never seen that a gull shifts a chick when it settles down on it to brood it. It seems therefore as if the first stimuli from the chick, either its movements or its squeaks, cause the parent to treat the pipped egg as a chick.

Of course this explanation is a tentative one. First of all, we should extend our statistics on egg positions. Further, the parents' reaction towards the end of the incubation period have been insufficiently studied. Also, there is no experimental evidence on the gravity responses in the chick. The problem certainly deserves further study.

CHAPTER 19

DEFENCE OF THE BROOD

The charge

Towards the end of the incubation period, the tendency of the gulls to defend their nest against predators is increasing, and shortly before the young hatch it reaches a peak, which will last until the young are several weeks old. At this time the birds show the magnificent " charge." When a dog, or a human intruder, comes near the nest, the gulls will swoop down on him again and again. Usually the birds do not actually touch the intruder, but occasionally they do. Even when they do not touch him, the whole manœuvre gives the impression of a preparation for real attack, for they lower their feet a fraction of a second before they flash past the enemy, and if they hit him, it is usually with the feet. When we made some slow-motion films of this attack, we noticed to our astonishment that most of the shots showed the bird extending only one foot (Figs. 25–27), though in some cases it stretched them both out. This, incidentally, is an observation on human psychology which I have made repeatedly. One may have studied an animal for years and years, trying to watch it as closely as possible, and yet one may overlook quite simple things like this. Sometimes it is the film that shows you something you had not seen before, sometimes another observer tells you. This is especially instructive when that other man is quite untrained. It teaches one to be very careful in claiming that this or that does not happen because one has never seen it oneself. Once your attention has been called to it, you may see it again and again, causing you to wonder why you had not seen that before. I have exactly the same experience when reading a foreign language. I have often

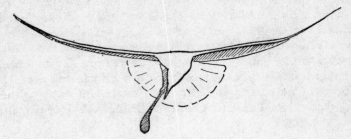

FIG. 25

The charge at a human intruder near the nest. (Taken from a slow motion film)

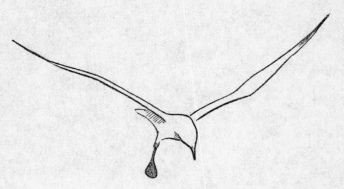

FIG. 26

Another charge from a slow motion film

FIG. 27

A charge in which both legs are used. (From a slow motion film)

stumbled upon a word or an expression I was sure I had never met with before. After I looked it up in the dictionary, and became aware of the word's existence, I met it several times in the next few weeks. Such experiences demonstrate the tendency to perceive the whole rather than its parts. Configurational perception makes you overlook details which may be quite obvious when an analytical effort has made you aware of them. Analytical vision *is* an effort, and the primary type of perception is configurational.

Alarm calls

The charge, though the most spectacular of defence reactions, is by no means the only reaction to predators. There are several preparatory reactions; they have very interesting aspects. When a gull sees an intruder—in our modern world this is usually a human being—it utters the alarm call, " hahaha! " This call can be uttered in many different grades of intensity, depending, amongst others, on the distance of the intruder. The lowest intensity is a scarcely audible " hehe " or " hehehe." With each syllable, the beak is opened widely. With increasing intensity, the call becomes deeper and louder, and the number of syllables increases to four or five. Also, a number of series are repeated in quick succession when the intensity is high. When the excitement is maximal, another call is uttered, a very sharp and high-pitched " Keew! "

These calls have an immediate and profound effect on the other gulls. At the slightest sign of unrest, the incubating gulls stretch their necks, and little is needed to make them stand up and walk or fly away. This wariness at the nest has undoubtedly to do with the fact that the gulls themselves are conspicuously coloured whereas the eggs have a cryptic coloration. Comparison of various species of birds shows that there is a certain correlation between wariness at the nest and the coloration of the bird and/or its eggs. This may be illustrated by comparing the Herring Gull (and other gulls and terns) as one extreme with the Nightjar as the other extreme. The Nightjar has rather conspicuous eggs but has a marvellous concealing coloration itself, and it usually sits on the eggs until it is almost touched. Of course, the correlation is not absolute, since there are a number of other factors involved, but I do not think there is reason to doubt that there is a relationship between wariness at the nest and coloration of adults and eggs.

Innate reactions to the alarm calls

The Herring Gull's reaction to the alarm call is innate. Even newly born chicks react to it. There is further a correlation between the differences in intensity of the alarm call and the differences in the intensity of the reactions elicited by it. The low-intensity call " hehehe " does not cause more than a mild restlessness among the neighbouring gulls. When a gull gets a sudden fright, for instance when the observer leaves his blind unexpectedly, it will fly up with a piercing " keew," followed by a hurried series of " hahahaha's," and this causes an instantaneous panic among all the birds around, even among those who did not see the danger themselves.

Learning

The statement that the reaction to the alarm calls is innate does not mean that experience plays no part in the reactions. It does indeed, for it may influence the intensity of the reaction. When once I was watching a group of nests from my blind for a period long enough to get thoroughly acquainted with the individual gulls in the neighbourhood, I was often struck by the indifference with which the alarm calls of some particular gulls were received. Soon I became aware that very nervous, panicky gulls, which uttered the alarm call at the slightest disturbance, were ignored by the majority of the other gulls, while an alarm call uttered by one who was " known " as a " reliable " neighbour was always taken seriously. In other words, the gulls learn whose alarm call means real danger and whose does not, or at least need not be responded to immediately. I think that this is a learning process of quite a high standard.

Differences between argentatus and fuscus

A study of the alarm call revealed one more fact of great interest. On the isle of Terschelling Herring Gulls and Lesser Black-backed Gulls are nesting together. When visiting the colony, it always struck me that the latter's reactions were different from the former's. The Herring Gulls usually reacted to our presence by the " hahaha " call mingled with occasional " keews," the Lesser Black-backs usually called the " keew " call and uttered the " hahaha " only rarely. Both calls are much hoarser in the Lesser Black-back than they are in the Herring Gull, but there is not the slightest doubt that they are the same calls. This suggests that, although both species have the same calls, the thresholds of the different calls for the degree of danger are different; the Lesser Black-back is much more ready to respond with the high-intensity " keew." Since the two species are so closely related that they are considered borderline cases between different species and different subspecies of one and the same species, this throws some light on the way in which behaviour may change during evolution. Subspeciation and subsequent speciation has, in this " super-species," not only led to the development of a difference in pitch of all calls, but also to a shift in thresholds of two intensities of one reaction. One could imagine this development to be continued a little while along the same line, and the result would be two species with entirely different alarm calls : the Herring Gull might loose the " keew " and the Lesser Black-back might loose the " hahaha."

Concluding this part, I hope to have shown that the brooding period offers a great many problems of behaviour and sociology which can be approached by observation and experiment in the field. Many of these problems have only just been touched by our work, and here again my report is in many ways a sketch of a programme rather than an enumeration of results.

Plate 25a. The chick is fed for the first time in its life

   b. Feeding a chick

Plate 26. The parents' alarm calls make the chicks crouch

CHAPTER 20

THE "GULL PROBLEM"

THE PREDATORY behaviour of the Herring Gull is interesting in several respects. Most if not all Herring Gulls eat eggs when they can get them easily. Whenever eggs of other Herring Gulls, or of other species nesting in the open, such as Lapwings, Oyster-catchers, Eider-ducks, are left unguarded, a Herring Gull, like a Crow, will eat them. Usually they are eaten on the spot, but sometimes they are carried away. This the Herring Gull does by taking the egg between the mandibles—unlike crows, which peck a hole in it, then put the lower mandible through it, close the bill, and carry it very expertly with the hole up, so as to waste not a single drop of the valuable contents.

A Herring Gull will with the same eagerness eat another Herring Gull's eggs. As soon as a nest in the colony is unguarded it is robbed. Even a slight waning of attention of the parent bird may provoke the catastrophe: like a flash a gull may swoop down from the air and peck at the egg, as I described in Chapter 17.

Egg-robbing as a local phenomenon

Usually, however, egg-robbing is not a prominent feature in the behaviour of a colony. In the Wassenaar colony, Oyster-catchers, Lapwings, Curlews, Pheasants, Partridges and Nightjars are nesting right in the Herring Gull colony, and they usually hatch their young and raise them. This is partly due to the vigorous defence of some of these species, which is intense enough to overcome the desire to rob their nests existing in the normal gulls of this colony. Egg-robbing on a large scale, and more especially robbing of chicks, has been reported from several colonies that have grown out of proportion as a consequence of the protection. These colonies, consisting of several thousands of birds, are found on the Frisian Islands, both in Holland and in Germany. It seems to me very probable that overcrowding and, as a result, food shortage has been the cause of this behaviour.

Van Dobben's work on gull control

We owe the most accurate data on the predatory behaviour of the Herring Gull to Van Dobben, who studied it on the islands of Vlieland and Terschelling (1934). His observations concern primarily their predation of Shelducks and Eider-ducks. On Vlieland, it is especially the Shelducks that suffer. When the

FIG. 28

Sheldrake attacking a gull that is swallowing one of its chicks in flight

parents walk with their young from the breeding grounds in the dunes to the mud-flats, and also while the families are living on the tidal flats, the parent Shelducks will furiously attack any approaching Herring Gull. However, sometimes the male overdoes the attack, singles out one of the gulls, and pursues it over such a distance that the mother Shelduck and the chicks are left unprotected. This is the moment at which other gulls may attack the family, and (the mother being rather timid) may pick up one chick after the other. This is not an easy job, because the chicks dive like a flash and swim considerable distances under water; but when they begin to do this, they scatter and thus lose what protection they still might have.

The Herring Gulls simply hover above the diving ducklings and pick them up just before they reach the surface again. Even then the mother may still be able to make a desperate charge at the gull. Occasionally this may cause the gull to release its victim;

Fig. 29

Eider-duck defending its brood against an attacking Herring Gull

but even then the duckling will not be left alone and will be picked up the next time it comes up : the mother's charge is of no avail, and the gull swallows the unhappy duckling.

The Eider-duck is much more efficient in its defence. Whenever a gull comes too near, the young gather under the mother, whose fierce and vigorous defence, soon discourages the gull. The danger comes from scattering, when the young may be too far away from the mother to reach her in time. On the whole the Eider-ducks are able to survive even on the Frisian Islands, and in fact are increasing rapidly on Texel, Vlieland and Terschelling.

Apart from these ducks, many other species breeding in open flat country are being decimated by the Herring Gulls. Common Terns have practically disappeared from Vlieland; Avocets, Kentish Plover and Ringed Plover have suffered severely. In order to keep the gulls in check and to prevent more damage, we must know first of all why the gulls increase in numbers at such a rate; and secondly, how we can stop that increase.

The increase is certainly due to the absence of predators. One of the natural predators of the Herring Gull has probably been the fox. When it decreased through human interference, Man took over its role as an egg-predator and thus kept the gulls in check. As a matter of fact, he did it better than the fox and nearly caused the Herring Gulls' local extinction. When protection began, human predation fell down practically to nil, with a quick increase of gull numbers as a result. When the damage began, many colonies were already badly overcrowded. The increase continued at a steeper rate and became more obvious when the enormous numbers of immature birds, representing at least three generations, grew up and settled in the breeding colonies. That was the reason why the first years of attempts at gull control by taking the eggs and by shooting yielded no obvious result.

Various control methods were tried out by Van Dobben (1934). He found that taking the eggs caused the gulls to scatter over a much wider area, with the result that the second clutches were very difficult to collect in mass. Shooting, unless done with considerable consistency, was also inefficient. Killing the eggs by pricking a small hole in them had the advantage that the gulls did not abandon the nest at once. However, they sometimes abandoned them after a week or so; also, sometimes the wound healed and the chicks hatched. A better method was shaking the eggs some days after the onset of incubation. The germ is killed, but the gulls incubate one or two weeks in excess of the normal period of four weeks. After this period they do not begin a second brood.

Van Dobben now combined the results of these various tests and developed what seems to be a very good method of control. A limited area in a colony is selected as the future site of the reduced colony. In this area all eggs are shaken, and outside the area all eggs are taken. Part of the outside gulls will start a new clutch in the same area, but part change over to the central area, where there is, from the limited point of view of the gulls, no egg-robbing. In this way it is hoped to discourage the gulls in the outside areas and to concentrate them in the central area. Here shaking can be continued until the numbers are down to a fair level. On the island of Terschelling, where the Herring Gulls nest over an area of about 0.5 x 4 miles, a small central area is protected but the eggs are shaken, while on the remaining part egg-collecting is allowed to the islanders. Since Herring Gull eggs are excellent food—and since a collecting trip to the attractive dune scenery in May or June, culminating in boiling or frying the eggs on a little fire of driftwood on the beach (or, better still, in scrambling them raw with some brandy and sugar) is great fun—the egg-collecting is taken care of by quite an efficient little army of helpers, who, instead of having to be paid for it, are glad to pay a guilder for permission to help in controlling the gulls. This procedure was interrupted by the war, when egg-collecting again became indiscriminate, but by now the situation seems to be well in hand again.

Gross (1951) reports on another successful method, which has been applied in the United States. It is based on the same principles as Van Dobben's method, killing the eggs without causing the gulls to abandon them. Instead of shaking the eggs, they are sprayed with an oil emulsion mixed with formalin; this kills 95 per cent of the eggs.

Gull tradition
However, even these methods leave us with one difficulty,

and from the point of view of the behaviour-student a most interesting one. There are indications that a population which has once begun to prey upon eggs and young birds wholesale does not give up the habit when their numbers are brought down to a reasonable level. I think that this is due to tradition, young gulls learning it in some way from the adults. The Terschelling colony did not show signs of starvation in 1948 and 1949 when I spent several weeks watching it. Yet there were many gulls which indulged in egg-robbing and especially in chick-robbing in their own colony. Many of these were immature gulls, probably in their fourth summer, or three years of age. Their secondaries were mottled with brown, they had no white on the wing-tips, and they usually had a brown tail-band; their heads were white as in the adult gulls. These gulls were seen regularly roaming about in the colony. In the beginning of the season, they earned a living by feeding on the remnants of the meals served by the males to their females. I watched several of these gulls closely from my blind, and found that they knew exactly places where each male used habitually to feed his mate. They went straight from one station to the other. Later, they gathered around the nests with newly hatched young. And then a most interesting thing happened. The parents reacted immediately to the presence of these scavengers by stretching their necks. Usually the male, if at home, walked up to them from a considerable distance, assuming the upright threat posture. The young gulls, however, behaved unlike any other gull would do. They did not assume the inferior attitude as a very young bird would. They did not flee. But they did not threaten back either, as an adult bird which owns a territory would do. They just stretched their neck, stepped aside a few steps whenever the attacking male came within a foot or two, and then walked round him in the direction of the nest. The male then again took a position between the nest and the stranger, but again did not actually attack. It was clear that he *could* not attack, because the intruder did not provoke it. Flight or hostile behaviour would at once have released attack, but this stealthy and yet determined

approach was beyond the defender's capacities; a Herring Gull
has no defence against it. Thus the intruder might come within
a few yards of the nest, and there it would remain, just standing
very quietly, often with the neck entirely withdrawn, and not
provoking more than mild threats. Whenever part of one of the
chicks, covered by the parent, became visible, the intruder
would show interest, and we actually saw on some occasions how
it made a sudden dash and, while the desperate parents tried to
check it, tore the chick from under them and flew away with it.
I never saw these things in the Wassenaar colony, which until
now consisted of no more than about 500 pairs, but on Terschelling it was a regular feature, and when we were filming at
one nest, we had to supply new chicks to the parents every day,
because although we left them with two or three chicks in the
evening, only one or none were left next morning. Because the
interval was so short, the chicks probably being taken early in
the morning, new chicks, provided they were of about equal age
as the original chicks, were readily accepted by the deprived
parents. We kept this up for several days, but did not stay to
try how long we could continue it.

PART FIVE

Family Life

CHAPTER 21

THE BEHAVIOUR OF THE CHICKS

In praise of birds

With the hatching of the chicks a most charming period begins. The hours spent at my observation post on the top of a high dune on fine early June mornings belong to the happiest of my life. The low sun casts long shadows over the undulating bronze-green hills, covered with millions and millions of glittering dewdrops. The air is heavy with the scent of privet, rose, honeysuckle and yellow bedstraw. From the patches of birch wood in the valleys come the calls of Orioles and the crowing of Pheasants. Apart from the distant alarm cries of a pair of Curlews all is extremely quiet and peaceful.

To a hasty visitor a Herring Gull colony is nothing more than a noisy place covered with the birds' fæces and half-digested food. All he remembers afterwards is a chaotic mass of screaming gulls, all flying excitedly round and round and occasionally swooping down and delivering either a blow or a disgusting load of warm, smelly and sticky substance.

To the patient watcher it is different. The gulls are standing in pairs on their territories, preening, sleeping or just keeping an eye on the observer. And on almost every territory there are greyish downy speckled chicks. They are not very mobile, and spend much of their time in just sitting or standing, preening their downy plumage in a clumsy way, losing their balance repeatedly in doing so. Now and then they take a few steps, only to squat on their tarsi immediately. And all the time they are growing at a tremendous rate.

Plate 27. At this age the young do not yet utter the trumpeting call

Plate 28a. Feeding a half-grown chick

   b. The young make attempts to fly long before their wings are fully developed

Covering the chicks

When the sun is hot, they seek refuge in the shadow of their parents. When the gullery is quiet it is difficult to imagine that there is an intricate web of relationships between all these gulls. Yet there still is the—now latent—hostility between neighbours, there is the attachment of each pair to their territory, of each bird to its mate. But with the appearance of the chicks a change has occurred in the parents. Incubation has stopped, and new behaviour-patterns, those directed to the chicks, have appeared.

During hatching and for at least some days after hatching the parents still cover the chicks, usually in the nest. However, the sitting posture is different from what it was during incubation. The most obvious difference is found in the wings; a bird brooding chicks has the wings slightly lifted. Also a bird, in settling down on young, no longer shows the waggling movements nor does it shift the chick as it did the eggs.

This tendency to brood chicks decreases in a few days. It can be released again by heavy rain, when even chicks three weeks old may occasionally be covered. This is no luxury, and it may even, though rarely, be insufficient as a measure to protect the young. I once watched a gull settling down on half-grown chicks during a sudden and extremely heavy rainstorm. Its position was rather awkward, halfway on a steep sandy slope. After about five minutes, when it was still pouring I saw the adult get up and walk away, and it started to preen at a few yards' distance from the chicks. When I went over to have a look at the chicks, I found them dead, and half buried by wet sand. This must have been washed over them while they were being brooded, for they were alive and perfectly normal when it began to rain.

During the first hours after hatching the chicks are continuously covered until their plumage is " dry " and fluffy. When the parent is disturbed during those critical hours and the young are exposed to the open air, the downy feathers do not spread but stick together. I am not quite sure what is the cause of this phenomenon. If the chicks are exposed too long in this phase they die.

The first feeding

When the chicks are a few hours old they begin to crawl about under the parent, causing it to shift and adjust its position every so often. Sometimes the parent stands up and looks down into the nest, and then we may see the first begging behaviour of the young. They do not lose time in contemplating or studying the parent, whose head they see for the first time, but begin to peck at its bill-tip right away, with repeated, quick, and relatively well-aimed darts of their tiny bills. They usually spread the wings and utter a faint squeaking sound. The old bird cannot resist this, and if only the chicks persist it will feed them. First the parent stretches its neck, and soon a swelling appears at its base. It travels upward, causing the most appalling deformations and the most peculiar turnings and twistings of the neck. All at once the parent bends its head down and regurgitates an enormous lump of half-digested food. This is dropped, and a small piece is now picked up again and presented to the chicks. These redouble their efforts, and soon get hold of the food, whereupon the parent presents them with a new morsel. Now and then the chicks peck at the food on the ground, but more often they aim at the parent's bill, and although this aiming is not always correct, it rarely takes them more than three or four attempts until they score a hit.

After the chicks have had one or two turns, they cease to respond and with an amazing promptness they fade away into a peaceful slumber. The parent may call once or twice more, standing patiently with food in its beak, but getting no response it swallows the food again. After that, it cleans its bill, partly with its foot, partly by thrusting it into the sand, and then the meal is over. One never gets tired of watching these first reactions of the chicks to their parents. Their remarkable " know-how," not dependent on experience of any kind but entirely innate, never fails to impress one as an instance of the adaptedness of an inborn response. It seems so trivial and common at first sight, but the longer one watches it the more remarkable it appears to be.

Both male and female feed the young. I cannot corroborate Goethe's statement that the male takes a greater share in the feeding of the chicks than the female. If there is a difference it is very slight and it is certainly not true that the female feeds the young only " occasionally," as Goethe claims.

The food presented to the young is different from the food taken by the adult birds before there were young. Whereas the males often feed quantities of bivalves to the female, such as cockles and edible mussels (a food taken all through the rest of the year by both sexes so far as we know), the young usually get fish, sometimes crabs, and, in the Wassenaar gullery, worms. Goethe reports the same, only on Memmertsand the chicks seem to get mainly crabs. These are fed only occasionally at Wassenaar and Terschelling : as far as my experience goes, crabs are less wanted and only taken during windy weather, when fish may be difficult to get.

Innate behaviour

The begging response is not the only innate behaviour-element shown by the newly born chick. I mentioned the preening reactions before. Although these are still clumsy, it is quite possible to recognise in them the movements of the adult birds. The photographs (Plate 5, p. 36) show the similarity. Also, the stretching movements (Plate 4, p. 13) and the yawning are present right at the beginning. It is often difficult for the very young chicks to keep their balance during these exertions and it is amusing to see them tumble in an attempt to scratch their head or to stretch one wing and one leg, only to get up and begin anew.

The chicks have their special calls as well. A faint squeaking note accompanies the begging. It is already uttered by chicks still in the egg. It gradually develops into the begging note of the adult, which is uttered by females begging for food in front of males, and by both sexes as an introduction to coition. A chick in distress utters a longer, vibrating note; I believe, though I cannot be certain, that this is the same note as the " hahaha " call of the adults. The chicks do not have the trumpeting call, a fact suggested by the picture on Plate 27 (p. 176).

The reaction of the chicks to the adults' alarm call is also innate.   Even when still in the egg a chick stops its squeaking when it hears the " hahaha " call.   We often had opportunity to make sure that the reaction to alarm is auditory, for chicks which we kept in our blinds where they could not see the adults outside usually crouched when the alarm call was given by the gulls outside.   We could even induce them to crouch by crude imitations of the alarm call.

Conditioning to the territory

The crouching reaction shows an interesting development. Chicks of only a few hours of age crouch in the nest.   Before they are a day old, however, they leave the nest during alarm and crouch some distance away.   This distance rapidly increases during the next days, and soon they select special shelters, each of them running to its own hiding place when the alarm is called.

The influence which the alarm call has on the chicks, and also on the adult birds, is very limited.   It tells them merely that there is danger, but it does not tell where it is.   This occurred to me the first time when I was sitting in my blind, taking photographs of a gull with three half-grown young.   By some carelessness on my part, the parent gull saw one of my movements and instantly called the alarm, running away from the hide with sleek plumage and stretched neck.   The chicks reacted to the alarm immediately : they stretched their necks and looked suspiciously around.   When the parent repeated the alarm call and flew up, the chicks ran to shelter.   Their shelter was my blind, and in the next instant I had three frightened chicks crouching in my tent, at the very feet of the predator who caused their parent to call the alarm.   Adult birds may react similarly. Although of course they do not crouch, they often run to a high look-out post when they hear the alarm call.   It has happened several times that a gull brooding ten or twenty yards away saw my movements when I was taking photographs from my blind.   Its excited alarm calls sometimes caused another gull to fly on to my tent, where it would stand with the neck outstretched, looking around for the announced predator.

The crouching reaction itself is part of the cryptic devices.

The colour of the chicks, brownish grey of about the shade of sand, their disruptive pattern, and their tendency to crouch under cover and keep entirely motionless, are all elements with the functions of concealment.

The attachment of the young to the territory is very strong. Goethe transported young over distances varying from 20 to 70 yards. Most of his birds returned quickly to their territories; one bird had to make a detour of more than 50 yards but had nevertheless arrived home after two days. In some of the cases the young reacted to their parents' calls, but according to Goethe this was impossible in other cases and the young must have found their way without help from their parents.

The territory itself is known to the young in detail. It is amusing to see the chicks running to their accustomed hiding places when the alarm is called. In whatever part of the territory they may be when the warning is given, they seem never to be in doubt and make straight for their shelter.

Maturation of flight

My observations on the later phases of the development of the chicks are very incomplete. Interesting and amusing are the incipient flight movements of the chicks, which begin long before they have functional wing-quills. A chick of ten days old, which is still covered with down and shows only hints of quills on its " wings," may suddenly be overtaken by a flying urge. It flaps its wings, jumping up into the air as it does so, and performs a series of most curious and inefficient evolutions. In the course of the next weeks, these flight attempts grow more and more co-ordinated and efficient until they finally develop into real flight. The regular and continuous performance of these attempts at flight, and their gradual improvement, would suggest that the chicks are practising, and that the improvement is due to learning. However, as far as we know, birds do not learn to fly. Incipient, gradually improving flight movements are observed in the young of many bird species. The decisive experiment, proving that the improvement is not due to learning, was done with pigeons. Grohmann (1939) raised two groups of young pigeons. One group, the " experimentals," were reared in narrow earthenware tubes, in which it was impossible for them to lift their wings. The other group, the " controls," were allowed to " practise " flight unobstructed. When, after some weeks, these controls began to fly, the experimentals were released from their confinement and were also allowed to fly, and their performances were carefully watched and compared with those of the controls. There proved to be no difference in flying ability between the two groups!

This can only mean that the controls had not had the least advantage from their " practising." What then is the significance of the gradual improvement during their nestling period? Clearly it is not due to learning but to an internal process which makes the flying ability grow, even in individuals that never get any opportunity to practise. Irrespective of performance something matures in the bird during development. The urge to fly appears before the executive organs such as wings, muscles, maybe nervous connections, are fully developed, and this early awakening of the urge is responsible for the early occurrence of the flight movements. Premature awakening of the urge and growth of the executive organs therefore are responsible for this curious phenomenon which so deceptively resembles learning by practice.

With about six weeks the young are full-grown and are well able to fly. They wear the well-known grey mottled plumage, and if we visit the gullery at this time, many go up into the air just as the adults. Some may still resort to crouching even though able to fly, and it is very surprising to see such a youngster submitting itself to touch and even handling as if it were still a helpless chick, and then take wing all at once and join the crowd in the air.

Submissive posture of large young as a defence against the parents

When the colony comes to rest again these young return to their territories. They are still dependent. In the presence of their parents they adopt an " attitude of inferiority " (Plate 29b, p .192). This attitude is in all respects the opposite of the self-assertive vertical threat posture. Instead of raising the front part of the body, stretching the neck and pointing the bill down, the young lower their shoulders, and withdraw their head and neck, the most emphatic opposite of preparation to attack. This attitude seems to be an adaptation which has the task of suppressing any aggressive tendencies the parents might have. Such tendencies would be understandable. First, there is, in this time, a certain recrudescence of sexual behaviour in the adults—the males, especially, are beginning to build new nests. This never develops into a real new cycle, it is true; it always remains a half-hearted affair, but it is accompanied by an increase in aggressiveness. Secondly, the full-grown young, though different from the adults in their plumage, have arrived at adult stature, and I believe that this loss of infantile stature considerably impairs the young's power to release parental behaviour. One gets the impression that the young at this stage combine properties releasing parental behaviour with properties releasing hostile behaviour, and that any means by which the young can appease the parents must have considerable survival value.

In this horizontal posture the young performs food-begging movements very similar to those of the adult female which I described in Chapter 12, p. 105. When the parent shows the least inclination to regurgitate food, the young launch a formidable assault on it. The poor parent, struggling to vomit in peace, is surrounded and almost overrun by a screaming, wing-flapping tangle. Before the food which it brings up reaches the ground it is swallowed by the chicks. They are a rather unpleasant lot now, and I could not help sympathising with the parents when I saw what I believed to be the first signs of their growing hostility towards their clumsy, noisy, and obtrusive offspring.

How the family actually breaks up, I do not know. The young seem to leave the colony of their own accord, and to begin earning their own living very soon after this. Although food-begging by the juveniles may be seen occasionally during late summer and even at the beginning of winter, I believe that the adult gulls very rarely if ever feed young after they have left the breeding colony, but I must admit that my observations on the first weeks are very fragmentary indeed.

CHAPTER 22

ANALYSING THE CHICK'S WORLD

The begging behaviour

The newly hatched chick's begging response offers the observer an unique opportunity to study an inexperienced animal's sensory world. Is it not amazing that such a tiny chick, just emerged from the egg-shell, not only "knows" how to beg and swallow food, but also where and when to expect it? It "knows" that the parent bird provides the food, and it "knows" that it must come from the bill-tip, for it is almost exclusively at the parent's bill-tip that it aims its persistent pecking. In the language of the behaviour student, the begging behaviour is a reaction to stimuli provided by the adult bird. The reaction is innate, and it is obviously released by very special stimuli which the parent bird alone can provide, and which enable the chick to distinguish the parent's bill-tip from anything else it may encounter in its world.

We naturally were interested in the nature of these stimuli. In the literature we had found some observations which seemed to show that here again was a reaction dependent on only very few " sign stimuli." The famous German ornithologist, Heinroth, who has raised nearly all Central European birds from the egg and studied their development and behaviour, wrote (1928) that his Herring Gull chicks had the habit of pecking at all red objects, especially when these were kept low, so that they could peck downwards. This pecking at red objects, he thought, showed that their natural food was meat, and the downward trend would fit with the adults' way of feeding them, by regurgitating food, which the chicks had to peck up from the ground. Here for once Heinroth's unusually keen biological intuition failed him.

Observation of Herring Gulls feeding their chicks in the wild have shown that although the parents do regurgitate the food, they usually do not let the chicks peck it up from the ground (although this is sometimes observed) but take a piece between the bill-tips and present it to the chick. Also, the food is never red; at least I never observed it to be so. It is always half digested, and whether it be fish, rats, kittens, starfish, earthworms, clams, or crabs (to mention some of the more common kinds of food), it is never red, although the earthworms may occasionally be served fresh enough to have a—scarcely perceptible—reddish hue.

The red patch on the parent's mandible

Another, and doubtless the correct, interpretation of the behaviour of Heinroth's Herring Gull chicks was given by F. Goethe (1937). Goethe, as a field observer, knew the Herring Gulls' way of feeding chicks, and seeing that the chicks' pecking was aimed rather accurately at the adult's red spot on the lower mandible, concluded that the tendency to peck at red objects was in reality a reaction not to food, but to the red patch on the bill-tip. He designed a simple experiment to test this. Taking the head of a dead adult Herring Gull, he presented it to a chick in about the same attitude as a parent bird keeps its head when feeding the young. The chick pecked at it as it would do at its own mother or father. Goethe now took another head and covered the red patch with yellow paint. When this was presented to the same chick, it did not peck at it so often, although it did not entirely ignore it. Goethe did this test with two chicks that were taken from the nest just after hatching. Together these two chicks pecked 66 times at the " normal " head, and, in tests covering the same time, only 26 times at the head lacking the red patch. Then, to make absolutely sure that this preference for the red was entirely inborn, he put two eggs in an incubator, and did the same test with the chicks hatched from these eggs. These chicks, which of course had never seen another Herring Gull, responded 181 times to the " normal " head, and 58 times to the head with the all-yellow bill.

The special sensitivity to red was further demonstrated by

the fact that Goethe could elicit responses by red objects of various kinds, and of an appearance that was rather different from a Herring Gull's bill: such as cherries, and the red soles of bathing shoes!

It seemed to us worth while to go into this problem a little deeper. That the chicks were responding to the red patch was obvious; however, as the bill without red did also elicit some response, there must be more in a parent bird's bill that stimulated the chick. Also, the downward tendency had to be explained. As regards opportunity for experimental work, the reactions to cherries and bathing shoes showed that it should be easy to design dummies capable of eliciting responses. Further, the very fact that reactions to crude dummies were not rare, showed that the chick's sensory world must be very different from ours, for we would never expect a bathing shoe to regurgitate food.

Method of dummy experiments

Therefore, when in the summer of 1946 no war conditions prevented us any longer from working in the field, I took my zoology students out for a fortnight's work in one of the Herring Gull colonies on the Dutch Frisian Isles. We carried with us an odd collection of Herring Gull dummies and thus started a study which was to occupy and fascinate us during four consecutive seasons. I will go into the results of this study in considerable detail, because I believe that we happened to choose an ideal object for a study of this type. It was relatively easy to find newly-born chicks every day, and all chicks responded eagerly to most dummies. They kept up their innate responsiveness for rather a long time, and although they changed their behaviour a little by learning, the few pitfalls due to disturbances of this kind could be avoided. This together ensured that we could get quite nice statistics on the relative effectiveness of the various models; in total, we registered over 16,000 pecking responses, and on some days we counted over 500 reactions.

The red patch acts through colour and contrast

Our first concern was to find out whether the coloured spot had to be red, or whether just any darkish patch would do. Having had the experience with the incubating birds' lack of interest in the colour of the eggs, this seemed a natural thing to do. We made a series of flat cardboard models of Herring Gulls' heads, natural size. One was in natural colours, but only very roughly: the bill uniform yellow without any detail except the red patch. In the other dummies only the colour of the patch was different: one was black, another one blue, one even white, and of course there was one model without a patch at all. Armed with these models, we collected some newly-hatched chicks. Because the chicks, after hatching, are brooded by the parents until they are dry, we were certain that by selecting almost dry chicks we got them before they would have had experience of what the parent's bill meant to them.

At first, we presented the chicks with our dummies while they were in the nest. This gave us some responses, but only very few, for the chicks crouched, presumably as a consequence of the alarm calls of the adult birds, which were flying around our heads all the time. We decided to carry the chicks to a quiet spot outside the colony. To be sure that passing gulls would not give the alarm-note and thus disturb our work, we put up a tent, and made ourselves and the chicks comfortable in it. The chicks proved to be very sensitive to temperature changes. They could not bear too hot sunshine, and were still more sensitive to cold. This meant that if the weather was not really warm, one of us had to keep the chicks warm by brooding them. This naturally was considered girl's work. The foster-mother would keep the young in her sweater, and the colder it was, the deeper the chicks were hidden in their comfortable lairs. The foster-mother was also responsible for distinguishing the various individuals. This was always possible on the basis of the variation in the pattern of the head-coloration, but it was not always easy, especially on one very productive day on which we worked with thirteen chicks!

We now presented one of our dummies to one of the chicks.

In order to stimulate their pecking drive, we always began an experiment by imitating three times the mew call of the adults. Then the model was kept in front of the chick and gently moved. One observer noted the time and told us when 30 seconds had elapsed, and another noted the number of pecks shown during these 30 seconds. The chick, after his performance, was given back to its foster-mother, who promptly produced another chick that then was confronted with another model. Next a third chick had its turn, and so on, until every chick had had the chance to react to every model. In the case of three chicks and six models this would mean a series of 18 experiments, each of 30 seconds' duration. The continuous changing of model was necessary because the chicks responded best at the very first test, and gradually became less eager the longer the tests went on. Later, when they became more hungry, the responsiveness would go up again. Now if we gave all the chicks one and the same model at their first test, this model would get more responses than it " deserved." Therefore we had to take care that every model got the same chances.

It was fascinating to watch the chicks peck at the dummies. Again and again they would look at them, follow their movements with the eyes, and peck. Sometimes they seized a model's bill tip between their mandibles, and the saliva would flow and sometimes spoil our paper dummies. Sometimes we could not resist the urge to do some other tests as well, such as to imitate the " hahaha " call. Upon this, they would crouch, or sometimes run to cover and then crouch. They were not at all shy, and would select one of us for cover. As long as they were kept in a nice warm spot they would not defecate. But when they were handled there were accidents. We found also that we could call the chicks towards us by imitating the mew call. Sometimes we had them run from one end of the tent to the other just by calling them in turn. They were fascinating little creatures.

After having contributed their—most essential—share to our investigation, they were put back into the nests from which we had taken them and soon received a good square meal.

The responses we got with the first series of dummies were

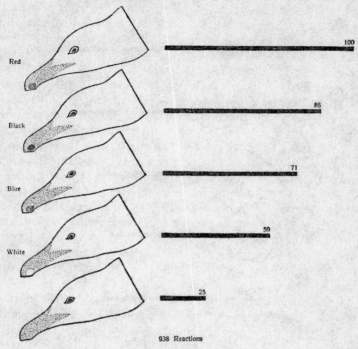

FIG. 30

Number of pecking responses to models with bill-patches of varying colour. (This and the eighteen subsequent drawings are all taken from Tinbergen & Perdeck, 1950)

divided among them as indicated in Fig. 30. The first conclusion that can be drawn is merely a confirmation of Goethe's work: the model with the red patch receives many more reactions than that with a yellow bill. But the other colours got many responses too: black, blue, and even white! This shows that contrast between the patch and the bill stimulates the chick. But if it were merely contrast and not colour, the black patch would have drawn more responses than the red patch, for the black certainly contrasts more strongly with the yellow than does the red. Therefore we were forced to conclude that the red patch acted

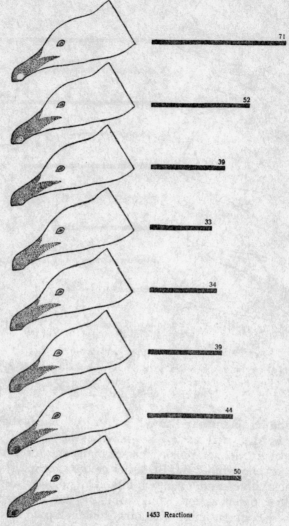

1453 Reactions

FIG. 31
The influence of contrast between bill and bill-tip patch

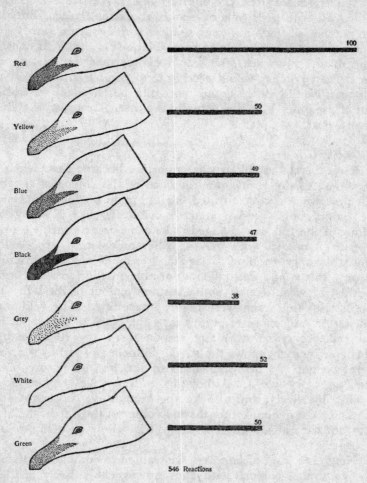

FIG. 32
The influence of bill-colour

both through its colour and through its contrast with the bill.

We decided to test the contrast first. We made a series of models all with grey bills of exactly the same shade. But they got patches of very different shades, running from pure white over a rather sliding scale to pitch black (Fig. 31). If contrast were of any influence, one would expect that the darkest and the lightest patches would receive most responses, and that the responses would be less, the more the patch shade resembled that of the bill. This was actually the case. Contrast, therefore, plays a part.

Bill-colour is ignored

That the red as colour was important became clear when we tried next to determine the influence of the colour of the bill. Till now we had concentrated our attention on the influence of the patch, but would it make much difference if the yellow colour of the bill was changed? In order to test this, we made a series of models with bills of different colours: red, yellow, white, black, green, blue. No patch was made on these dummies, because this would introduce a variable in the form of varying contrast between it and the background colour of the bill. The results with this series were highly interesting. The yellow bill did not get any more responses than the black or the green bill. But red got twice as many responses as any of the others. This convincingly shows the strong influence of red as a colour. Here we got the first indication of the limited nature of the chick's sensory world. Although the deep yellow colour of the bill is, objectively, and also for the human eye, no less characteristic or conspicuous than the red colour of the patch, the chick does not care at all whether the bill is yellow or black or blue or white.

Next, as a kind of side step, we wanted to compare the model in " natural " colours with that having an entirely red bill. As we had expected, the latter model got slightly fewer responses than the former. This was certainly due to the fact that in the former model not only the colour was right but the contrast between patch and bill too.

Plate 29a. The submissive posture of the full-grown young

b. A chick pecking at a cardboard head model

Plate 30a. Chick pecking at the lowest of two " bills "

b. Chick pecking at " cock's head "

Head colour

Now that the colour of the bill evidently had no influence, we wanted to know whether the head-colour might be important. Our next series therefore had differently coloured heads. The bill was yellow with a red dot in all models. The results here got somewhat complicated because evidently the varying degree of contrast between the bill and the head played a certain part. But it was clear that a white head did not stimulate more than a black or a green head. The head-colour therefore did not make any difference either. As far as colour was concerned, therefore, all that seemed to matter was the bill-tip and its immediate

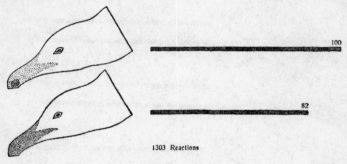

1303 Reactions

FIG. 33
Red bill tip versus red bill

environment. The contrast between the graphs of Figs. 30 and 31, and those of the graphs on bill- and head-colour (Figs. 32 and 34) is striking, and the negative evidence supplied by the latter graphs emphasises the evidence on the important function of the red patch.

We could not help being amazed by this find. Although by our studies of other animals we were accustomed to this phenomenon of selective sensitivity to only very few " sign stimuli," yet in each new case encountered one is surprised at the apparent " blindness " for so many other features of the environment. And one naturally wonders whether perhaps the eyes of our little gulls were still so poorly developed that they simply could not

H.G.W.   O

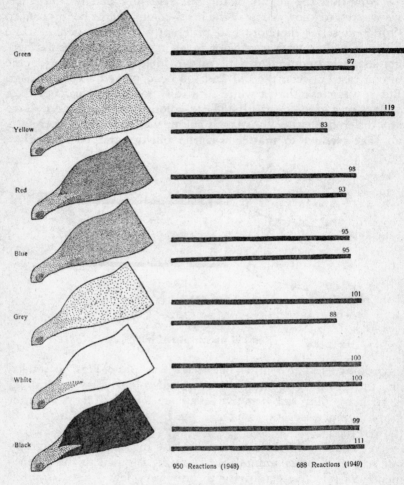

Green

Yellow

Red

Blue

Grey

White

Black

97

119

83

98

93

95

95

101

88

100

100

99

111

950 Reactions (1948)   688 Reactions (1949)

FIG. 34
Two series on the influence of head-colour

see more than just the red patch right in front of them. It could be, for instance, that they were simply extremely short-sighted, so that only the objects in their immediate vicinity could be seen at all. Or it could be that their field of vision was still confined to a small central area. But other observations showed that this could not be true. For instance, it occurred not infrequently that a chick would peck at something much farther away than the bill-tip, such as the corner of the mouth, or even the eye of the parent bird. And when we made the dummies represented in Fig. 35, where the red patch was painted at the wrong spot, somewhere on the forehead, we found that the chicks would divide their pecks between the bill-tip, the corner of the mouth, and the red patch. It was clear therefore that their eyes were not at all so poorly developed. And so again, as in so many other cases, we were forced to the conclusion that the restriction of the response to the red patch on the bill-tip had nothing to do with the capacities of the eyes, but with those of the nervous system. The eye received a relatively detailed

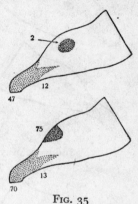

FIG. 35

Number of responses aimed at bill tip, bill base and red patch in an abnormal place

image—how detailed we do not know—and the selecting or sieving out of the sign stimulus was done somehow by the central nervous system.

Head-shape

So far, we had only been studying the influence of colour. But we saw that the chicks still responded, though on a lower level of intensity, to a dummy lacking the patch. This meant that it must be guided by some characters of shape, since the yellow colour of the bill was of no influence whatsoever. Therefore, our next attempts were directed at finding those form characters. The first step was to make just an oddly shaped model

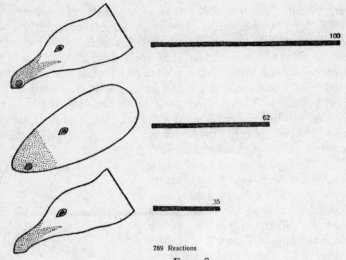

789 Reactions

Fig. 36

Influence of red patch and bill-shape compared

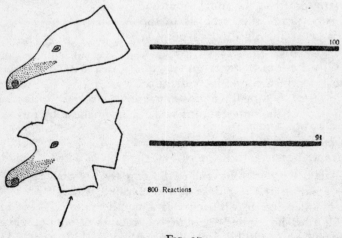

800 Reactions

Fig. 37

Influence of head-shape. Arrow indicates orientation of some of
the reactions

and compare its influence with that of a dummy of normal shape. We made a kind of large egg-shaped " head," with roughly the right colour-pattern (Fig. 36). It received fewer reactions than the " standard " model, but considerably more than the yellow-billed head. The inferiority of the egg-shaped head might be due to inferiority of the bill or of the head. In order to test this, we designed the " cock's head " pictured in Fig. 37. And sure enough, although the shape of the head was highly abnormal, it was scarcely less influential than the standard head! This meant that it was the shape of the bill that mattered, and not,

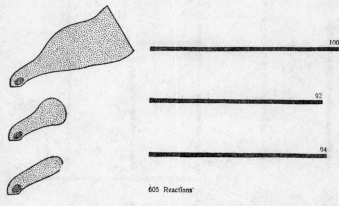

100

92

94

605 Reactions

FIG. 38
The presence of a head has little influence

or almost not, the shape of the head. This was well in line with the results of the colour tests: not only the head's colour, but also its shape was of no interest to the chicks. We then took a somewhat bolder step. Suppose the head did not matter at all ? Suppose a mere bill would be sufficient for the chick? The fact that we did not confine ourselves to a comparison of a complete head and a bill, but, as Fig. 38 shows, inserted a kind of intermediate dummy too, shows our hesitation in taking our supposition seriously. Yet the chicks did take it seriously, for the bill as such was not so much inferior to the complete head.

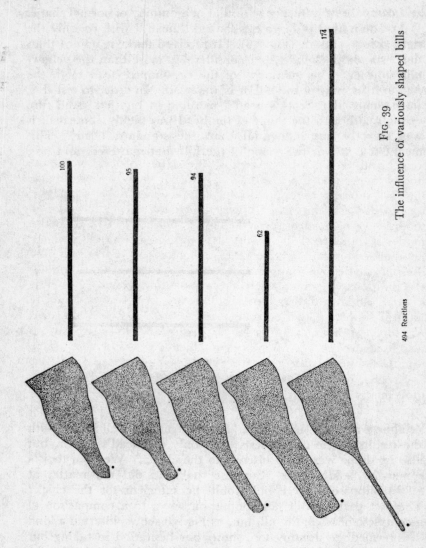

494 Reactions

Fig. 39

The influence of variously shaped bills

Bill-shape is important

We now proceeded to study the influence of the bill's shape more closely. Because the handling of the complete head dummies was easier than that of a bill, we used complete heads with bills of various shapes. We expected that the exact pointed shape of the bill would not matter much, and that the elongate shape would be more important, and therefore we made, besides a dummy of standard bill-shape, one with a rounded bill of the same general proportions, and then varied the shape of this generalised bill. This was done by making it longer, higher, longer-and-higher while keeping the same proportions, and finally longer and much thinner. I do not know why we made that last dummy; presumably for completeness' sake, or maybe we just had a brain-wave. But as the results show, this very last model gave us a surprise by being far more effective than the model of standard shape. This was puzzling again, and now for another reason than in any of the previous cases. For up till now the most effective dummies were always those that, among the dummies presented, were the most natural ones. But here a quite unnatural bill seemed to be more effective than the natural shape. Closer consideration showed, however, that this was only apparent. In order to understand this, we had to watch again the very first feed a chick gets in its life. This usually happens while the chick is still being brooded. As soon as a chick dries, it becomes restless. The parent reacts to its movements by standing up, and often by giving the mew call. In most cases the chick will react to this by begging, and the parent will feed. Often the parent will feed even before the begging of the chick begins. The chick then comes from under the parent, walks towards the bill, and pecks at it. In this situation the chick views the parent's bill from behind, and, as Fig. 40 shows, it sees the bill, which is laterally compressed, as a very thin rod. Although at most of the subsequent feeds the chick is no longer confined to the nest, and approaches the parent from any angle, and therefore rarely views the bill from behind, the innate response is adapted to the very first occasion on which it is going to be used.

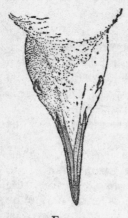

FIG. 40
A Herring Gull's bill as
the chick sees it

A study of the results with the other dummies shown in Fig. 40 proves that the shape of the bill is not, or at least not exclusively, determined by its proportions, for the large bill of normal proportions elicits far fewer responses than the bill of the same proportions but normal size.

The dummies of Fig. 41 were designed to try whether there is a minimum length of bill. That is indeed the case. Therefore our general conclusion must be, that the bill must not be shorter than the normal length, and that it has to be thin. Or in other words: in addition to being elongate, it must be above a certain length and under a certain thickness. A curious mixture of relational and " absolute " properties!

There remained another problem to be solved. Why does the chick aim at a special part of the bill, viz., the bill-tip? In the normal bill, this is partly due to the presence of the red patch. For the red patch not only releases the pecking response, but it also directs it. This is shown clearly in Fig. 35 where about half of the total responses was aimed at the red patch, although it was in an abnormal position. When the red patch is moved still farther away from the bill-tip, it draws far less pecks at it, and relatively more are directed at the bill-tip, as is the case with practically all the pecks released by the yellow-billed model without a red patch anywhere. This shows, first, that the influence of the red patch diminishes, the farther away it is from the bill tip. Further, the bill-tip as such must provide some sign stimulus of great importance.

Here various guesses were possible. It could be that the chick reacted to the ends of the elongate bill. But then: why to one end rather than to the other? Or, as the parent bird, and, in imitation, our dummies, always kept the bill-tip pointing down, the chick might react to the lowest part of the bill. Lastly,

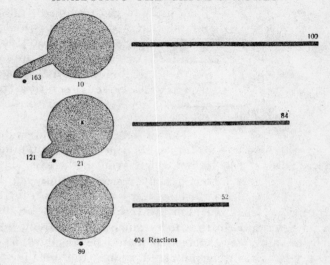

FIG. 41

Influence of bill and of " lowness "

the bill-tip usually is the part of the bill closest to the chick, and " nearness " might also be an effective sign stimulus.

Lowness

" Lowness " was tried first. This was done by presenting two white, red-tipped sticks at equal distances but one below the other (Plate 30). The chicks invariably aimed at the lower stick. Also, we made a model consisting of a circular " head " with two " bills," identical but for position (Fig. 42). Of the 102 reactions elicited by this model, 94 were directed at the lower of the two bills. A still simpler model showed the influence of " lowness " still more clearly. A circular disc was presented to the chicks, and the part at which they aimed their pecking was determined by noting to which of the four quadrants indicated in Fig. 43 they aimed. Of 109 responses, 107 were aimed at the lowest quadrant of the disc's red edge.

" Lowness " also acted in another way: the lower a dummy

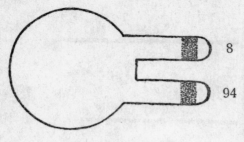

8

94

FIG. 42
The lower of two " bills " is preferred

was presented, the more reactions it elicited. Fig. 44 illustrates how the same model was presented, in successive tests, now at a height of 11 cm. above the ground, now at 5 cm. above the ground, then at an intermediate level. The higher the bill was held, the fewer responses did it get.

Nearness

It is obvious, therefore, that this reaction to " lowness " was, at least partly, responsible for the aiming at the parent's bill-tip. In much the same way " nearness " could be tested. The same two red-tipped sticks were presented, now at the same level, but one nearer the chick than the other (Fig. 45). Again, the results show that our guess had been right: the responses practically all went to the nearer of the two sticks.

Position of the bill

By accident we stumbled upon another important stimulus. When we presented one of the rather weak models, such as a head of the standard shape but without a bill-patch, in a horizontal position instead of with the beak pointing downwards, it seemed to rouse only slight interest. It therefore occurred to us that " lowness " might well act in a relative way too, in such a sense that if there were not an evidently lowest part the whole model might be unattractive. This was tried out by presenting, in successive tests, a white, red-pointed stick in such a way that its tip was always at the same spot but the stick was

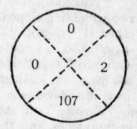

FIG. 43
The influence of " lowness " demonstrated by responses to a circular disk

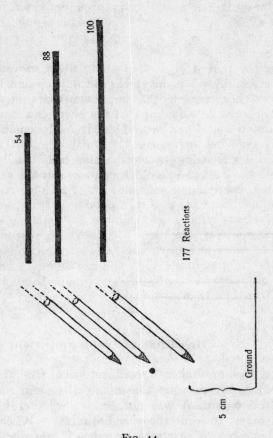

FIG. 44

The influence of lowness on the total number of responses. The black dot
indicates position of the chick's bill-tip in all experiments

kept either horizontal, or vertical, or in an oblique position
(Fig. 46). The result was indeed striking: the bill must be
vertical, or at least must point downward, exactly vertical being
the most favourable position. The same result was yielded by
a short test in which we used an all-white head of standard

shape. Here the horizontal head apparently left the chicks entirely at a loss.

Other sign stimuli

Because the parent bird often made slight movements with the head, especially when the chicks did not respond to the food presented, and because we got the impression that such movements stimulated the chicks, we compared the effect of a dummy when kept motionless and when moved slowly. Movement was thus proved to have some influence.

Another possible stimulus was the mew call. As I mentioned above, the mew call made a chick run towards the gull uttering it, or to the experimenter imitating it. But after running, the

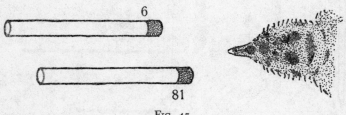

FIG. 45
The influence of " nearness "

chick would look around as if to expect visual stimuli. While it was, therefore, obvious that the mew call caused the chick to approach the parent, it was not certain whether it increased its responsiveness towards the visual stimuli. When we compared the number of reactions to a head presented while we uttered the mew call at short intervals with those to the head presented in silence, a slight stimulating influence of the call was found.

It seemed to us that we had now reached a stage where we could list most if not all of the sign stimuli that influenced the chick's begging response. The object that releases the pecking (i.e. the bill of the parent bird) is characterised for the chick by (1) movement, (2) shape (elongate, not too short, thin),

(3) lowness, (4) downward-pointing position, (5) nearness, and (6) the bill-patch, which must be (*a*) red and (*b*) differing, by contrast, from the ground-colour of the bill. It is striking how many of these properties are not easily measurable, that is to say, they are not quantities of something, but they are relationships. This shows that even this selective responsiveness to only few sign stimuli, relatively simple as it may be as compared with more complex phenomena of sensory stimulation, yet must be dependent on very complicated processes in the central nervous system, for " relationships " cannot exist in an indivisible unit, but only in an organised system.

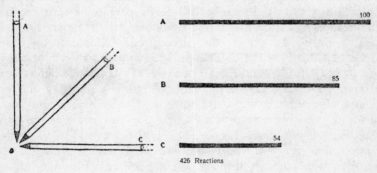

426 Reactions

FIG. 46

The influence of the bill's " attitude "

We were still a little uncertain about one problem. All our dummies had been highly schematic: they were flat, and all the structural details of bill and feathers were lacking. Although the eagerness of the chicks' responses rendered it improbable that they missed much of essential value in our dummies, yet the possibility could not be excluded as long as it was not deliberately tested. We therefore constructed a dummy of plaster which, while it did not show more detail than the flat dummies, was three-dimensional (solid) and had the rough shape of a Herring Gull's head. This dummy did not get more responses than our standard flat dummy. The final test was a comparison of our flat standard dummy with the head of a fresh dead Herring Gull, and even here the difference was negligible. Neither three-dimensionality nor details other than the red patch therefore formed part of the hungry chick's world.

The expression " the chick's world " has only limited value. Our observations do not mean that the six sign stimuli enumerated above are the only properties of the outside world that exist for the chick. They are the properties that exist for the chick when it is in a mood to beg for food. There are other stimuli that influence the chick's behaviour, and that therefore are part of its world, but they are linked to other parts of the behaviour-pattern. For instance, the parents' alarm call is such a stimulus. But it does not call forth pecking responses, but behaviour of quite another type: crouching by the newly-hatched chick, running for cover and subsequent crouching by older chicks. In this way the chick's world is built up by a number of such sets of stimuli, each releasing a part of the chick's behaviour-pattern. The strange thing, difficult to comprehend for the human observer, is that the various properties of the same object in the objective outside world are not projected by the chick into one object. It is entirely irrelevant for the chick whether the red patch and the alarm call are provided by its own father, or whether the red patch is presented by one human experimenter, and the call by another. There is no indication whatsoever that a chick in this phase synthesizes the sign stimuli as belonging to one object. This occurs, as we will see, at a later stage, and is the result of a learning process.

Constructing a super-gull.

When we had discovered that so many of the sign stimuli to which the chick responds are of a relational character, such as " as low as possible," " as near as possible," and, with regard to the patch, " contrasting with the bill-colour as much as possible," it occurred to us that it might perhaps be possible to improve upon nature, that is to say, to make a dummy that would stimulate the chick still more than the natural object, viz., the parent's head. The most promising point of attack seemed to us the contrast of the patch with the bill. Contrast is a matter of different colours or shades separated by a borderline. To the human eye, contrast is strongest when the difference in shade is largest and when the boundary line is sharp. We improved upon the contrast between patch and bill by making a red patch which was surrounded by a white ring, which again was surrounded by a red ring. This red-white-red patch was made to compete with a red patch of the same total area (Fig. 47), so that, in fact, the amount of red was larger in the all-red patch. Yet more pecks were aimed at the "super-patch" than at the more normal patch. Using this, and some of the other results already mentioned, we took a long thin red rod, at the end of which we painted three white rings. This dummy, for the human eye rather dissimilar to a Herring Gull's head, was compared, in successive tests, with the plaster head, one of the best dummies we had, and in fact inferior to neither the flat standard dummy nor the natural head. The rod beat the three-dimensional head by 126 to 100.

What should we call this phenomenon? At first we called it, thoughtlessly, "super-optimal stimulus," a contradiction in terms, since "optimal" by definition cannot be exceeded. "Supernatural" would be a good term, if it were not used already in another sense. We have, therefore, chosen the term "supernormal." The possibility of supernormal stimuli has been found in other animals too. In a series of choice experiments we found, for instance, that an Oystercatcher, which normally lays a clutch of three, and sometimes four eggs, prefers five eggs if the choice is between three and five. Still more astonishing was the reactions of a number of Oystercatchers

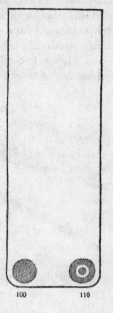

100   116

253 Reactions

FIG. 47

A "supernormal" patch, made by increasing the number of contrast lines to a giant egg, a wooden dummy painted in natural colours, and measuring 14.5 x 10 cm. When they were faced with this giant egg and one of their own eggs, they usually went to the giant egg and made frantic attempts to sit upon it (Fig. 49). Another case was found by Koehler & Zagarus (1937) in the Ringed Plover. This bird is more strongly stimulated by a white egg with large black dots than by its own eggs, which are buff with small brownish dots (Fig. 50).

I think the phenomenon is not so unreal as it seems to be when we realise that similar observations may be made with our

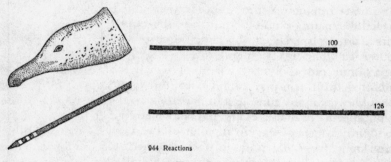

944 Reactions

FIG. 48

A thin red rod with three white bands provides a stronger stimulus than an accurate three-dimensional plaster head

own species. I believe that the lipstick is an instrument serving to provide supernormal stimuli. If one doubts whether this has anything to do with the phenomena discussed above, let him tell why women paint their lips various shades of red, and not green or gold. Also, I think the excessive baby characters of Walt Disney's *Bambi* are justified because they are an exaggeration of the baby features releasing maternal reactions in man which are portrayed in Fig. 58.

Returning to the Herring Gull, the red patch on the bill seems to be a genuine social releaser, or *Auslöser*, as Lorenz—the first to draw attention to such structures—called them. But the other properties of the parent's bill, its elongated shape, for instance, or its thinness, or its being pointed downward, can scarcely be called releasers. For it is not only inherent in the concept of releaser that it releases an innate response in a fellow member of the same species, but also that it is an organ especially

FIG. 49

An Oystercatcher prefers a giant egg model to its own egg and a Herring Gull's egg. (After Tinbergen, 1951)

adapted to this purpose. This holds for many calls of birds, and probably for many conspicuous morphological features such as the wing specula of ducks, or the red colour of a stickleback male. It evidently is true of the red patch at the Herring Gull's mandible too, for we have not been able to find any other use for it. The downward pointing of the bill seems to be part of the actual regurgitation and feeding, but it might well be that it has under-gone some adaptation towards a releaser function, because the parent keeps the head down for such a long time, longer perhaps than necessary for the feeding itself. But the shape of the bill of course has been evolved according to the demands of feeding methods; it is not elongated and laterally compressed as an adapta-

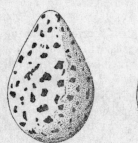

FIG. 50

A white plaster egg with large black dots stimulates a Ringed Plover more strongly than a real Ringed Plover's egg (right). (After Koehler & Zagarus, 1937)

tion to the chick's demands. It is probably rather the other way round: the chicks' reactiveness is modelled upon the shape of the bill.

In view of these problems, it would be very much worth while to make a comparative study of sign stimuli releasing the chicks' begging in other species of gulls. How would the chick of the Common Gull react, where the parent cannot boast a red patch? And how would the chick of the Black-headed Gull react to bill-colour—and to head-colour? And, although the terns do not feed their young by regurgitation, young terns do beg by pecking at the parents' bill-tip, even when these have no fish at hand. Would it be just accident that so many species of terns have a conspicuously coloured bill tip? Here is a fine opportunity for experimenting in the field, a type of study which, as I hope the reader will agree, may lead to exciting and unexpected discoveries.

It should be said, however, that great care has to be taken against disturbance of breeding colonies. If done carefully and with regard for the birds, the work might be done without causing accidents either directly, or indirectly by disturbing normal colony life and causing the chicks to wander and get lost.

CHAPTER 23

SIGN STIMULI IN OTHER ANIMALS

IT HAS BEEN known for a long time that innate behaviour in animals can easily be released by abnormal conditions that resemble the normal conditions in some respects. It is the *result* of such " mistakes " that have always been emphasised, and it was usually pointed out that " instinct " was " blind " and rigid, and made the animal behave very stupidly when confronted with unnatural situations. An analysis of the fact itself, viz., the dependence on only part of the environmental features, has only rarely been made, and the relatively few systematic experimental studies of the phenomenon are very recent. Not all these studies are equally thorough and complete, some are even very fragmentary, but together we have now a good deal of evidence for various animal types, and the more that becomes known the more clearly do we see that the dependence on " sign stimuli " is a general characteristic of innate behaviour. It is worth while to review some of the most striking work thus far done. As I have tried to show in the report on the chick's pecking response, it is important not only to show what the animal is responding to, but also to which parts of the environment it is not paying attention. This is rarely done, but usually the ineffectiveness of environmental features can be concluded indirectly from the evidence presented.

The gaping of thrushes

As a case more or less parallel to our study of the gull chick's begging response the work by Tinbergen & Kuenen (1939) on the gaping response of nestling thrushes (Blackbird and Song Thrush) may be cited first. Here too, the releasing stimuli as well as the directing stimuli were studied. During about a week after hatching, the birds are blind. They then respond by gaping, particularly when the nest is jarred. They do not respond to the parents' calls, except that the alarm call inhibits their gaping, and makes them crouch in the nest. Gaping is directed by gravity. The birds gape vertically, independent of where the parent bird is. When the nest is suspended from a string, and swung around, thereby adding a horizontal component to

FIG. 51
Gaping of young thrushes released but not directed by human finger.
(After Tinbergen, 1951)

gravity, the birds gape in the direction of the resultant, which is indicated by the inclination of the string.

When the eyes are open, visual stimuli of a very vague nature release gaping, in addition to the still effective jarring. By manifold experiments it was found that any object, provided it is not too small (we found a lower limit of about 3 mm. diameter), which moves, and which is above the horizontal through the nestlings' eyes, releases gaping. Any piece of cardboard, human fingers, a stick, were equally effective. Again, this vagueness of the total situation, or, in other words, the dependence on these few sign stimuli, was not due to restricted capacities of the eye. For instance, when the object was moved below the horizontal, the birds would look at it and follow it with their eyes, but they did not gape. Whereas the visual stimuli could easily release the gaping, they did not direct it during the first few days. The gaping was still entirely vertical, even when the object that had released it was not at all above them, but only just above the horizontal. Fig. 51 shows gaping released by a finger, yet the chicks' necks point upwards, as if they were ignoring the " parent " that was taken seriously enough to respond to it. Only after one to three days did visual stimuli begin to play a part in directing the gaping; the birds began gradually to gape

FIG. 52

Various models of Blackbirds which induce the nestlings to gape at the " heads," as indicated by arrows. (After Tinbergen & Kuenen, 1938)

towards the head of the parent bird. This made it necessary to study the directive influence of the head. The shape was of not much importance: anything protruding from the body would do, as is clearly demonstrated in Fig. 52. Any interruption, however insignificant, could draw the necks towards it, provided it was external, not internal, and provided it was more or less on top of the body. When two sticks were presented above each other, just as in our Herring Gull test, the nestlings would always gape towards the upper one, just contrary to what the Herring Gulls did. Also, nearness played a part, but not in the same sense as in the Herring Gulls. Last, but not least, size was important. However, it was not so much the absolute size of the head that mattered, but the relative size. This is shown best in the tests with double-headed dummies. The two dummies shown in Fig. 53 have the same set of heads. In the dummy with the small body gaping was directed to the small head, the responses to the large dummy were directed towards the large head. It is head-size in relation to body-size therefore that matters.

Defence in the Bittern

Reactions to a head happen to have been studied in some other cases too. As long ago as 1921, Portielje did some highly interesting work on the European Bittern. As is well known, this bird adopts an extremely upright and stretched attitude when surprised by a predator among the reeds, and this posture together with its cryptic coloration makes it well-nigh invisible. If the predator nevertheless perceives it and makes an attempt to

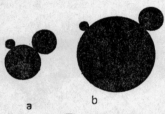

a   b

Fig. 53

Two models of Blackbirds with two heads each. Further explanation in text

catch it, the stretched attitude is at once abandoned and the bird crouches back, bending its heels as if it were ready to jump, withdrawing the beak and pointing it towards the enemy, ruffling all its feathers and spreading its wings. Instead of concealing itself, it makes itself appear as formidable as possible, and prepares for defence by force. When the predator comes still closer, the formidable bill will flash out and deliver a terrific peck at the enemy's head as soon as it comes within reach. What enables the bird to single out the head? Just as in the thrushes, one of the sign stimuli is the interruption of the body's outline. When Portielje withdrew his head as far as possible between his shoulders and covered himself up with a coat so as to have head and body appear as one solid object, he could approach the Bittern as closely as he wanted, and when moving gently, he could even seize the bewildered bird's feet.

When, in his crouched position and covered by the coat, Portielje mounted a cardboard disc of roughly head size and shape on top of him, the Bittern would peck at this cardboard head dummy.

Whether here too there is a fixed relationship between body-size and head-size, and whether the head must preferably be on top of the body, and whether nearness plays a part too has not yet been ascertained. The tests do show, however, that a very schematic imitation of a head on top of a body is sufficient to elicit the defence reaction, and that any detail in a head, eyes for instance, does not play an important part. Incidentally, Portielje says, and his experiments seem to confirm his opinion, that the story that the Bittern will aim at the eyes of an enemy is just a story.

Reactions to birds of prey

Lastly the head plays a part in recognition of flying birds of prey by many birds. Most birds, especially those living in the open, react to a bird of prey flying overhead by some type of alarm: they crouch, or run to cover, or at least keep a careful watch on it. In social birds, a special warning cry is often released. It is not difficult to test this reaction with dummies, for many birds react readily to flat cardboard imitations of a

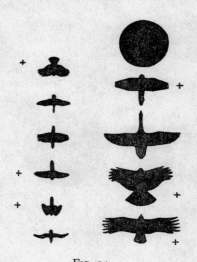

FIG. 54

Various models used by Lorenz & Tinbergen for the study of predator-reactions in young fowl. Those marked released escape responses. (After Tinbergen, 1948)

bird of prey sailed overhead. Lorenz and I did some work with his hand-raised young birds of various species. It soon became obvious that here again the reaction was mainly one to shape. When the model had a short neck so that the head protruded only a little in front of the line of the wings, it released alarm, independent of the exact shape of the dummy (Fig. 54). This, incidentally, shows why so often the same alarm reactions are released by flying swifts and by a flying nightjar. At first sight

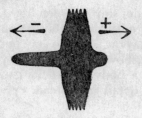

FIG. 55

Model which gave positive responses when sailed to the right but none when sailed to the left. (After Tinbergen, 1948)

one would expect that the alarm reactions to a cuckoo would also be explained by its resemblance to a bird of prey, but the alarm reactions to a cuckoo seem, at least partly, different from those to a sparrow-hawk (Edwards, Hosking & Stuart Smith, 1948).

How complex this reaction to the shape of the head is, appears from a test which has been carried out both by Lorenz and me, and by Krätzig with Ptarmigans. It is quite possible to make a dummy with symmetrical wings and with head and tail shaped in such a way that either front or rear may be regarded as head or as tail (Fig. 55). This model, when sailed to the right, has a short neck and a long tail and is more or less hawk-like. When sailed to the left it gives the impression of something like a goose, with a long neck and a short tail. Now it is surprising that both Lorenz's and Krätzig's hand-raised fowl reacted very differently to this model, depending on how it was moved. When sailed to the right it caused alarm, when sailed to the left it only aroused mild interest or was ignored.

During these experiments, we saw some amusing examples of the birds' power to learn by experience. In order to sail our models, which crossed a meadow where the birds were feeding or resting, at a height of about 10 yards along a wire, running from one tree to another 50 yards away, either Lorenz or I had to climb the tree and mount the dummy we wanted to test out. One family of geese (which also reacted to some of our dummies) very soon associated tree-climbing humans with something dreadful to come, and promptly called the alarm and walked off when one of us went up.

Of course, shape is not the only sign stimulus that characterises a bird of prey. Geese are sensitive to any slowly sailing object, that is to say any object that moves across the sky slowly in relation to its own size. A downy feather sailing with the wind raised suspicion just as much as a slow large aeroplane. And when jackdaws or pigeons began to soar instead of hurrying over, they caused alarm among the geese. The most terrifying movement is a fast downward dive. When one of our models—a circular disc which was practically ignored by all our birds—happened to fall down when it was halfway along its course from one tree to the other, it caused a wild panic. And many birds, for instance waders feeding on the tidal flats, may be seen to start in panic and form dense flocks, zigzagging over the flats, as soon as a new arrival comes dropping down from the sky like a stone. In most birds, the reactions to predators are variable, from first preparations, released by a distant predator, to an emergency dive into cover, or freezing on the spot, as a reaction to the sudden appearance of a predator. Many species even have different alarm calls for the different occasions.

Alarm reactions of Jackdaws

A very specialised case of an alarm reaction to a predator has been reported by Lorenz. His tame Jackdaws gave the alarm call and even fiercely attacked him when he had caught one of them in his hand. His best " friend " among them, the famous *Tschock*, a female which had been hand-raised by him, never objected to being handled. But as soon as Lorenz took one of a group of newly arrived young Jackdaws in his hand, *Tschock* uttered the alarm call and within a second had pecked at and injured the hand carrying the bird. By accident the nature of the sign stimulus was found: once when Lorenz, coming back from a bath in the Danube, stood on his roof, surrounded by his Jackdaws, he discovered that he had quite forgotten to take the wet bathing suit out of his pocket. He took the black suit out, and in the same instant was surrounded by a cloud of panic-stricken Jackdaws, all uttering the alarm call and attacking him.

Carrying about his black reflex camera, however, had no influence, but waving black strips of paper from the film-packs promptly released attack. A half-hearted attack was even released in spring when one of the Jackdaws of the colony, like all others very well known personally to the members of the colony, carried a black feather to its nest. " Something black and dangling being carried " seems to be a fair description of the stimulus situation, and it clearly is relatively irrelevant by whom it is carried. Interestingly enough, there is no other innate reaction to predators in this social bird; the " knowledge " of special predators has to be acquired, and under normal conditions always is acquired, because the parents, during the long period of family life, warn the young when a predator appears, and this quickly conditions them.

Another interesting case, not analysed as yet, but perhaps open to analysis, has been reported by Makkink in the Avocet. Avocets have a special warning signal for one special group of predators: the gulls. So far as we know, this is unique, although we must not forget that we know precious little about these things.

In other cases of sign stimuli the emphasis is still more on movement, and on type of movement. Heinroth relates how his hand-raised Peregrine falcons lived in one room together with various other birds, such as pigeons and Partridges, both, as every field observer knows, potential prey of the Peregrine. However, the falcons did not make any attempt to catch them, expecting food only from Heinroth, until one day a pigeon happened to fly away from about the place where one of the Peregrines was. And then, like a flash, the falcon had caught it, not being able to resist the stimulus " something flying away from me."

The red breast of the Robin

The most fascinating types of sign-stimuli are those in which colour plays a part, as is the case with the red patch in the Herring Gull. A clear-cut and extreme instance is provided by the Robin, so well known by the thorough studies of Dr. David Lack. In defending the territory, a male Robin performs a threat display in front of intruding Robins, and even attacks them. The threat consists of ruffling the red breast and turning it towards the opponent. When a stuffed Robin was placed

in a territory, the owner
promptly approached it
and displayed. This was
elicited by the red breast,
for a mounted young speci-
men, in which the breast
is dull brown instead of
red, was ignored. Yet a
mere tuft of red breast
feathers was treated in
many cases as an enemy,
that is, the birds reacted to
it by showing the threat
display in front of it. Comparison of the effects of the
mounted young Robin and
the tuft of red feathers
shows that "something
red" is a much more
powerful releasing situation
than all the other characters
of a Robin together. This
is quite similar to the chick
Herring Gulls' reactions to
the dummies shown in Figs.
36 and 48.

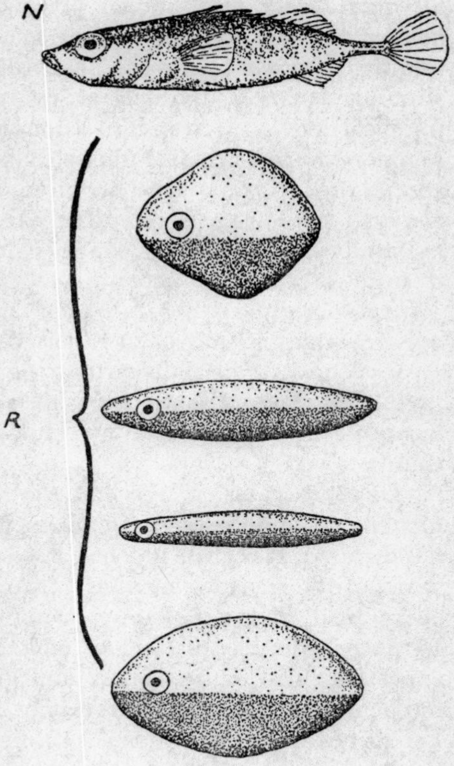

Experiments of much
the same kind have been
done with "lower" animals

FIG. 56

Stickleback models of "N" and "R"
type. Further explanation see text

too. The state of affairs in the Three-spined Stickleback is in
many respects similar to that in the Robin. In this little fish,
the male takes up a territory in spring, much as some birds
do on the land. The fish, being unable to sing, advertises
its presence by briskly swimming around and by gorgeous
nuptial colours: red on throat and breast, greenish-blue on
the back; its large eye is brilliant blue. Trespassers into the
territory, especially other males in spring colour, are furiously

attacked.   Here again it is possible to release attack by bringing
dummies into the territory, and much as in the Robin, the red
colour is the main sign stimulus.   All kinds of crude imitations
of sticklebacks are attacked, provided they are red underneath.
But little attention is paid to complete sticklebacks in neutral
colours.   Of the dummies pictured in Fig. 56 all were attacked
except the top one.

The Grayling butterfly

Even in insects, which have a nervous system that is organised
along quite other lines than that of the vertebrates, essentially the
same phenomena are found.   The work done with the Grayling
Butterfly is particularly illuminating in this respect.   Of this
species the male has an elaborate courtship display.   The first
reaction to a passing female is the sexual pursuit flight.   This is
followed by a series of ceremonies on the ground, during which
the male stimulates the female by means of a specialised scent-
organ on the fore-wing.   The first reaction, the pursuit, is released
by visual stimuli from the female, and, because it is dependent
on few such sign-stimuli, it can again be analysed by dummy
tests.   It was found that the passing female stimulates the male to
follow it (" is recognised ") by the following characters: it must
be dark, and it must be fluttering and not sailing, " fluttering "
being recognised by the ups and downs, and by the continuous
changes in apparent shape due to the rhythmic folding and
unfolding of the wings.   Size, colour, and general shape do not
matter and may vary within very wide limits.   The ineffectiveness
of colour is significant in connection with other parts of the
behaviour-pattern of the same species.   When the very same
male that follows red, yellow, green and black paper butterflies
with equal perseverance becomes hungry—and leaves the
females alone to pay his attention to nectar-giving flowers—he
shows preference in favour of yellow and blue flowers.   This
behaviour can also be tested with dummies, for instance by
putting out sheets of paper of many different colours, and also of
many shades of grey, in the neighbourhood of the flowers usually
visited.   Under certain circumstances the butterflies will visit

these papers, and their choice on such occasions is definite: the yellow and blue papers are practically the only ones visited, while all the others are ignored. Giving the frequency of reactions to the various colours in the form of a graph, as is done in Fig. 57, shows the difference between the two responses at a glance. In the sexual pursuit colour does not play any part, but shade matters: the darker the better. In the feeding behaviour it is wave-length that counts. On the other hand, the feeding reaction does not respond very precisely to particulars of shape: the unnaturally shaped papers, just rectangles of several inches' side length, obviously were quite attractive.

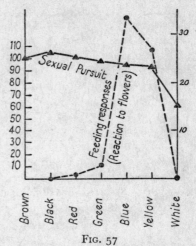

FIG. 57

Reactions of male Grayling butterflies to colours. Drawn line: during pursuit of a female. Broken line: during feeding on flowers. (After Tinbergen, Boerema, Meeuse and Varossieau, 1942)

Only, the feeding behaviour being a chain of activities, the butterflies did not actually alight on the paper except on rare occasions, and usually they did not really attempt to suck honey. Other stimuli, presumably of an olfactory nature, are necessary to release the next link in the chain of activities.

The Water-beetle

As a final example (which is still more striking because it shows that a whole sense organ may be left unemployed in certain parts of the behaviour pattern) I will cite the feeding behaviour of the water-beetle, *Dytiscus marginalis*. This lugubrious scavenger finds its food primarily by means of scent. Two visual dummies, one giving off the scent of meat of any kind, the other chemically indifferent, are treated differently; while the latter is ignored, the former is seized. Whereas live tadpoles, small fish,

FIG. 58

Objects which release parental responses in man (left) and objects which do not (right). (After Lorenz, 1943)

earthworms, etc., are rarely refused and their smell is detected from some distance, the beetle never reacts to them when they are presented behind glass. This total lack of visual responsiveness in the hungry insect is the more astonishing, as it has highly developed eyes. During feeding, however, these eyes, are entirely unemployed; probably they are used during flight alone.

Sign stimuli in human life

This selection of instances may show that the Herring Gull chicks do not stand alone with their strangely organised " world." It is difficult to imagine how it must be subjectively to have one's world divided up into " signs " from one that object are not united into a total mental picture of that object. Yet we might get some idea of it if we could make a more thorough and unbiased study of our own species. For deeply rooted in man is the same type of reactivity, and however deeply it may be covered by all types of higher mental processes, on some occasions these innate foundations of our sensory world become visible. Lorenz has pointed out that in the life of man some sign stimuli play a part in a similar way as in animals. By dummy experiments on a huge scale (the doll industry, the film industry, and the raising of pet animals) some of the sign stimuli provided by the human baby, and irresistible especially to the adult female, have been brought to light. A glance at Fig. 58 shows that the ideal baby face must have a small facial part and a large brain part of the head.

Moreover, its cheeks must be fat and rounded. The baby's crying, and its clumsy movements, are also necessary to make it really cute.

CHAPTER 24

PERSONAL TIES

Indiscriminate response to young chicks

When we had discovered that the adult birds recognised their mates and even their neighbours individually, we naturally wanted to know if gull parents could recognise their own young. Also, it seemed possible that the chicks learned to recognise their own parents.

There were some indications suggesting that parent gulls might be reluctant to extend their parental care over strange chicks. We often saw chicks cross their territory's boundary. The more mobile chicks of at least ten days of age were especially liable to do so. This always had the most sensational consequences: the neighbouring gulls pecked at them and often killed them. These hostile reactions to strange chicks are the cause of much of the chick mortality in gulleries which are frequently visited by man. Human intrusion and especially handling of the chicks causes them to run away and stray into strange territories where they are attacked.

The hostile reaction points to individual recognition. However, gulls occasionally attack and kill their own young, as has been recorded, for instance, by Moreau (1923). As far as my experience goes, such events take place during confusion caused by human intrusion, but nevertheless their occurrence throws some doubt on the interpretation of the killing of strange young. Conversely, gulls may occasionally adopt strange young. Therefore, the only way to decide the problem of recognition seemed to be experiment. By interchanging young of about the same age but belonging to different pairs and watching the parents' behaviour towards the strange young we tried to obtain objective

224

information. We did this several times, with quite interesting results. I will first give some details:

I. *29th June, 1935.* A nest with one egg and two chicks of about one day old is watched from a hide O 20 yards away. We put two strange chicks of the same age (S¹ and S²) near the nest's two own young (O¹ and O²); all chicks crouch at about a foot's distance from the nest.

11.0. S¹ squeaks continuously, walks to the left and is soon invisible from the blind. One of the O parents alights (♂ or ♀?), no reaction of the young is seen. S² walks past O¹ and through the nest to the parent and begs, then returns and sits by the side of O¹.

11.10. The parent utters the trumpeting call. O¹ and S² run towards it, S¹ joins them. The parent gives the mew call. The three chicks come in its shadow, O² remains where it was. The parent stands still, quietly picking up some insects.

11.30 Alarm, the test is broken off.

The next test is taken immediately afterwards. We leave O¹ and S¹ and give O² and S² to another pair. O¹ and S¹ are watched from the hide. The O parent alights; after two minutes it walks towards O¹ giving the mew call, passing S¹ on its way. It then comes back to S¹ and gives the mew call. The chicks do not react, and the parent walks on, and begins to preen about 3 yards away. S¹ walks towards O¹; the parent joins them, utters the mew call and regurgitates. Both chicks are fed. They then sit in the parent's shadow. After a few minutes the parent walks away, then returns, giving the mew call, and both young respond.

This experiment is typical for all the tests, in total twelve, which we did with chicks of one or a few days old. In all cases the strange young were accepted. It was not of any importance whether the strange young were exchanged or simply added to the nest's own young.

Hostile behaviour to strange chicks develops within a week

II. The same nest as in I, *3rd July, 1935*. The egg has hatched, we find only two young but do not search the dense vegetation around the nest where the third young probably hides. The same strange chicks S¹ and S² are again placed near the nest. At 8.45 one of the parents alights near one of the S-chicks. It gives the mew call, then pecks at the S-chick.

There are some disturbances in the colony. Both O-parents are intermittently on the territory. One of the parents feeds the chicks; we cannot make sure whether one of the S-chicks is fed or not.

9.57. Two O-chicks and one S-chick are sitting close together. A parent comes down, uttering the mew call. It pecks at the S-chick. The chick runs away, whereupon the parent follows it and pecks at it again and again, then leaves it alone.

We now take one O-chick and one S-chick away.

10.20. The parent alights.

10.30. The S-chick walks towards the parent. The latter flies up even before the chick has reached it, pecks at it, the chick runs away.

This test shows that the same chicks four days later were not readily accepted and even had to endure repeated attacks. The attacks were not severe, and the parent seems to meet the strange chick by a curious mingling of parental and aggressive tendencies. However, the difference from test I is striking. Tests involving chicks five days old and older were much more difficult to arrange than those with very small chicks because the older chicks were much more mobile and often disappeared from sight. Nevertheless, we have done six exchange experiments with chicks five or more days old; in all these cases the strange chicks were not whole-heartedly accepted; usually they were chased.

III. *3rd July, 1935*. A pair with three chicks about 2½ weeks old are given a strange chick of the same age. The S-young is put down at a place which the O-chicks frequent regularly.

One of the O-parents comes towards the young at once, and hovers over it. The chick walks slowly over the territory. The parent dives down upon it and charges three times. The parent then chases a neighbour away, returns to the chick and alights near it. The chick crouches. The parent walks away but remains on the territory. The chick shakes its head and at once the parent reacts by stretching its neck. When the chick begins to move away, the parent charges immediately. The chick leaves the territory.

Here again the young was not accepted. It must be noted, however, that it did not beg or show any positive reaction to the strange parent. It is possible that the foster-parent noticed the anxious attitude of the chick and attacked it for that reason.

IV. *12th July, 1935.* A pair with four young of about 2 weeks old. We do not know why this pair had four young, but we had observed them several days and had seen that these four young were all treated by the pair as if they were their own. We add one chick about 3 days old.

10.5. One of the adults alights. Two O-chicks begin to beg at once, the S-chick runs towards them. When it is still more than a yard away, the parent walks over to it and pecks at it. The chick does not run away but begs; yet it receives a number of pecks. Then the parent takes it in its bill and shakes it violently.

This experiment suggests that the attitude of the parents in rejecting strange young is not so much dependent on the stranger as on their own young. As soon as the parents know their own young they react to strangers as " not their own young." Each chick that is different is attacked, even if it is of an age when chicks are not yet recognised by their parents.

We are led to conclude therefore that the Herring Gulls learn to know their own young during the first few days after hatching. It seems that this knowledge is acquired in about five days. In ethological terms: in the first few days after hatching the Herring Gull reacts to all newly-born young on the territory by directing all parental behaviour to them. This parental behaviour-pattern becomes conditioned to the parents' own young after five days at the most. From then on this whole behaviour-pattern no longer reacts to stimuli presented by any chick, but the parent is now only sensitive to a much more restricted situation, for only the stimuli characteristic of the parents' own chicks can release the parental responses.

Which stimuli are involved?

How do the parents recognise their young? Which are the stimuli that play a part in this remarkable " conditioned reaction "?

Goethe has shown that gull parents react to the call of their own chicks, even when they cannot see them, while they do not react to the calls of strange chicks under the same conditions. He therefore concludes that voice is an important factor. Both he and I noticed further that the pattern of dark dots on the chick's head is very different in each of several young, and it seems possible that the parents learn these patterns. Both he and we coloured chicks entirely black. The results were not very clear. The parents noticed the change, as one could expect, but they did not show definitely hostile behaviour. It is possible that the chick's voice was more decisive than its visual properties. Here certainly is an interesting field for experimental work.

Individual ties in other birds

Individual recognition of chicks has also been found in other birds. Watson & Lashley (1915) studied the behaviour of Noddy and Sooty Terns, two tropical species. The Noddies, nesting in trees, do not recognise their young at any age, whereas the ground-nesting Sooties are very similar to Herring Gulls in that they learn to recognise their own chicks in the course of about 4 days. As in the Herring Gull, recognition seems to be based on both auditory and visual clues, and the authors even think that touch stimuli may play a part.

Dircksen (1932) found evidence of individual recognition of young in the Sandwich Tern. In this species the social organisation seems to be somewhat different from that in the Herring Gull. Several authors report that the young often unite into large groups, and evidently assuming that the parents involved take care of these chicks indiscriminately, compare this with the " crèche " system as found in some penguins. However, I am not at all sure that feeding is really indiscriminate in the Sandwich Tern; I often watched such groups during migration in August when they were resting on the sea shore, and I saw numerous indications of careful selection of individual chicks by adults returning with food.

In the Black-headed Gull there is, according to Kirkman, the same ferocious hostility against strange chicks as in the Herring Gull. It is not clear from Kirkman's account, however, whether the very young chicks are also attacked or whether they are tolerated indiscriminately.

After our study of brooding behaviour, which showed that a gull does not learn to know its own eggs even after four weeks of incubation, the quick conditioning to the chicks is striking. Why does a gull learn to " know " its own chicks, and why does it not learn to " know " its own eggs?

The two types of reaction are not so diametrically different as they seem to be. For in reality a gull knows its own eggs quite well, but it recognises them by their location and not by other properties. Chicks are not recognised by location: at least they are recognised anywhere on the territory. It is not a matter of recognition or no recognition, but rather of two different types of recognition, in which the emphasis lies on different aspects of the situation. Yet the problem remains: why these two different types of recognition?

The only thing I can say is that evidently the two types of recognition fit very well with the properties of the objects concerned. Eggs do not move about and when a gull learns to know the locality of the nest it will be able to brood the eggs even if it has only the most sketchy " knowledge " of eggs. Chicks, on the contrary, move continuously, and a mere knowledge of the nest site would not help the parents to find the chicks. Why, however, a general knowledge of the type of a Herring Gull chick on the basis of a few sign stimuli would not be enough, and personal ties between parents and chicks have evolved, I don't quite understand.

Chicks recognise their parents

I have only very few observations bearing on the problem of recognition of the parents by their young. We have often seen, of course, that half-grown chicks do not beg food from strange adults. But in most of these observations the chicks were on strange territory, and, knowing how very well the chicks know their territory, we might assume that strangeness of surroundings inhibits begging altogether. However, chicks at least some weeks old seem to distinguish quite well between their own parents and strangers on their own territory. Our own observations are too few to justify any definite conclusion, but Goethe's data do not leave much doubt; he even reports that chicks are able to recognise their parents' voices.

CONCLUSION

AT THE END of this report on our study it may be good to pause and consider where it has carried us, in order to see what we have gained, and what new prospects may have been opened.

In retrospect, one feels a curious mingling of satisfaction and embarrassment. Satisfaction, and gratitude, because of the intense delight the field study of birds has given one; embarrassment about the shocking discrepancy between the number of man-hours spent in the field and the paucity of the yield in terms of scientific results. Yet the embarrassment is usually of short duration; I would be a hypocrite not to confess that I feel I understand the Herring Gull better than I did twenty years ago, and I don't regret for a moment that I have spent so many hours of my life in the gullery.

It is often difficult to make others understand why we enjoy doing this kind of thing. A rational explanation may make people understand in a way, but cannot make them share the joy. That is, I believe, because our true motives are entirely irrational. We bird-watchers feel that the steel-and-concrete environment we are creating all over the world satisfies only part of our habitat demands. City-dwellers, and deprived of our original, green, living habitat, we seem to develop a craving for it, and we go out now and then to seek it.

But just being in our ancestral habitat does not entirely satisfy us; sightseeing soon bores us; we want to do something. That again is only natural, for after all the human male is a hunter. And I strongly feel that our bird study is sublimated hunting, as is bird photography. All aspects of hunting: habitat selection, stalking our quarry, trying to outwit it, and finally experiencing intense satisfaction in getting what we want, are present in both bird watching and bird photography. I know through introspection that scientific bird study and bird photo-graphy give me exactly the kind of experiences and satisfactions as I once found in hunting seal on the arctic ice. It is subjectively the same to me whether I outwit the seal in order to shoot it or the bird in order to discover something about its behaviour. Even the trophy is an essential part of both. I am not in the least ashamed to confess that my photographs and this book are my trophies, and I am sure my fellow bird-watchers will agree with me.

The discovery, this triumph and trophy of the scientist, can be of very different calibre. Again, a true understanding of its meaning cannot be reached along rational ways. But the reader of this book may have recognised sympathetically what we have felt when we saw our ringed pairs return to their breeding territories of previous years, and when we discovered that Herring Gulls learn to know their own young, and when we saw a gull take a wooden egg up into the air and drop it, thereby revealing that this behaviour was a response to hard food. Discoveries of a larger calibre were the unravelling of the drives underlying threat behaviour, and the recognition of the function of the Herring Gull's territory.

Which were our main discoveries? A brief discussion might help to see the results in perspective and also to outline plans for future study.

The most obvious thing about the gulls' behaviour is their lack of insight into the ends served by their activities, and into the way their own behaviour serves these ends. A rigid, almost automatic dependence on internal and external conditions is revealed every time an analysis is made. Thus the chick responds again and again, up to hundreds of times, to a crude dummy in spite of the fact that the dummy never provides it with food; it just cannot resist the few " sign stimuli." The adults often behave in the same " stupid " way: the wooden egg was carried up and dropped just because it was hard; there is no sign of any insight into the function of dropping hard food, for when the gulls have the choice between soft mud or water and hard rock, they do not select the rock, and even do not learn to do so after many disappointments. The egg-rolling shows a similar rigidity; it never occurs to the gulls to use their wings or feet, which certainly would be better instruments than the narrow bill. Such instances could be multiplied.

These facts helped us in giving up the naïve, anthropocentric way of explaining animal behaviour in terms of our own experiences, and made us turn to a study of true causes. Thus we were led to experiments with models. We did such tests systematically in only two cases: the incubation response to eggs, and the chick's begging response. Our work on the former problem is no more than a very crude beginning, but with the latter problem we made some progress, although the work could and should be expanded. In both cases the inborn tendency to react was shown to be dependent on few, relatively simple " sign stimuli." The character of these sign stimuli was usually " configurational," that is, they could not easily be described as quantities of something, but had to be described in terms of relationships, such as the degree of contrast between the colour of the bill and that of the patch, or the nearness, or the lowness of the bill, which were found to be " stimuli " releasing the chick's begging. Therefore, such studies lead to a peculiar result: while they satisfy us to a certain extent because they show us causes of behaviour, they challenge us by presenting us with a new and even far more perplexing problem: what happens in the eyes and the nervous system of a chick when it appreciates " lowness," or " contrast," or " nearness "?

Further our studies reveal a striking contrast between sign stimuli and " conditioned," or learnt, stimuli. The reactions of adult birds to their mates—and to their chicks once they have learned to know them—become so selective that no other individual can release them. This can only mean that after this learning process they are sensitive to such fine details that the very slight differences between the birds' own mate and other birds, and between their own chicks and strange chicks, are sufficient to prevent responses to strangers.

The learning processes so far discovered reveal amazing capacities of the gulls. This leads to another puzzle. We see that the learning capacity of a Herring Gull is excellent. Yet it is only applied in special cases and not in others. Why does a gull learn so little about its own eggs even when they are strikingly different from other eggs? The problem is really of a more general nature. The eyes of a Herring Gull are excellent, probably even better than ours. Why does not it use its eyes always to the limits of their capacity? Why, for instance, does it brood a cylinder? Also, its executive organs could be used much more extensively, as we have seen in the egg-rolling. All such considerations make one increasingly aware of the limitations of the central nervous system. This might seem to be rather a negative conclusion, yet it seems to me to be of extreme importance; all this type of work forces one to the conclusion that behaviour, however variable it may seem to be at first sight, is dependent on mechanisms in the nervous system, mechanisms with strictly limited functions. Here, as in so many other cases, nature has only developed what is necessary, and no more. I think the bearing of this conclusion is insufficiently realised, particularly in human psychology.

Turning from the external stimuli to the internal states that determine behaviour, it is clear that the birds' behaviour is governed by a set of relatively few drives, or internal urges. Dependent on which of these drives is most active at the moment, a bird will search and find situations in which it can satisfy these drives by expressing them in the appropriate movements. For instance, the father of a clutch of eggs may be brooding them for hours. Gradually the brooding urge is used up by the very act of incubating. At the same time his feeding drive may be rising. These changes render him more and more susceptible to the expressions of broodiness in his mate. When the female finally becomes so broody that she walks up to the nest as a preparation to settling on the eggs—a type of behaviour which is the outcome of her internal brooding urge, which she has to obey—he is quite willing to leave, and nest-relief occurs. The male then leaves for the beach and starts foraging. When his foraging is done, his brooding drive gains power once more and sends him back to the colony.

Apart from these short-range fluctuations in drives there are also long-term changes. All through the winter the reproductive drives are at a low ebb, and the birds consequently leave the gullery alone. But in early spring they return to it, and select territories, they fight and mate.

Together with the awakening of a drive and the movements towards certain situations dictated by the drive, there is an increasing sensitivity to special stimuli and the urge to react by special types of behaviour. A very instructive example of this is the change in attitude towards eggs which takes place shortly before the incubation phase begins. While an egg, even a Herring Gull's egg, is eaten when it is encountered early in the season, it is responded to by brooding as soon as the bird's brooding urge awakes. Another instance: in the beginning of the incubation phase a pipped egg releases nibbling at the cracks —which will probably kill the chick—but these very same stimuli release the new pattern of chick brooding and feeding when administered towards the end of the brooding phase.

I think the story of the Herring Gulls will have made it clear —as would the life-history of any bird—how inadequate and incorrect it would be to describe the behaviour as a mere bundle of immediate responses to external stimuli. Not only does the condition of the bird determine which stimuli will be influential at a certain moment and what behaviour shall be released by them, but, in addition, the internal condition causes the bird to go and search for special situations which can provide the right stimuli for the release of the behaviour belonging to the urge that is activated at the moment. In psychological terms: a bird's " needs " vary; they are dependent of the nature of the drive that is activated, and these drives cause " spontaneous " behaviour.

To anybody who has watched animals this is just a common-place observation, just a simple descriptive statement of what actually happens. Yet it is not a matter of common knowledge, even in professional circles. This is due to the deplorable fact that so few people ever pause to look at what happens, and to investigate why it happens. Animal behaviour is in the same position as politics and medicine: almost everybody feels entitled to have an opinion about it. Worse still, there are not a few learned men who put these opinions in print, without being aware of their ignorance of simple observational data. Ignorance of another type is often found among scientists who focus attention on one special part of behaviour and study this in the laboratory. While this tendency has led to splendid research and has yielded important results—I may point, for instance, to the work of Pavlov and his school—it cannot be denied that as a method it is insufficient for acquiring an understanding of behaviour as a whole. Patient observational study of the whole behaviour-pattern is necessary. The analysis has to start at this level and must work its way down, step by step, to the lower levels.

A crucial point at the start of the analysis is the recognition of the drive underlying the behaviour at a given moment. It is easy to understand that we determine the state of an incubating bird as " broody," and that we conclude that a copulating bird acts under the influence of the sex drive, because we see it sit, and we see it mate. But the greater part of a bird's time is spent in half-hearted, incomplete movement which breaks off before any unambiguous, overt act is performed. The layman who accompanies us in the field is often sceptical when we tell him that this bird is aggressive, that one is broody, and another again is under the influence of its mating drive. Yet for the trained observer it is possible to recognise slight indications of the activation of a drive with great certainty. This recognition is based mainly on two criteria: (1) a knowledge of graded scales of intensities of movements, and (2) a correlation between type of movement and type of external stimulation. Perhaps this abstract statement needs some explanation.

In the case of the incubation drive, long observation shows that one can observe all intermediates from a mere looking at the eggs to actual incubation. Such intermediates are: walking towards the eggs; uttering the mew call; standing at the nest and slightly fluffing the ventral feathers; extreme ruffling of all the ventral feathers; bending the legs and almost settling down on the eggs.

Apart from this intensity scale of the reaction, which the observer can follow from the complete act to less and less complete movements, acquiring increasing powers of judgment with growing experience, there is the correlation between all incubation movements and the situation " nest with eggs on territory." Incubation does not always and invariably occur when the bird is in this situation, but, conversely, whenever the bird incubates, it is in this situation.

I have chosen incubation as an example because it is a very simple behaviour-pattern. In less simple activities the value of the criteria is more obvious. The low intensities of the upright threat posture are, to the beginner, difficult to recognise; the experienced observer, however, knows the sliding scale of intensities, and he knows that they are released by the situation " intruder on or near the territory."

It is especially the second criterion that has led to the correct interpretation of displacement activities, for the most obvious thing about them is that they occur under conditions which lead the observer to expect behaviour belonging to quite another drive. Application of the second criterion showed for instance that "grass-pulling" gulls must be in an aggressive state. Grass-pulling was then seen to be different from autochthonous collecting of material. " Choking " was more difficult because it occurred in two different situations, and the only possible interpretation was that it could indicate either aggressiveness (namely when it is a reaction to strangers) or nest-building activity (when it was done with the mate in the centre of the territory and in the absence of intruders). Especially this last case shows that there is still another criterion: the interpretation of choking as aggressive behaviour was supported by the fact that it usually alternates in quick succession with other types of aggressive behaviour. Thus the consistency of behaviour is often, though not always, a considerable help. Prolonged observation of any animal reveals that it is difficult for it—as it is for man—to shift suddenly from one type of activity to another. This tendency to stick to one type of action (to the activities of one instinct) is dependent on the intensity of the activation: the stronger the drive, the more difficult it is to change.

The recognition of displacement activities and of intention movements enables us to understand much more clearly how the fundamental drives are acting. It makes it possible for us to understand, for instance, the various strange movements performed during boundary clashes and to see that they are the results of the simultaneous activation of two drives, aggressiveness and flight. Further, it reveals the origin of movements commonly labelled as " displays " or " ceremonies." I should like to point out that this again has only been possible by studying the behaviour pattern as a whole. If we had limited our attention to fighting only, without studying nest-building as well, we would have been entirely at a loss with grass-pulling and choking, we would not have discovered the principle underlying displacement activities, and our final conclusion about the drives underlying the various threat ceremonies would never have occurred to us. Also, we would not have gained the slightest insight into the problem of the origin of the ceremonies. Sticking to broad observation and suppressing one's natural desire to concentrate on one special aspect may seem a waste of opportunities in the beginning, but it pays tenfold in the long run.

Now the more we probe into these problems of the causation of the social behaviour of gulls, and discover that the organisation is (in comparison with that of our own social behaviour) relatively simple, the more we are impressed by the efficiency of their social system; by the fact that in spite of all the limitations of the gulls' nervous system, they manage to build up their society every spring, and make it function. In this respect they attain as much, and perhaps even more, than man, who is becoming a serious threat to his own kind.

It is scarcely necessary to stress the differences in type of organisation between human societies and those of gulls. It is clear that much in the gull society is organised on a purely instinctive level, and in that respect differs from human society. In the gulls we find infinitely greater rigidity, and an almost complete lack of adaptability. There is no insight, no foresight —or at the most very little.

But it is more urgent at present to emphasise the similarities between man and animals. The student of animal behaviour cannot help believing that modern man is much too apt to overlook the fact that he too is urged by drives, that he too has his innate responsiveness in all spheres of life, that he too is very much limited by his nervous system. Man likes to consider himself a rational being; he not only fails to recognise his instincts, he even scoffs at instincts and considers them inferior. This attitude makes him fall a victim to them much more easily than is necessary. The student of behaviour is struck by the deeper similarity between man and animals; he recognises himself only too often in an animal. Also, he has rather a higher opinion of instincts; for instance, he recognises that they are at the bottom of his subjective experiences. And he has his doubts about the all-controlling power of reason, for he sees its limits too often.

Finally, a few words must be said about the problem of the relation between the community as a whole and the individuals as elements of it. Among sociologists there is a certain tendency to stress the importance of the whole, and to minimise the importance of the composing parts, the individuals. I think our study can contribute something to this problem. There is, of course, no doubt that a gull society is organised in another way from human society because it is built up by gulls and not by humans. In causal terms, a gull colony as it is and works to-day is a function of the properties of the individual gulls. Because of the almost complete lack of adaptability of the individuals, changes in the demands of society cannot be met by the individuals. It is true that humans are often capable of meeting new demands of a changing community, and this has probably led to the emphasis on the importance of the society as a whole as a formative agent in the life of the individual. Yet I must again emphasise the fact that the adaptability of human individuals has very obvious limits, and these limits are perhaps seen more clearly by the student of animal behaviour than by the human sociologist.

When we consider the history of the communal organisation of the gulls, we have to do with the survival value of organisational systems. A system built up by gulls which could not feed their young, or by gulls which could not be monogamous and thus would not take their due part in the incubation of the clutch, would not work and would produce no offspring. In an evolutionary sense therefore the gulls have been moulded by what their community must achieve. In this sense the whole has determined the properties of its component elements.

It seems therefore that in one respect the elements determine the qualities of the whole, and that in another respect the whole determines the qualities of the individual elements. To stress either one aspect unduly is to stress part of the truth.

Although I hope to have shown that this type of study leads to interesting results, I should once more emphasise and specify its incompleteness. There remain many problems to be solved. For instance, the stimuli provided by the eggs have not been studied in enough detail. Also, we did not find out on what stimuli individual recognition is based. Further, our study of the internal changes which bring a bird into the incubation phase, or into the next phase of care of the young, has scarcely begun. All these problems still require a considerable amount of experimentation, and probably our descriptive knowledge will have to be refined in the course of such work.

Other problems are in a still less satisfactory state. The origin of choking is obscure. Also, the begging behaviour as an introduction to coition is still ill-understood. The begging of the male is particularly puzzling.

Such problems, all of them concerning the causes, the functions, the origin and the evolution of courtship and threat display, and all of them of considerable interest to human psychology, might be solved by extending our study to related species, for comparison is a powerful tool in all studies of the origin and evolution of behaviour. The main result of our Herring Gull work therefore is not to be found in the conclusions drawn, but rather in the sharper formulation of the problems. It is only natural therefore that we have now begun to study related species.   The generous support of the Nuffield Foundation has enabled a team of behaviour students to start a study of the Black-headed Gull, the Kittiwake, and the Arctic Tern.   Colleagues in Holland and Finland are concentrating on related species, and all the observers are in close touch with each other. All this shows that the work done so far is only a beginning.

I know people often wonder whether it is worth while to spend so much time and energy in watching the ways of wild birds while there are so many urgent problems of human sociology to be solved.   I am convinced it is.   The utilitarian might be convinced when we remind him of the practical value this kind of work will have for human psychology and sociology—a value which is still seriously underrated.   Therefore I feel we are justified in following our irrational, non-utilitarian urges.   But even if this were not so, and if I myself could not see any use in watching gulls, I am afraid I would not leave them alone. Blood is thicker than water.

LIST OF PLATES

BIBLIOGRAPHY

ARMSTRONG, E. A. (1944). White plumage of sea-birds. *Nature, 153:* 527. (1946) The coloration of sea-birds. Why does white plumage predominate? *Birds of Britain, 2:* 15-19. (1950) The nature and function of displacement activities. *Symposia Soc. Exper. Biol., 4:* 361-87.

AUSTIN, O. M. (1949). Site tenacity, a behaviour trait of the Common Tern (*Sterna hirundo* L.). *Bird Banding, 20:* 1-39.

BAYLISS, H. A. (1949). Gulls dropping metal objects on glass. *Brit. Birds, 42:* 191.

BENT, A. C. (1921). Life Histories of North American Gulls and Terns. *Bull. U.S. Nat. Mus.* No. 113.

BIERENS DE HAAN, J. A. (1947). Animal psychology and the science of animal behaviour. *Behaviour, 1:* 71-80.

BOESEMAN, M. J., VAN DER DRIFT, J., VAN ROON, J. M., TINBERGEN, N. and TER PELKWIJK, J. J. (1938). De bittervoorns en hun mossels. *Levende Nat. 43:* 129-36.

BOYD, A. W. and THOMSON, A. LANDSBOROUGH (1937). Recoveries of marked swallows within the British Isles. *Brit. Birds, 30:* 278-87.

BROEKHUYSEN, G. J. (1935). Gedragingen van nog niet geslachtsrijpe doch reeds zelfstandige Zilver en Grote Mantelmeeuwen (*Larus argentatus* Pontopp. et *Larus marinus* L.). *Ardea, 24:* 239-50. (1937) Gedragingen van geslachtsrijpe en nog niet geslachtsrijpe Zilver-en Grote Mantelmeeuwen buiten de broedtijd. *Ardea, 26:* 159-72.

BROWN, D. H. (1949). Glaucous Gulls diving for food. *Brit. Birds, 42:* 95.

BRÜCKNER, G. H. (1933). Untersuchungen zur Tiersoziologie, insbesondere der Auflösung der Familie. *Z. Psychol. 128:* 1-120.

BURCKHARDT, D. (1944). Möwenbeobachtungen in Basel. *Orn. Ber., 41:* 49-76.

CRAIK, K. J. W. (1944). White plumage of sea-birds. *Nature, 153:* 288.

CREUTZ, G. (1949). Verfrachtungen mit Kohlund Blaumeisen (*Parus m. major* L. und *Parus c. caeruleus* L.). *Vogelwarte, 2:* 63-78.

CULEMANN, H. W. (1928). Ornithologische Beobachtungen um und auf Mellum vom 13. Mai bis 5. Sept. 1926. *J. Orn., 76:* 609-53.

CUMMINGS, S. G. (1914). Herring Gulls diving. *Brit. Birds, 7:* 201-2.

DAANJE, A. (1941). Ueber das Verhalten des Haussperlings (*Passer d. domesticus* (L.)). *Ardea, 30:* 1-42. (1950) On locomotory movements in birds and the intention movements derived from them. *Behaviour, 3:* 48-99.

244

DARWIN, C. (1890). The Descent of Man (2nd edition). London, Murray.

DAVIS, D. E. (1942). Number of eggs laid by Herring Gulls. *Auk, 59:* 549-54.

DENSING, M. (1939). The Herring Gulls of Hat Island, Wisconsin. *Wilson Bull, 51:* 170-75.

DICE, L. R. (1945). Minimum intensities of illumination under which owls can find dead prey by sight. *Amer. Nat. 79:* 385-416.

DIJKGRAAF, S. (1946a). Die Sinneswelt der Fledermäuse. *Experientia, 2:* 438-49. (1946b) Over het orientatieprobleem bij vogels. *Proc. K. Ned. Akad. Wet., 49:* 690-98.

DIRCKSEN, R. (1932). Die Biologie des Austernfischers, der Brandseeschwalbe und der Küstenseeschwalbe nach Beobachtungen und Untersuchungen auf Norderoog. *J. Orn., 80:* 427-521.

VAN DOBBEN, W. H. (1934). Bijdrage tot het meeuwenvraagstuk. *Org. Club Ned. Vogelk., 7:* 63-78. (1937) Zilvermeeuwen-anecdoten. *Levende Nat., 40:* 353-61.

DROST, R. (1949). Zugvögel perzipieren Ultrakurzwellen. *Vogelwarte, 2:* 57-59.

DROST, R. and SCHILLING, L. (1940). Ueber den Lebensraum deutscher Silbermöwen, *Larus a. argentatus* Pontopp., auf Grund von Beringungsergebnissen. *Vogelzug, 11:* 1-22.

DUTCHER, W. (1902). Results of special protection to gulls and terns obtained through the Thayer fund. *Auk, 19:* 34-63. (1904) Report of the A.O.U. Committee on the protection of North American birds for the year 1903. *Auk, 21:* 97-208.

VAN ECK, P. J. (1939). Farbensehen und Zapfenfunktion bei der Singdrossel, *Turdus e. ericetorum* Turton. *Arch. néerl. Zool., 3:* 450-99.

EDWARDS, G., HOSKING, E., and SMITH, S. (1948). Aggressive display of the Oystercatcher. *Brit. Birds, 41:* 236-43.

ELLIOTT, H. F. I. and MOREAU, R. E. (1947). Start of incubation by Herring Gull. *Brit. Birds, 40:* 286.

FARNER, D. S. (1945). The return of robins to their birthplaces. *Bird Banding, 16:* 81-99.

FISHER, J. (1952). The Fulmar. London, Collins, *New Nat.*

GEYR VON SCHWEPPENBURG, H. (1938). Zur Systematik der *fuscus-argentatus* Möwen. *J. Orn., 86:* 345-65.

GOETHE, F. (1937). Beobachtungen und Untersuchungen zur Biologie der Silbermöwe auf der Vogelinsel Memmertsand. *J. Orn., 85:* 1-119. (1939) Ueber das "Anstoss-Nehmen" bei Vögeln. *Z. Tierpsychol., 3:* 371-87.

GRIFFIN, D. R. (1943). Homing experiments with Herring Gulls and Common Terns. *Bird Banding, 14:* 7-33. (1944) The sensory basis of bird navigation. *Quart. Rev. Biol., 19:* 15-31.

GROHMANN, J. (1939). Modifikation oder Funktionsreifung. *Z. Tierpsychol., 2:* 132-44.

246 BIBLIOGRAPHY

GROSS, A. O. (1940). The migration of Kent Island Herring Gulls. *Bird Banding, 11:* 129-55.

GROSS, A. O. (1951). The Herring Gull-Cormorant control project. *Proc. X. Int. Orn. Congr. Uppsala 1950:* 532-36.

VON HAARTMAN, L. (1949). Der Trauerfliegenschnäpper. I. Ortstreue und Rassenbildung. *Act. Zool. Fenn., 56:* 1-104.

HARBER, D. D. and JOHNS, M. (1947). Great Black-backed Gull dropping Rat. *Brit. Birds, 40:* 417.

HAVILAND, M. D. (1915). Feeding habit of the Black-headed Gull. *Brit. Birds, 9:* 72-73.

HAZELWOOD, A. (1949). Agile Flight manœuvre of Herring-Gull. *Brit. Birds, 42:* 159.

HEINROTH, O. (1911). Beiträge zur Biologie, namentlich Ethologie und Psychologie der Anatiden. *Verh. 5. Int. Orn. Kongr. Berlin, 1910:* 589-702.

HEINROTH, O. and HEINROTH, M. (1928). Die Vögel Mitteleuropas. Berlin, Bermühler. (1941) Das Heimfinde-Vermögen der Brieftaube. *J. Orn., 89:* 213-57.

VON HOLST, E. (1950). Die Arbeitsweise des Statolithenapparates bei Fischen. *Z. vergl. Physiol., 32:* 60-120.

HOWARD, H. E. (1929). An introduction to the study of bird behaviour. Cambridge University Press. (1935) Territory and food. *Brit. Birds, 28:* 285-87.

HUXLEY, J. S. (1914). The courtship habits of the Great Crested Grebe (*Podiceps cristatus*); with an addition to the theory of sexual selection. *Proc. Zool. Soc. Lond. 1914:* 491-562. (1923) Courtship activities in the Red-throated Diver (*Colymbus stellatus* Pontopp.); together with a discussion on the evolution of courtship in birds. *J. Linn. Soc. Zool. 35:* 253-92. (1934) A natural experiment on the territorial instinct. *Brit. Birds, 27:* 270-77.

ISING, G. (1945). Die physikalische Möglichkeit eines tierischen Orientierungssinnes auf Basis der Erdrotation. *Ark. Mat. Astr. Fysik. 32A:* 1-23.

KENDEIGH, S. C. (1941). Territorial and mating behaviour of the House Wren. *Ill. Biol. Monogr. 18:* 1-120.

KIRKMAN, F. B. (1937). Bird behaviour. London & Edinburgh, Nelson.

KOEHLER, O. and ZAGARUS, A. (1937). Beiträge zum Brutverhalten des Halsbandregenpfeifers (*Charadrius h. hiaticula* L.). *Beitr. Fortpfl.-biol. Vög. 13:* 1-9.

KORTLANDT, A. (1940a). Eine Uebersicht der angeborenen Verhaltungsweisen des Mittel-europäischen Kormorans (*Phalacrocorax carbo sinensis* Shaw & Nodd.); ihre Funktion, ontogenetische Entwicklung und phylogenetische Herkunft. *Arch. néerl. Zool., 4:* 401-02. (1940b) Wechselwirkung zwischen Instinkten. *Arch. néerl. Zool. 4:* 442-520.

KRAMER, G. (1949). Ueber Richtungstendenzen bei der nächtlichen Zugunruhe gekäfigter Vögel. In: Ornithologie als biologische Wissenschaft

BIBLIOGRAPHY 247

(Festschrift E. Stresemann), 269-83. (1952) Experiments on bird
orientation. *Ibis.*, *94:* 265-85.

KRÄTZIG, H. (1940). Untersuchungen zur Lebensweise des Moorschnee-
huhns, *Lagopus l. lagopus*, während der Jugendentwicklung. *J. Orn. 88:*
139-66.

KÜHN, A. (1927). Ueber den Farbensinn der Bienen. *Z. vergl. Physiol.*, *5:*
762-801.

LACK, D. (1939). The display of the Blackcock. *Brit. Birds, 32:* 290-303.
(1940a) Pair formation in birds. *Condor, 42:* 269-86. (1940b) Courtship
feeding in birds. *Auk, 57:* 169-79. (1943) The life of the Robin. London,
Witherby.

LACK, D. and LOCKLEY, R. M. (1938). Skokholm Bird Observatory homing
experiments I. *Brit. Birds, 31:* 242-28.

LOCKLEY, R. M. (1937). Black-backed and Herring Gulls and Ravens
feeding on ants. *Brit. Birds, 30:* 325-6.

LORENZ, K. (1931). Beiträge zur Ethologie sozialer Corviden. *J. Orn., 79:*
67-120. (1935) Der Kumpan in der Umwelt des Vogels. *J. Orn. 83:*
137-213, 289-413. (1941) Vergleichende Bewegungsstudien an Anatinen.
J. Orn., 89 (Festschrift Heinroth): 194-294. (1943) Die angeborenen
Formen möglicher Erfahrung. *Z. Tierpsychol. 5 :* 235-409.

MAKKINK, G. F. (1931). Die Kopulation der Brandente (*Tadorna tadorna*
(L.)). *Ardea, 20:* 18-22.

MEINERTZHAGEN, R. (1935). The races of *Larus argentatus* and *Larus fuscus*
with special reference to Herr B. Stegmann's recent paper on the subject
Ibis, (13) *5:* 762-73.

MEISENHEIMER, J. (1921). Geschlecht und Geschlechter im Tierreich. Jena.

MEYKNECHT, J. (1940). Farbensehen und Helligkeitsunterscheidung beim
Steinkauz (*Athene noctua vidalii* A. E. Brehm). *Ardea, 30:* 129-74.

MOREAU, R. E. (1923). Herring Gull eating its own chick. *Brit. Birds, 16:*
221-22.

NICE, M. M. (1937). Studies in the Life History of the Song Sparrow. I.
Trans. Linn. Soc. N.Y.4.

NOBLE, G. K. and VOGT, W. (1935). An experimental study of sex recognition in birds. *Auk, 52:* 278-86.

NOBLE, G. K. and WURM, M. (1943). The social behaviour of the Laughing
Gull. *Ann. N.Y. Acad. Sci. 45:* 179-220.

OLDHAM, C. (1930). The shell-smashing habit of gulls. *Ibis*, (12) *6:* 239-44.

PIRENNE, M. H., and CROMBIE, A. C. (1944). White plumage of sea-birds.
Nature, 153: 526-27.

PORTIELJE, A. F. J. (1921). Zur Ethologie bzw. Psychologie von *Botaurus
stellaris*. *Ardea, 15:* 1-15. (1928) Zur Ethologie bzw. Psychologie der
Silbermöwe, *Larus a. argentatus* Pontopp. *Ardea, 17:* 112-49. (1944)
Dieren zien en leren kennen. Amsterdam, Nederlandse Keurboekerij.
4th ed.

PUMPHREY, R. J. (1948). The sense organs of birds. *Ibis, 90:* 171-99.

RÄBER, H. (1949). Das Verhalten von gefangenen Waldohreulen (*Asio o. otus*) und Waldkauzen (*Strix a. aluco*) zur Beute. *Behaviour, 2:* 1-96.

RAND, A. L. (1942). *Larus kumlieni* and its allies. *Canad. Field-Nat., 56:* 123-26.

RICHDALE, L. E. (1941). Sexual Behavior in Penguins. Lawrence, University of Kansas Press.

RINTOUL, L. J. and BAXTER, E. V. (1925). Report on Scottish Ornithology in 1924. *Scot. Nat. 1925:* 73-88, 109-30.

RUITER, C. J. S. (1941). Waarnemingen omtrent de levenswijze van de Gekraagde Roodstaart, *Phoenicurus ph. phoenicurus* (L.). *Ardea, 30:* 175-214.

RÜPPELL, W. (1936). Heimfindeversuche mit Staren und Schwalben 1935. *J. Orn., 84:* 180-98. (1940) Neue Ergebnisse über Heimfinden beim Habicht. *Vogelzug, 11:* 57-64. (1944) Versuche über Heimfinden ziehender Nebelkrähen nach Verfrachtung. *J. Orn., 92:* 106-32.

RUSSELL, E. S. (1934). The behaviour of animals. London.

SCHUYL, G., TINBERGEN, L. and TINBERGEN, N. (1936). Ethologische Beobachtungen am Baumfalken, *Falco s. subbuteo* L. *J. Orn., 84:* 387-434

SCHÜZ, E. (1941). Bewegungsnormen des weissen Storches. *Z. Tierpsychol., 5:* 1-36. (1949) Die Spät-Auflassung ostpreussischer Jungstörche in West-Deutschland durch die Vogelwarte Rossitten 1933. *Vogelwarte, 2:* 63-78.

SELOUS, E. (1933). Evolution of habit in birds. London, Constable.

SEREBRENNIKOV, M. K. (1931). Der Rosenstar (*Pastor roseus* L.); seine Lebensweise und ökonomische Bedeutung in Uzbekistan. J. *Orn., 79:* 29-57.

VAN SOMEREN, V. D. (1930). Curious changes of diet in Black-headed and Herring Gulls. *Scot. Nat. 1930:* 132.

STEGMANN, B. (1934). Ueber die Formen der grossen Möwen ("Subgenus *Larus*") und ihre gegenseitigen Beziehungen. *J. Orn., 82:* 340-80.

STEINBACHER, G. (1937). Das Wiedererkennen des Geleges bei der Silbermöwe (*Larus a. argentatus* Pont.). *Beitr. Fortpfl.-biol. Vög., 13:* 23-25. (1938) Beiträge zür Brutbiologie einheimischer Möwenarten. *Ber. Ver. schles. Orn., 23:* 42-65.

STEINIGER, F. (1952). Bilder vom Tauchen der Silbermöwe. *Vogelwelt, 73:* 157-59.

STRONG, R. M. (1914). On the habits and behaviour of the Herring Gull, *Larus argentatus* Pont. *Auk, 31:* 22-50, 178-200.

THOMSON, A. LANDSBOROUGH (1924). The migration of the Herring Gull and Lesser Black-backed Gull: results of the marking method. *Brit. Birds, 18:* 34-45. (1931) On "Abmigration" among the ducks; an anomaly shown by the results of bird-marking. *Proc. VII Int. Orn. Congr. Amsterdam, 1928:* 382-89.

TINBERGEN, L. (1935). Bij het nest van de Torenvalk. *Levende Nat.*, *40:* 9-17. (1939) Zur Fortpflanzungsethologie von *Sepia officinalis* L. *Arch. néerl. Zool.*, *3:* 323-64.

TINBERGEN, N. (1932). Vergelijkende waarnemingen aan enkele meeuwen en sterns. *Ardea*, *21:* 1-13. (1934) Enkele proeven over het ei als broedobject. *Ardea*, *23:* 82-89. (1935) Field observations of East Greenland birds I. The Behaviour of the Red-necked Phalarope (*Phalaropus lobatus* L.) in spring. *Ardea*, *24:* 1-42. (1936) Zur Soziologie der Silbermöwe, *Larus a. argentatus*. *Beitr. Fortpfl.-biol. Vög.*, *12:* 89-96. (1936) Waarnemingen en proeven over de sociologie van een zilvermeeuwenkolonie. *Levende Nat.*, *40:* 262-80. (1939a) Field observations of East Greenland birds II. The behaviour of the Snow Bunting (*Plectrophenax nivalis subnivalis* (Brehm)) in spring. *Trans. Linn. Soc. N.Y.5.* (1939b) On the analysis of social organisation among vertebrates, with special reference to birds. *Amer. Midl. Nat.*, *21:* 210-34. (1940) Die Uebersprungbewegung. *Z. Tierpsychol.*, *4:* 1-40. (1948) Wat prikkelt een scholekster tot broeden? *Levende Nat.*, *51:* 65-69. (1949) De functie van de rode vlek op de snavel van de Zilvermeeuw. *Bijdr. Dierk.*, *28:* 453-65. (1951) The study of instinct. Oxford University Press. (1952) "Derived" activities: their causation, biological significance, origin and emancipation during evolution. *Quart. Rev. Biol.*, *27:* 1-32.

TINBERGEN, N. and BOOY, H. L. (1937). Nieuwe feiten over de sociologie van de Zilvermeeuwen. *Levende Nat.*, *41:* 325-44.

TINBERGEN, N., BOEREMA, L. K., MEEUSE, B. J. D., and VAROSSIEAU, W. W. (1942). Die Balz des Samtfalters, *Eumenis* (*Satyrus*) *semele* (L.). *Z. Tierpsychol.*, *5:* 182-226.

TINBERGEN, N. and VAN IERSEL, J. J. A. (1947). "Displacement reactions" in the Three-spined Stickleback. *Behaviour*, *1:* 56-63.

TINBERGEN, N. and KUENEN, D. J. (1939). Ueber die auslösenden und die richtunggebenden Reizsituationen der Sperrbewegung von jungen Drosseln (*Turdus m. merula* L. und *T.e. ericetorum* Turton). *Z. Tierpsychol.*, *3:* 37-60.

TINBERGEN, N. and PERDECK, A. C. (1950). On the stimulus situation releasing the begging response in the newly hatched Herring Gull chick (*Larus a. argentatus* Pontopp.). *Behaviour*, *3:* 1-38.

VANDERPLANK, F. L. (1934). The effect of infra-red waves on Tawny Owls (*Strix aluco*). *Proc. Zool. Soc. Lond. 1934:* 505-07.

VERWEY, J. (1928). Het gedrag van de Zilvermeeuw. *Leven en Werken, 1928:* 815-30. (1930) Die Paarungsbiologie des Fischreihers. *Zool. Jb, 48:* 1-120. (1949) Habitat selection in marine animals. *Folia biotheoretica, 4:* 1-120.

WACHS, H. (1933). Paarungsspiele als Artcharaktere; Beobachtungen an Möwen und Seeschwalben. *Verh. Zool.-Bot. Ges. Wien, 1933:* 192-202.

WALKER, A. B. (1949). Herring Gull "paddling" on grass field. *Brit. Birds, 42:* 222-23.

WALTER, W. G. (1943). Some experiments on the sense of smell in birds. *Arch. néerl. Physiol.*, *27*: 1-73.

WATSON, J. B. and LASHLEY, K. S. (1915). Homing and related activities of birds. *Publ. Carneg. Instn.*, No. 211.

WITHERBY, H. F. et al. (1938). The Handbook of British Birds. London, Witherby.

YEAGLEY, H. L. (1947). A preliminary study of a physical basis of bird navigation. *J. Appl. Physics, 18:* 1035-63.

YEATES, G. K. (1934). The life of the Rook. London, Allan.

ZAHN, W. (1933). Ueber den Geruchssinn einiger Vögel. *Z. vergl. Physiol., 19:* 785-96.

INDEX